HIGHER GROUND

HIGHER

SALLY L. KITCH

Women in Culture and Society
A series edited by Catharine R. Stimpson

GROUND

*From Utopianism
to Realism in American
Feminist Thought
and Theory*

THE UNIVERSITY OF CHICAGO PRESS
CHICAGO AND LONDON

SALLY L. KITCH is professor of Women's Studies and Chair of the Department of Women's Studies at the Ohio State University. She is the author of *Chaste Liberation: Celibacy and Female Cultural Status* and *This Strange Society of Women: Reading the Letters and Lives of the Woman's Commonwealth*.

The University of Chicago Press, Chicago 60637
The University of Chicago Press, Ltd., London
© 2000 by The University of Chicago
All rights reserved. Published 2000
Printed in the United States of America

09 08 07 06 05 04 03 02 01 00   1 2 3 4 5

ISBN: 0-226-43856-2 (cloth)
ISBN: 0-226-43857-0 (paper)

Cover image courtesy of Susan Fillin-Yeh, with thanks to David Krapes for the color transparency. Cartoons reprinted by permission from the following sources:

Page 18: "No, Lad, We Aren't Movers. We're Just Shakers," *The New Yorker*, Feb. 15, 1999, p. 71. © The New Yorker Collection 1999 Mick Stevens from cartoonbank.com. All rights reserved.

Page 149: "Despite My Best Efforts, You're Still the Man and I'm Still the Woman," *The New Yorker*, Aug. 19, 1996, p. 104. © The New Yorker Collection 1996 Edward Koren from cartoonbank.com. All rights reserved.

Page 162: "Thank You for Backing Up Your Opinions with Hard Data," Mischa Richter and Harald Bakken. *Chronicle of Higher Education*, July 26, 1996, B6.

Page 253: "I'm Leaving You and the Kids to Join the Promise Keepers," *The New Yorker*, Nov. 24, 1997, p. 104. © The New Yorker Collection 1997 Peter Steiner from cartoonbank.com. All rights reserved.

Library of Congress Cataloging-in-Publication Data
Kitch, Sally.
  Higher ground : from Utopianism to realism in American feminist
thought and theory / Sally L. Kitch.
     p. cm.
  Includes bibliographical references and index.
     ISBN 0-226-43856-2 (cloth : alk. paper)—ISBN 0-226-43857-0
(pbk. : alk. paper)
     1. Feminism—United States—History. 2. Feminist theory—United
States—History. 3. Utopias—United States—History. 4. Feminist
fiction—History and criticism. 5. Utopias in literature. I. Title.
HQ1410.K59 2000
305.42'0973—dc21   99-055605

CONTENTS

FOREWORD

by Catharine Stimpson

The poet E. E. Cummings once warned his readers not to pity the human species, "this busy monster," for it is far too capable of cruelty, power trips, and arrogant self-delusion. After this diagnosis, he concludes:

> We doctors know
> a hopeless case if—listen: there's a hell
> of a good universe next door; let's go[1]

Cummings pungently captures the utopian spirit, another human capability. If life seems awful, let's imagine another place that shimmers with promise. Or, if life seems like hell, let's light out for a hell of a good universe elsewhere.

The word utopia arose in the early modern period. Sir Thomas More, the English writer and statesman, coined it in the early sixteenth-century, combining Greek words for "place," "good," and "no." A utopia then is a good place that is no place. More then published *Utopia,* his narrative of a fantasy island, in 1516. However, the apparently deep and unquenchable need to construct utopias existed well before

1. E. E. Cummings, "Pity This Busy Monster Mankind," *A Little Treasury of Modern Poetry English and American,* rev. ed., ed. Oscar Williams (New York: Charles Scribner's Sons, 1952), 366.

More and has outlasted him. The power of this need, and the dangers of gratifying it, especially for feminism, are the great subjects of *Higher Ground,* Sally Kitch's bold, radical, and striking new book.

Kitch is well-known for her work on American utopian communities. She carefully distinguishes among "utopianism," a thought process and social activity; "utopists," who practice one or both; and "utopias," actual or fictional communities. Utopias contrast sharply with both the grimy muddles of everyday life and dystopias, which are actual or imagined communities of evil—for example, George Orwell's *1984*. She is aware of how pervasive feminist utopianism has been, how many feminist utopists there have been, and how many utopias feminists have created. A significant proportion of women's utopian works in nineteenth-century America are feminist in tone and content. In general, as Kitch tells us, utopists are interested in gender arrangements. Ironically, many male utopists have been idealistic and unconventional in all but their picture of gender. Perhaps not surprisingly, dystopists have also feared the loss of conventional gender roles. Because Kitch has come to doubt utopianism, the fact of its pervasiveness in feminist action, theory, and pedagogy deeply concerns her. The explicitly or implicitly utopian feminist theorizing she most closely examines takes up central issues—gender differences, the linguistic construction of gender and its connections to postmodernism, the causes and consequences of differences among women. She argues that a utopian valorization of motherhood led to distorted theories of sexual difference and an inadequate recognition of the differences among women. In brief, the utopian virus infects the heart of feminism.

Having read much of what Kitch has read, having attended some of the same conferences and classrooms that she has, I know how well and yet how tactfully she has mapped this terrain. Interestingly, she extends her critique to such other contemporary movements as multiculturalism; the culture wars, fought in part over multiculturalism; and the Promise Keepers, the fusion of a muscular evangelical Christianity and American masculine norms. Indeed, Kitch suggests that learning how to measure utopianism in feminism can help to build a "utopia detector" to apply to other movements. Although feminism has played a role in multiculturalism and the culture wars, it has cast a mostly cold eye on the Promise Keepers. For Kitch, all of them display ultimately dangerous features of Utopianism. Naively, it assumes that good societies inevitably shape good people in a triumph of benign social conditioning over malign human tendencies. Arrogantly, it presumes that advance planning can anticipate human need and values, a triumph of benign social engineering over life's unpredictabilities, surprises, and contingencies. Erroneously, it conflates social criticism and programs for social change, an equation of "problem identification with problem solution." Believing in the reality of that hell of a good universe next door can be as sweetly innocent as cheering on Peter Pan in a pantomime, but it can also be as murderously stupid as following a thug with a machine gun carrying out ethnic cleansing.

Significantly, Kitch is not a dystopian curmudgeon. Her spirit is courageous and resilient. She is aware of the attractions and strengths of utopianism, and she is respectful of the feminist artists, writers, and scholars who have argued for its value. Nor is Kitch a feminist-basher who hopes that she will gain fame, power, and glory by heaving Molotov cocktails at women's studies. Her overarching ambition is to contribute to our emancipatory thinking about politics, society, and culture. She believes, legitimately, that emancipatory thinking about gender and women in all their differences is essential if this ambition is to be served. In part, her book works to repel the virulent strain of utopianism from feminism. In even greater part, it offers an alternative to utopianism, a "higher ground." Kitch takes the phrase from a gospel hymn, "Lord, plant my feet on higher ground / New heights I'm gaining every day."

Gaining higher ground demands a way of thinking and acting that is hopeful but grounded. It is implicitly linked to two intellectual traditions: first, to a strand of feminism, most famously associated with Mary Wollstonecraft, that values reason, and second, to a strand of American pragmatism that asks us to test ideas against reality. Kitch also identifies and codifies a strand of thinking about gender—the work, for example, of the sociologist R. W. Connell, the feminist theoretician Drucilla Cornell, or the literary critic Rey Chow—that is compatible with her own. *Higher Ground* envisions and embodies a mature feminism that is a site of conceptual struggle, criticism, and self-criticism. It permits multiple theories, ideas, identities, and voices. Although they bear a "family resemblance" to each other, they neither echo nor imitate each other. This feminism is realistic and reasonable, aware that every action has unintended consequences and costs and that real debate is complex, contradictory, and difficult. Finding higher ground may be arduous, but a sense of purpose and necessity animates the quest.

Higher Ground is the result of years of interdisciplinary reading and inquiry, but one of the passages I most cherish is a rare autobiographical moment. It pictures a young woman who has spent the day in her office and classroom, now at home in her kitchen, toddlers at her feet, getting dinner for the family. She is hard-working, harassed, doing her best, juggling several lives, moving between ideas and the banalities, at once demanding and delicious, of children who must be fed. She dreams, but she must also earn a living and help her babies grow. She has succeeded at both, and is now publishing still another important book. It is at once her diagnosis of a dreamer's potential disease, utopianism, and a well-reasoned, deeply-felt guide to a journey to a better universe. This universe, of course, will not exist next door unless we have the wit, patience, and strength to build it on higher ground than we now occupy.

Catharine R. Stimpson
New York University

INTRODUCTION

If you want to make God laugh, tell her your plans.
—Anne Lamont, *Bird by Bird*

Feminists love a utopia. At least many of us do. And why not? In order to think about feminist ideas and goals, we are almost forced, like utopian planners, to imagine societies that have never existed. Besides, utopias offer hope and fuel the imagination. They present near-perfect feminist worlds and new social contracts based on "feminine" qualities or achievements. They promise to transform human nature itself through feminist social revolution.

If a utopian approach to feminism sounds self-evident to you, dear reader, it is because utopianism and American feminism have been so closely associated for so long. Such an approach sounded self-evident to me during the years I spent exploring the gender arrangements and symbolism of American utopian societies and feminist utopian fiction. I embarked on that work convinced that planning for a feminist future meant restarting humanity from scratch. How else to eliminate eons of gender prejudice, exacerbated as it has long been by racial, class, and ethnic hierarchies? How else but by redesigning the human condition to persuade those who benefit from women's oppression to relinquish the perquisites of their power? What better models for social change than utopian ones, like those offered in the rich genre of feminist utopian fiction?

I remain fascinated with utopian designs in both experimental communities and fiction, but I no longer consider utopianism the best approach for conceptualizing feminist social change, and I no longer consider feminist utopian fiction or designs the primary sources of responsible and constructive feminist theory. By *utopianism* I mean a compendium of attitudes about and strategies for social change that share the characteristics of utopian designs and visions. Those characteristics include a belief that good societies produce good people and that human needs and social values are constant and can be anticipated through careful advanced planning. Utopianism also involves insightful social criticism that often suggests programs for social change. Some feminist thinkers regard those beliefs, assumptions, and connections as virtually synonymous with feminism itself, but I argue in *Higher Ground* that the equation does a disservice to feminist thought and theory. It is not necessarily the case, for example, that insightful social criticism guarantees effective planning for social reorganization. The transformation from observation to action equates problem identification with problem solution, a step that may mistake the tip of the iceberg for the whole. Feminist theorizing needs strategies for discovering more than the obvious issues and concerns and for going beyond contemporary analyses of them.

Throughout *Higher Ground,* I shall propose other definitions and hazards of utopianism, as well as strategies for reducing utopianism in feminist thinking. In the process, I want to distinguish between *utopianism* as a thought process and utopian practice by *utopists.* The former can but does not necessarily lead to the latter; that is, utopianism as a mode of thought may or may not produce utopian experimentation. The distinction allows us to recognize the achievements of particular utopian societies, as well as the courage some utopists have shown in risking their fortunes and sometimes their lives in order to enact their principles, without necessarily embracing utopianism as an approach to social change. The distinction also allows us to appreciate utopian fiction, including and especially feminist utopian fiction, as representations of dreams and desires for a better, more humane, and more principled future. We can celebrate that fiction's fascinating, clever, even brilliant ideas without necessarily concluding that such fiction can or should be the primary source of feminist thought and theory.

Higher Ground develops the distinction between utopian practice and utopianism and asks whether the latter can truly accommodate the complexities of feminist concerns—gender difference, differences among women, or the intersection of sex, race, and class with various social domains. It considers whether utopian thinking takes feminism to the higher ground it promises.

Although answering that question occupies much of *Higher Ground,* the book's analysis will demonstrate that the legacy of utopian thinking, however inspirational, ultimately proves inadequate to the task of feminist theorizing. Indeed, the utopianism that seems to inspire feminist thought can often limit it and even threaten its survival. To explore that paradox, *Higher Ground* first considers explicitly utopian fictional works that propose ideal societies or social systems and then examines feminist theorizing that has little or no connection to utopian practice.

EMBEDDED UTOPIANISM

Some readers may be surprised by my claim that utopianism pervades feminist thinking, even that which does not entail designing an ideal society. Surely, they might think, most feminist theorists toil in the vineyards of life's brutalities—its violence, poverty, racist sexism, and sexist racism—with their feet planted firmly on the ground, not with their heads in utopian clouds. But throughout this book we shall see that, even in addressing the earthiest of issues, many feminist thinkers and writers have—often inadvertently—embraced utopian approaches to the problems they address.

Examples of such utopian approaches can be found in the earliest rhetoric of the current women's movement—in, for example, the slogans of the 1970s. "Sisterhood Is Global!" and "Let a Woman Do It!" were rousing and inspiring imperatives in their day, but they were also utopian constructions that muted the complexities of women's lives and obscured the implications of gender in various contexts and relationships. They were utopian in their assertion—or implication—that being a woman means possessing qualities and talents that can save the world. They served a purpose by proclaiming women's value at a time when such value was rarely recognized or asserted, but almost thirty years later, as the twenty-first century dawns, such slogans can sound silly.

Most who hear them now would call them naïve, or imperialist, or "essentialist" rather than utopian. Such slogans might embarrass feminists who recognize that the inequities of today's global economy situate women very differently around the world and create different needs and perspectives in their wake. Such slogans do not match our experience with leaders like Margaret Thatcher or even Benazir Bhutto or with several decades and years of "the woman." We have learned that letting a woman do any "it"—hold political office, head a company or a university—does not necessarily produce better (or even remotely feminist) policies, institutions, or products. But whatever else can be said of them, the slogans were also utopian at their base—falsely optimistic, idealizing, lacking self-reflection, and binary in their conception. They confused problem identification with problem solution. Like many utopian notions, they created more dissension and disappointment than they did harmony.

Higher Ground suggests that deficiencies in feminist theory that have been called by various other names can often, in fact, be attributed to hidden utopianism, which inspires not only idealizations but also a preference for solutions and answers over questions and continuous analysis. It argues that some of feminism's utopian expectations, such as claims about women's inherent virtues, have sown the seeds of feminism's declining popularity and internal discontent.

It is sometimes easier to identify utopianism and recognize its dangers in the thinking of feminism's detractors than it is to see it in our own thought. One example is a "right to life" TV ad from a few years ago. The ad's utopian tone was established through a male voice-over that defined the terms of the issue. "Many people are making room at life's table," the voice intoned, while the camera's eye focused on the belly of a pregnant woman apparently floating (since it was both headless and feetless) beside a table set with china and silver in the dining room of a comfortable white family.

The ad's invitation to women to express their "true" natures by welcoming all offspring depends, of course, on an idealized view of motherhood, children, and family life that obscures the real-life context for childbearing decisions. It leaves unasked and unanswered many thorny questions: What about the thirteen-year-old who has been impregnated by her uncle? What about the poor woman who has weakened her body and compromised her future with too many pregnancies and too many babies? What about the mind, heart, and dreams of the woman whose face is hidden from view? In reducing the complex issue of unwanted pregnancy to a single issue of generosity, the ad raises an implicitly utopian question: "Since this view of the world works for some, why can't it work for all?" That form of utopianism, which simplifies, idealizes, and appeals to easily evoked emotions, helps to explain the effectiveness of many right-to-life campaigns. It also helps to explain the relative ineffectiveness of pro-choice rhetoric, which necessarily complicates issues and emotions and challenges romantic ideas of motherhood. It's not surprising that utopia eclipses reality for many who hear its call.

Because of its appeal, utopian thinking has also attracted many feminists as they, too, have sought to create a better world from a feminist perspective. Betty Friedan's 1963 classic, *The Feminine Mystique*, is a representative case. Despite its landmark status, the book has accumulated numerous detractors, who have called it variously classist, racist, and heterosexist. I would argue that many of those deficiencies actually resulted from Friedan's utopianism, which directed her toward certain conclusions without also directing her to consider the lives, experiences, and desires of women outside the group of middle-class white housewives she studied. Her problem was utopian myopia. For example, in exploring the "problem that has no name," Friedan proclaimed that a fulfilling career is the "only way for a woman, as for a man, to find herself, to know herself as a person" ([1963]1984, 344). Rather than focusing on the continuing need to manage households and raise children, Friedan predicted that domestic responsibilities would be whittled down to a manageable size once women abandoned their obsession with domesticity in favor of their significant careers.

Friedan's projection of one problem as *the* problem and her subsequent construction of a single life course for women as a group projects the characteristics of a part onto the whole, what logicians call a *metonymic fallacy*, which can easily infect utopian thinking. Some women became all women to Friedan. Also typical of utopianism is Friedan's disregard for possible unintended consequences of her prescribed social change. Thus, she both ignored working-class and poor women and women of color and overlooked the possible problems full-time careers might generate even for the middle-class white women who accepted her invitation to "have it all." The latter utopian oversight has produced perhaps the most egregious unintended consequence of all—the specter of Friedan's original readers' *daughters* still struggling to balance home and work almost forty years later.

It is tempting to think that more recent feminist theorizing, with its greater sophistication and more careful attention to matters of race, class, sexuality, and other markers of difference among women, has outgrown utopianism. Such a conclusion, however, is itself utopian, since only in utopia is the present or future necessarily an improvement over the past. *Higher Ground* argues that sensitivity to difference and other advances in feminist thinking have not, in fact, eliminated utopianism from feminist thought, nor have they obliterated its problematic influence. Today's utopianism, as we shall see, has its own characteristics and produces its own negative consequences. For example, recent ideas about differences among women sometimes both reify and idealize particular groups, demonize others, and privilege certain standpoints for knowledge. Although the locus of privilege has changed, those are traditional utopian ideas in modern dress.

THE UTOPIAN SELF

While they are not equivalent, utopian practice can, of course, produce utopianism, and vice versa. That is, fascination with utopian practices can easily lead to utopian thinking. I have made this transition myself, so I know its appeal as well as its pitfalls. Years ago, I became convinced that feminism could best be advanced by the wide-scale construction of kitchenless houses, connected in clusters to communal dining facilities. Such a model was one proposal of the domestic feminists of the 1920s, with whom Charlotte Perkins Gilman, also the author of numerous utopian fictional works, was associated. Not coincidentally, my conviction about the kitchenless house developed when I had two hungry toddlers hanging on my legs as I prepared dinner every evening, still dressed in the working-woman's clothes and shoes I had no time to change. I committed the metonymic fallacy of thinking that all women's "liberation" depended on the kind of change in domestic life that might appeal to certain professional women with small children.

My love of utopia had become utopianism. Like Friedan, I could not recognize the limits of my views. I might have been right about a particular solution for myself or a particular group of women, at least during a certain phase of life, just as Friedan was right to identify careers as one way for educated women to pursue self-fulfillment and contribute to society. But like Freidan I was wrong to think that my ideas were fundamental to feminism for all women—or even to my own life—for all time. Indeed, a kitchenless house did not appeal to me for very long and would now not suit me at all.

Such myopia translates into another utopian fallacy, the "present focus," which is the weak underside of the utopian genius for social critique. Social criticism is often perversely tied to the situation it analyzes. Even when social criticism is accurate it may not be comprehensive. Friedan's analysis of the "feminine mystique" was insightful, but it missed lots of women who were already working and overlooked the significance of many other factors besides the boredom of house-wives that produced women's unhappy lot in the 1950s and 1960s. Friedan needed to consider work structures, employment prospects, credit and wage policies, women's educational opportunities, the avail-ability of birth control and child care, cultural prohibitions against "unfeminine" behavior, and other aspects of 1963 society, many of which were as invisible to contemporary eyes as the "problem with no name." Likewise, my obsession with domestic architecture prevented me from seeing additional important factors contributing to women's (and even my own) role stress, such as androcentric work structures that ignore all workers' domestic responsibilities. Simply undoing or reversing the situations that we observe and critique can exacerbate rather than solve the larger problem of which they are a part.

That certain ideas once considered utopian are now commonplace in American life does not in and of itself obviate the pitfalls of utopi-anism. Women now have careers, serve in public office, and run busi-nesses, as many nineteenth-century feminist utopian writers imag-ined. Fast-food restaurants have rendered many an American house virtually kitchenless. But the assimilation of those once-utopian ideas does not necessarily reflect the triumph of utopianism as a thought process. Indeed, it may reflect the opposite, as such reforms often produce decidedly different outcomes—unintended consequences—than those their utopian planners might have envisioned. Domestic feminists did not have McDonald's takeout in mind when they pro-moted the kitchenless house. Nineteenth-century utopian fiction writ-ers supported women's participation in nontraditional careers as a way to establish gender justice, which that participation has not produced. By the same token, those writers did not anticipate the sexual harass-ment that has been such a common feature of women's experience in such jobs. In addition, there is no evidence that such "advances" in modern life actually reflect the influence of utopian ideas. Indeed, there are many more compelling explanations for their development in everyday life.

Despite these criticisms of utopianism, however, I do not intend to discourage feminist interest in utopian experiments or the thinkers who have conceptualized, fictionalized, or created idealized worlds. Nor do I want to prevent feminists from reflecting on and learn-ing from utopian designs. I believe that there is much to learn from utopias and utopianism (although not necessarily what utopists might intend). Throughout this book, I shall consider an ongoing tension between utopian desires and solutions and (an)other way(s) of conceptualizing feminist social change. Like other feminists, I cannot avoid entirely a utopian reflex response to certain issues: violence against women, rape, racist sexism, sexist racism, genital mutilation, the glass ceiling, the sticky floor, and even the tenure woes of women in my own profession. They evoke both my rage and my utopian rhetorical impulses: "If women were in charge, by God, none of this would happen." "Let's just lock up *all* the men and then watch the world improve." "Why can't we all just *get along?*" Occasionally, such invocations have some validity: a critical mass of women legislators *does* affect the policy emphasis of government. But the utopian strategies they represent seldom produce effective solutions. *Higher Ground* explores the utopian heritage in American feminist thought that prompts such reactions. It offers a perspective on that legacy that helps us understand its limits and hidden repercussions. It warns against relying too heavily upon utopianism in the formulation of feminist thought.

FROM UTOPIANISM TO HIGHER GROUND

Having rejected utopianism as the best approach to feminist theorizing—defined as the process of explaining and correcting women's symbolic deprecation and material disadvantages in most societies—*Higher Ground* seeks to define alternative ways of transforming ideas into social reality. Achieving higher ground entails recognizing that all plans for social change can harbor unforeseen consequences. On higher ground, no principle or ideology, including feminism, can be immune from scrutiny. Even our sacred ideals must be tested for their potential to backfire or to metamorphose into something quite unlike themselves—like those funny plastic transformer toys that turn from truck to robot with the twist of an axle. On higher ground, we must recognize that feminist wishes fulfilled can disappoint as well as satisfy.

The term that I have selected to capture the qualities of that higher ground for generating and enacting feminist thought is *realism*. I use it in full recognition of its long and conflicted history in a multitude of disciplines and social arenas, a history that I will explore more fully in chapter 5. Even my own utopian sensibilities bristle as I introduce the word. Yet I believe it is well chosen, not in opposition to *utopianism*, which would create a dualism more characteristic of utopian than of realistic thinking, but in contrast to it, a thought process that both converges with utopianism and diverges from it in significant ways. Thus, the realism developed in *Higher Ground* is post-utopian in the way of many other contemporary ideological "posts," such as "post-structuralism" and "postmodernism." That is, *realism* both builds upon and critiques *utopianism.* Post-utopian realism need not insist that people never dream or discuss "what if." Nor does it prescribe a single or simplistic view of human virtue or the existence of objective, undisputed reality. Rather, the realism in this book represents a framework for conceptual struggle, self-reflexive scrutiny, and ideological give-and-take within which plans for the future can be assessed. Instead of the utopian certainty of knowing, it *approaches* knowledge and welcomes revision.

For the purpose of comparing the two concepts, we can associate *utopianism* with the desire to improve the human condition through the invention of perfected social systems. Utopianism typically presents (or assumes) a paradigm deemed sufficient to the challenges of life's complexity. It articulates ideals, sometimes relentlessly, but unlike *idealism,* in the philosophical sense, it does not assume that thought alone constitutes truth or that ideas alone motivate or determine human behavior (Schmitt 1997, 63). It generally prefers massive to incremental change, rejecting rather than embracing the past. Utopianism often determines its own values in response to large-scale social trends or "evils." Urban consumerism inspired many nineteenth-century rural ascetic utopian communities, for example, while the concept of patriarchy has motivated much feminist utopian thought. A typical utopian response to evil, as we have seen, is reversal—from consumerism to asceticism, from patriarchy to matriarchy or female rule. Those reversals, in turn, institute large-scale values that also resist challenge.

Also stated simply, *realism,* though variously and sometimes conflictingly defined, puts less stock in principles and ideals alone; it interjects the complexities and vagaries of human action and interpretation into the functioning of abstractions. Legal realists, for example, believe that law exists more in judges' rulings than in legal codes and statutes. Realism sees that some truths lie beyond human comprehension; therefore, it regards uncertainty and contingency as inevitable and often valuable. If utopianism maps primarily uncharted territory, then realism functions mostly in the known, pluralistic, confusing, and inevitably imperfect world. It is immersed in history.

There are many ways to compare the two worldviews, and that comparison will occupy us throughout *Higher Ground.* A few are worth emphasizing, however. One is their different approaches to ideals. As we have seen, neither utopianism nor realism constitutes *idealism,* in which ideas and principles are considered sole or self-sufficient motivators of human behavior. But whereas utopianism selects ideals that then determine all human behavior through moral suasion, realism expects and even invites the surprising creative forces of human perceptions and behaviors that lie beyond social control to shape ideals. Thus a utopist is likely to make rules enforcing and preventing the infringement of predetermined ideals, while a realist typically constructs her ideals in response to innovations, forces, and circumstances that acknowledge human independence from and resistance to social manipulation. Realism, therefore, suggests a process of ideological-historical give-and-take.

Another important contrast between utopianism and realism involves their views of good and evil. Utopianism typically distinguishes between the two as separate forces, often on religious grounds, and imagines that evil can be fully isolated, confronted, and eliminated so that good can triumph. Realism, on the other hand, recognizes the confusing interconnection that often exists between the two, the maddening link between the forces that promote life and happiness on the one hand and those that destroy them on the other, like the life-producing human hormones that also fuel death-producing cancers.

Such differences motivate me to articulate the dangers of utopianism for feminist thought and theory. Seeing that human complexities must inform feminist analyses and incorporating within feminist thought the realistic interconnection between good and evil, friend and enemy, solution and problem are essential to formulating truly responsible and constructive political and personal ideologies and social-change strategies. Feminism needs to occupy that realistic but difficult higher ground if it is to flourish and endure.

Human beings' interaction with nature offer numerous instances of those complex connections. For me, the Jemez Mountains in New Mexico provide a compelling example. The Jemez have a long history as the home of the Anasazi, ancestors of modern Native American tribes, who built and carved shelters in the sandstone cliffs of Puyé and the Frijoles Canyon and eked crops from the sandy soil of the mesas above them. On a bright summer's day, as they stand tan and deep green soaking up the southwestern sun, the Jemez beckon visitors to enjoy their trails and streams and to ponder the lives of their ancient inhabitants.

At dusk, the mountains seem quite romantic, as the setting sun behind them spreads a purple stain on the eastern slope. Particularly alluring is the strand of tiny lights that appears partway up the center peak, defining a tilted mesa. All illusions of romance are shattered, however, when the viewer realizes that those lights define the road to Los Alamos, birthplace of the atom bomb and home, since the 1940s, to weapons' research operations of the United States government. Then the mountains' sun-soaked daytime mantle and purple evening cloak are revealed as camouflage for the production of man-made agents of destruction. Robert Oppenheimer, who had vacationed in New Mexico as a child, understood that function of the Jemez landscape when he selected the site for the secret Manhattan Project.

Utopian sensibilities are horrified by modern man's introduction of destructive forces into the mountains' wooded landscape and near-sacred Indian terrain at Puyé and Bandelier. They recoil in horror at the defilement of the ancestral homes of today's Keres-speaking peoples of the Cochiti, Santo Domingo, and San Felipe pueblos. But that sense of the mountains' desecration by Los Alamos, understandable as it is, coveniently overlooks other important realities about the Jemez. That is, the mountains have always been the site—both simultaneously and by turns—of the inseparable forces of good and evil, splendor and destruction, protection and danger. The land that once sustained the Anasazi also somehow failed them, forcing them to abandon their craggy settlements some four hundred years ago. Perhaps the once-friendly climate changed, or the once-fertile soil lost its nutrients; today's anthropologists can only speculate. Equally possible, the rocks and forests that once protected them from their human enemies may eventually have sheltered and hidden invading tribes that finally drove the Anasazi from their dwellings (Hoard 1983, 3).

Stripped of utopian lenses, we must see that even before the bombs that horrify us, tension between forces of nurturance and destruction had long shaped the history of the Jemez, in the natural cycles of storm and drought, the perils of flood, snakebite, and avalanche, and the human conflicts among the groups cohabiting there. Those alternating forces have coexisted for millennia with the mountains' beauty and historical significance. Realistic feminist thinking must recognize similar inherent contradictions and conflicts at the core of its issues and goals. We ignore those contradictions at our peril, constricting our purview and reducing the value of our analyses.

Although feminist thought has long been compatible with utopianism, it does not need utopianism to flourish. Indeed, as this book endeavors to explain, without utopianism feminist thought and theory can more easily embrace its mission and celebrate its diversity. It need not pretend, as utopianism sometimes does, that all problems can be named and solved and all evils identified and exorcized. Without utopianism feminism can more readily recognize contingent truths, inevitable conflicts, and complex motivations and loyalties, as it addresses the problems it can name. Realistic feminist thought can embrace the serendipity and vagaries of human life, identity, relationships, and institutions. It can avoid exclusivist or separatist metaphors and replace them with tropes of coexistence. It can embrace self-criticism and ideological tension. It need not risk utopianism's proclivity for idealization, demonization, and false dichotomies. It need not breed the disappointment that inevitably results from unfulfilled utopian promises and unrealized utopian ideals.

In short, *Higher Ground* argues that, without utopianism, feminism becomes a richer and more dynamic system of thought. It allows the continual interplay of simultaneously held but diverse and sometimes contradictory "truths" about women's lives and the concept of gender, gender differences, equality in the face of difference, difference in the face of equality, and scores of similar contingencies.

Happily, the vast body of contemporary feminist thought and theory already contains an array of alternatives to utopian thinking: in work that acknowledges the inevitability of change without deprecating the past; tolerates, even welcomes, ambiguity; insists on subjecting first principles to continual scrutiny; recognizes the limitations of language and the complexity of meaning; and takes controversy as the starting point for knowledge and understanding. It is the task of this book to identify and analyze such realistic feminist thought as it also investigates implicit and explicit utopianism in other writings. The critique of feminist thought and theory that follows is dedicated to the proposition that feminist theory can function as the "head" rather than merely the "arm" of the women's movement and that a good head on its shoulders constitutes the best insurance that the feminist corpus—multiaxial, multilobular, and multiloquent as it rightly is—will stay healthy for many years to come.

CRITIC OR DETRACTOR?

Although *Higher Ground* can properly be labeled a critique of feminist thought and theory, it should not therefore be identified with the host of feminist detractors who have come out of the woodwork in the last two decades, determined to discredit feminism itself (or its corollary, women's studies). Their names are legion: Camille Paglia, Christina Hoff Sommers, Germaine Greer, Daphne Patai, even Betty Friedan. Each in her way has found in feminist ideas or practice an evil (once hidden from her) that is so abhorrent it can only be eradicated by the eradication of feminism itself. And each, in her way, has committed the metonymic fallacy of finding her own analysis so compelling that it overcomes all other depictions of feminism.

For example, after producing a 1970 feminist classic, *The Female Eunuch,* Greer decided in 1984 that the sexual freedom she once touted was a mistake and suggested that women revisit the model of the peasant wife, confined to home and hidden from public view. In 1990, Greer criticized her own mother (as a symbol of other devouring mothers) for emasculating her father, who was consequently largely absent from her life. Also in 1990, Paglia declared that feminists had become whiners who missed the fact that women haven't really accomplished much for civilization. She claimed that date rape was feminist nonsense and that feminists had overlooked the key life force of traditional heterosexual relationships. (Her real complaint may have been with feminists who had not sufficiently recognized her talents.) In 1994, Sommers (whose work is funded by conservative groups like the Olin Foundation) accused the "homely" women in women's studies of getting revenge for their poor chances in the marriage marketplace by blaming men and deploring sex. She identified as "gender feminists" anyone who thinks that women are not as free as democratic rhetoric leads us to believe we are.[1]

Patai and her coauthor, Noretta Koertge, also chose 1994 as the moment to condemn all of women's studies because of the arrogant moral certainty displayed by certain "students who stomp in seminars" and demand "political purity" from their professors (1994, 13, 17). Their *Professing Feminism: Cautionary Tales from Inside the Strange World of Women's Studies,* like many such critiques, both identifies important issues and exaggerates and demonizes them. In their case, the methodology is so poor it is difficult to judge the significance of their observations. They based their condemnation on anonymous anecdotes from people allegedly connected with the field—only about

1. For a discussion of these and other feminist detractors, see Susan Faludi (1991) *Backlash: The Undeclared War against American Women,* 318–24. See also Christina Hoff Sommers's *Who Stole Feminism? Women Who Betrayed Women* (1994); Betty Friedan's *The Second Stage* (1981); Germaine Greer's *Sex and Destiny* (1984) and *Daddy, We Hardly Knew You* (1990).

thirty in all. Sommers also makes extravagant claims based on minimal or distorted information (Hirschman 1994).

In a dramatic reversal, Betty Friedan led the way for this spate of feminist denouncement with her book *The Second Stage* (1981), in which she replaced her 1963 focus on the "feminine mystique" with a swipe at the "feminist mystique." She criticized feminism for overlooking important intrinsic differences between men and women and for overemphasizing women's rights rather than recognizing the greater challenge of establishing better intimate and familial relationships. (Like Paglia, Friedan may have sought a kind of revenge on feminists who, along with the media, had largely ignored her after her retirement from NOW in 1970.)

My critique of utopianism in feminist thought and theory falls into a category different from these examples. It does not constitute a condemnation of the universe of feminism (a metonymic fallacy in and of itself). That I find something to criticize does not suggest that I believe feminism or feminist thinking has failed altogether. I seek feminism's refinement, not its obliteration.

THE BOOK'S ORGANIZATION

Higher Ground pursues three large and, by some measures, overwhelming topics—feminist thought, utopianism, and realism. To reduce these topics to reasonable proportions and bring them into meaningful juxtaposition with one another, I have developed several organizational and analytical strategies in *Higher Ground*.

One is the grouping of selections from contemporary feminist theoretical texts into three major categories. The grouping is not meant to suggest that the categories are mutually exclusive but rather to highlight characteristics of contemporary feminist thought that are particularly susceptible to the hazards of utopian thinking.

The first category, the discourse of gender difference, includes various theories about the putative differences between the sexes and/or about particular characteristics typically associated with maleness and femaleness, masculinity and femininity. Feminist gender difference theories, like their misogynist counterparts, can easily exploit romanticized or demonized concepts of the sexes and can easily fall prey to the temptation to overlook differences within each sex category. Thus feminist gender difference theories are susceptible to utopian assumptions about the differences they mean to prove.

The second category, the discourse of differences among women, addresses distinctions among women because of race, ethnicity, class, sexuality, and other characteristics. Like the previous category, this discourse often imputes idealized characteristics and particular powers to one category or another, generally in response to unfair hierarchies or the erasure of differences. But sometimes the cure is worse than the disease. Identity politics and epistemic privilege are two utopian theories within the discourse of differences that (paradoxically) can obscure rather than illuminate particularity among women.

The third category, the discourse of linguistic construction, includes but is not limited to postmodern theories of sexuality and gender that emphasize the controlling power of language to the exclusion of all else. Within this discourse, some theorists claim that gender itself is simply a linguistic construction. At that point utopianism infuses works in this category by reducing the complexities of gender and sexuality to their discursive characteristics alone.

Another strategy for managing the large themes of *Higher Ground* is the organization of the book into four parts, which, by turns, define and apply the analytical categories of utopianism and realism. Part I, "The Utopian Roots of American Feminism," explores the utopian context within which American feminist theorizing has evolved. It contains two chapters that demonstrate feminism's close ties to utopianism. Chapter 1, "The American Utopian Landscape," presents a brief and selective history of utopianism in Western thought, American intellectual history, and the settlement of the North American continent. While tracing a general utopian heritage in the United States, the chapter highlights examples of hidden boomerangs, ironies, and occasional tragedies, especially for women, within the American utopian experimental and theoretical legacy. Chapter 2, "Feminist Utopias," surveys the three-hundred-year history of feminist utopian fiction, starting with French *précieux* novels of the seventeenth century but focusing primarily on trends in and selections from American novels of the nineteenth and twentieth centuries. As with utopian experiments, fictional utopias have offered feminists many appealing models, but they have also entailed certain paradoxes and limitations that must enter into any assessment of feminism's fascination with utopianism. In addition, chapter 2 explores the utopianism inherent in much feminist criticism of that fiction, which has created a kind of sacred space for utopian visions in feminist theory. Both chapters 1 and 2 also explore the particular pitfalls of utopianism, especially for feminist thought.

Part II, "Utopianism in Feminist Thought and Theory," moves the analysis from explicit to implicit utopianism. Chapter 3, "Detecting Utopianism," focuses on general utopian analyses in feminist thought, including the idealization and romanticization of both women and women's groups and the quest for feminist purity. Chapter 3 also explores certain epistemological flaws that characterize utopian thought, including foundationalism, confirmation bias, and the myth of the truth teller. Chapter 4, "Utopian Discourses," analyzes specific examples of feminist utopian thought within the three discourses—gender difference, differences among women, and linguistic construction. Of particular concern are utopian constructions such as enforced gender dichotomy, identity politics, epistemic privilege, and performativity.

Part III, "Toward Higher Ground: Realism in Feminist Thought and Theory," is composed of two chapters that define and apply realism as a concept for feminist theorizing. Chapter 5, "Searching for Realism," introduces the concept of realism in various disciplines and defines more specifically the term's meaning for feminist theory. Chapter 6, "Toward Realistic Feminist Discourse," applies the concept of realism to feminist theorizing in the three categories—gender difference, differences among women, and linguistic construction of gender. Chapter 6 also offers substitutes for utopian constructions, such as a body-based/social constructionist theory of motherhood, theories of coalition that accommodate the "internal multiplicity" of individuals, and theories that link material and discursive constructions of sexuality and gender.

Part IV, "Beyond Feminism," concludes the book with chapter 7, "Confronting the Culture of Utopia." Chapter 7 discusses the hidden utopianism that shapes the controversies surrounding today's "culture wars" and debates over "political correctness" in both society at large and higher education. Chapter 7 also analyzes the Promise Keepers as an organization whose utopianism actually undermines its goals. The chapter ends by formulating strategies for a realistic feminist approach to social change.

I THE UTOPIAN ROOTS OF AMERICAN FEMINISM

"No, lad, we aren't movers. We're just Shakers."

INTRODUCTION

S o much about America's utopian heritage is captured in this little
cartoon. A child from "the world" instantly knows a Shaker when
he sees one, chipping away at a simple, elegant table, against a background of equally simple, elegant chairs hanging on the wall. The
Shaker himself is familiar enough with "the world" to recognize the
pun embedded in the question the child has apparently asked him. He
also seems to take enough pleasure in being his kind of Shaker not
to want to be the world's kind of mover. At the same time, the cartoon pokes ironic fun at the confusion in the American collective
consciousness, represented by the naïve young boy, between a group
called "Shakers," which exists apart from mainstream life, and the
"movers and shakers" who presumably drive the engines of American
politics and commerce. We smile because we know that, although
their names may sound the same, the Shakers of the furniture and
boxes have little in common with the (movers and) shakers on Capi-
tol Hill or Wall Street.

To me, this cartoon reveals a utopian core at the heart of American
life while also exposing the culture's careless misunderstanding of
utopianism's deeper meaning. The cartoon suggests that, like many
appropriations in American popular culture, the motivations and values of utopian commitment are easily co-opted as sound bites and
puns. At the same time, however, it illustrates that Americans treasure
and identify with a utopian heritage that continues to shape our understanding of ourselves and our society.

American feminists have shared in the American utopian heritage, in both our political strategies and our literary imaginations. But, in the spirit of the cartoon, that legacy has created some confusion. Lost on many of us, as on the boy in the cartoon, are important—even crucial—distinctions between the lure of utopia and the realities that must concern us.

The chapters in this part of *Higher Ground* survey various characteristics and examples of both the American utopian heritage and the American feminist utopian heritage. Chapter 1, "The American Utopian Landscape," suggests how utopianism has infused Americans' self-concepts through an incomparable record of experimental communities that have flourished on American soil. It also defines utopianism as a mode of thought and compares it to realism as an alternative way of approaching social change. Chapter 2, "Feminist Utopias," explores three hundred years of feminist utopian fiction, with an emphasis on nineteenth- and twentieth-century American works. It also discusses utopianism in feminist critical responses to that fiction.

Without attempting to present a complete history, these chapters provide specific examples of utopian thought, utopian experiments, and utopian imaginative texts that illustrate the potent American utopian legacy affecting us all, especially feminists. These chapters also introduce and analyze both the appeal and the hazards of the utopian thinking which underlies that legacy.

ONE   *The American Utopian Landscape*

Among the Shakers none are overworked, and none ever want a day's labour; none live in luxury, and no man, or woman, or child, lacks anything.
—John Finch, quoted in *Shaker Furniture: The Craftsmanship of an American Communal Sect*

One should see, as I did, the Shaker community at Canterbury, New Hampshire, on a glorious day in early summer. From the visitors' center, the land tumbles down a slope in voluptuous contours, contained, in true Shaker form, by a pristine white board fence that organizes grass, trees, houses, and the fields beyond into an ordered, utilitarian grid. Large clapboard buildings hug the landscape with the famous Shaker sense of proportion that allows structures larger than ordinary houses nevertheless to exude hominess and warmth from their shuttered, multipaned windows and inviting doorways. The scene suggests a godlike cleanliness, peace, harmony, and domesticity. To breathe the morning air is to inhale Shaker values: order, integrity, balance, spirituality, communality. To see what the human hand can do not to dominate but to complement nature is to understand the Shaker principle of work as God's love made manifest, as well as the Shaker quest to live according to the heavenly order.

My own deeply felt response to the Shakers is by no means unique. Many people who have observed Shaker communities, furniture, tools, and believers (either in person or through their writings) during the group's more than two-hundred-year history have felt respect and even awe for the Shaker way of life. To observers like John Finch, writing in 1844, the communities' "neatness, cleanliness and order . . . and the cheerfulness and contented looks of the people" suggested social perfection (Andrews and Andrews 1964, 56–57). Since the earliest days of the nineteenth century, scores of artists and writers and thousands of ordinary working Americans have appreciated, if not emulated, the Shaker gifts of celibacy, simplicity, utility, and spiritual surrender as antidotes to the vainglory, bustle, and complexity of ordinary American life. The list of distinguished visitors to and observers of Shaker communities includes Presidents James Monroe and Andrew Jackson, Charles Dickens, Secretary of War Edwin Stanton, New Harmony founder Robert Dale Owen, and other American utopists, such as Martha McWhirter of the Woman's Commonwealth. Shaker publications were translated into many languages, including Russian and German. Leo Tolstoy corresponded with Shaker Elder Frederick Evans at the end of the nineteenth century. Shaker doctrine and lore influenced literary works by William Dean Howells, Nathaniel Hawthorne, Catherine Sedgwick, and Herman Melville (Andrews 1963, 221).

As the best known and perhaps most successful of the hundreds of utopian experimental communities in the United States over the last two centuries, the Shakers have captivated Americans and Europeans as an example of what a sense of order, adherence to principle, and commitment to spiritual communality can do for human society. Far in excess of their numbers, the Shakers have inspired generations of Americans with the fruits of their labors in God's vineyards: artifacts in which the unity of form and function constitute art. Even today, I suspect that more Americans can identify a Shaker box or rocking chair than can name the Justices of the Supreme Court.

America's love affair with the Shakers, then, is a good place to begin the process of analyzing *utopianism*—the mind-sets, attitudes, assumptions, and goals associated with utopian social-change strategies —as it intersects with the activities of *utopists* (those who start or participate in utopian experiments) and with *utopias* (the actual or fictional communities established on utopian principles). Starting with an enduring utopian community like the Shakers enables us to see utopia's appeal. There is much to like about Shaker dreams of spiritual perfection (a term they favored) and desire to create a social system that would help human beings avoid sin and pursue life's fundamental values. Such utopian visions do help humanity escape the prison of today, construct tomorrow with intentionality, and seize control of human destiny (Manuel 1966, ix–xxi). They promise to replace societies that have grown haphazardly with those designed specifically for producing the good life (Walsh 1962, 57). Utopian visions are also a form of social protest, since they typically react to current, unsatisfactory social conditions—sin, materialism, injustice. They present positive alternatives to such conditions. As the Northampton (Massachusetts) community's constitution explained, "'It is impossible to survey the present condition of the world . . . without perceiving [that] the great evils that afflict humanity . . . [are] the direct consequences of existing social arrangements'" (quoted in Kesten 1993, 28). Northamptoners dedicated their community, which lasted only from 1842 to 1846, to improving education and eliminating sectarianism, war, government corruption, and the tyranny of religion (ibid., 32). Since the real world is so flawed, why should we not applaud those who dream of and establish a better one?

AMERICA AS UTOPIA

The appeal of such utopian approaches is even more understandable in the context of American history. Indeed, the United States itself was once touted as a utopia, and various portions of it, like California and the mineral-rich West, were actually advertised as utopias from the 1840s through the 1930s. Certain American suburbs were designed and marketed as utopias as recently as the 1950s. The great seal of the United States, *Novus Ordo Seclorum*— a new order of the ages— also reflects a kind of utopian mission. Many immigrants to the United States still regard their new country as a utopian retreat from the persecutions and poverty of the old, wherever it was. Even if they no longer expect American streets to be paved with gold, aspiring immigrants endure the harsh conditions they face here because they expect better things to come.

From the fifteenth century on, European exploration of the North American continent was often based on utopian promise. Spanish explorers of the sixteenth century were certain they would find untold riches and even the fountain of youth in the New World. Cortez's minions marched through what is now New Mexico, perilously close to the Jemez Mountains, in search of hidden cities of gold. White European settlers of the American northeast intended their new homes to represent a new beginning for human society. In 1614 John Smith compared the New England coast to Eden. John Cotton compared land charters in the New World to "the grand charter given to Adam and his posterity in Paradise" (Eliade 1966, 265). Settlers of the Massachusetts Colony expected New England to be "the place where the Lord will create a new Heaven and a new Earth" (Hinds 1973, v–vi).

It is not surprising, therefore, that a substantial number of eighteenth- and nineteenth-century Europeans fleeing persecution, seeking a better life, or waiting to welcome Christ's second appearance chose American soil as an ideal site for locating experimental communities (Hinds 1973, v–vi). One of those was the Society of Believers in Christ's Second Appearing, known as the Shakers. A small band of Believers arrived from England on the shores of New England and settled in upstate New York in 1774, a year after their leader, Ann Lee, was divinely inspired to relocate the group to America. For the Shakers, the new land represented an opportunity to establish on their own terms a heavenly order on earth, just as it had for the Labadists, Pietists, and the Ephratans who preceded them.

American citizens have also organized utopian communities, having been inspired, perhaps, by utopian immigrants as well as by their own recognition that the American dream was as yet unfulfilled. Among them were Bronson Alcott and Charles Lane, who founded Fruitland, Massachusetts, in 1843; John Humphrey Noyes, who founded the New York Oneida Community in 1848; and Frances Wright, who founded Nashoba in Tennessee in 1825.[1] The utopian urge did not stop with the nineteenth century, however. It surged again in the twentieth century, inflamed by the social upheavals of the late 1960s and 1970s, which reintroduced the familiar sense that America had not yet fulfilled its promises. By then, longtime Americans were the ones establishing self-contained experimental communities such as Twin Oaks in Virginia and Walden Three in Rhode Island, as well as such lesbian separatist communities as Adobeland, Silver Circle, and Green Hope Farm. Although some of these communities have lasted twenty years or more, most, like their nineteenth-century predecessors, survived only a few years. But many of the themes driving their sometimes conflicting pathways to an authentic

1. Oneida was by far the most long-lived of this group of communities. Noyes first organized a community in Putney, Vermont, in 1840, and moved his Perfectionists to Lenox, New York, in 1848. The community developed several branches, including one at Wallingford, Connecticut, founded in 1851. There were 288 members in 1880 (Kanter 1972, 246). In 1881, the community was reorganized into a joint-stock company known as Oneida Community Limited. It exists today as an industry known as Oneida Limited. Frances Wright was born in Scotland, but came to the United States as a child.

American dream are surprisingly similar to those of previous centuries: sexual reform, celibacy, communism, and vegetarianism.

Contributing to America's utopian associations was the influence of Native American culture, hidden as that influence may be in white Europeans' version of American history. Indian ideas of democracy and women's political and economic rights were not identified in and of themselves as utopian, but their existence in this "virgin" land convinced some European newcomers, including women, that the land itself must somehow embody and support such values, which were almost unthinkable on European soil. Democratic ideas had traveled to Europe, along with Indian tobacco, peanuts, and corn, long before massive European emigration to the "New World." Thomas More was influenced by the democratic constitution of the Iroquois Confederacy in the composition of his *Utopia*, as was John Locke, who extracted from it some of his own views of tolerance, natural equality, and women's rights. Early historians of the New World were impressed with Native American ideas of liberty, as well as with the absence from their societies of crime, jails, and greed, which were all too familiar in Europe. The colonists' ideas for confederation, as well as for the eventual Constitution of the United States (and even later, the United Nations charter), were clearly influenced by Native American practices, especially those of the Iroquois, whether or not those practices were thoroughly understood. Benjamin Franklin's Albany Plan of Union, for example, reflects years of talking with Indian leaders and of planning for confederation. European settlers were also impressed with the combination in Indian democratic tradition of fierce individualism and concern for community (Johansen 1982, 13–20; Jacobs 1992, 188). Indeed, the new nation chose the Iroquois symbol of the bald eagle to illustrate the Latin motto on its great seal. Clutching a bundle of arrows, the Iroquois eagle also appears on dollar bills, recalling in that guise a 1775 meeting between the Twelve United Colonies and the Iroquois, as well as the Iroquois Confederacy's Great Law and the unity of the Iroquois confederacy (Grinde and Johansen 1991, xxi).

The suffrage movement also owes a debt to Native American democratic practices and ideals. Both Matilda Joslyn Gage and Elizabeth Cady Stanton found inspiration for their principles of gender equity and women's sovereign control of their own lives in the practices of the Six Nations of the Iroquois Confederacy, the Haudenasaunee, whose lives they studied in upstate New York during and before the 1870s. Gage was even adopted into the Wolf Clan of the Mohawk nation

(Wagner 1992, 118–20). Among the Iroquois, suffragists observed the equal division of power between the sexes, the primacy of the mother-child bond (in contrast to white women's disqualification from legal custody of their children), the intolerance of rape, and women's freedoms within marriage, among other egalitarian practices. Indeed, Iroquois women actually feared the prospect of American citizenship because they knew they would lose such rights and status (ibid., 123–25). The Iroquois influence also inspired feminist utopian thinking; Gage and Stanton equated women's rights with an American legacy more compelling than their own European heritage, whose laws and practices denied women's political and economic rights. Through the Iroquois, America itself seemed to promise gender justice.

In addition to basic principles of democracy and sexual equality, Native American religious views about their homeland could well have influenced utopian European reformers who came to American shores. Whereas European Christians saw Eden as a lost haven waiting to be regained *somewhere else,* Native American tribes believed that they already occupied "Eden," that the North American continent was the perfect land for which the gods had intended them. Discovering that Native American belief might have reinforced the Europeans' idea that they had come to the right place to find the perfection they had lost, even as they ignored Indians' rights to the continued occupation of that land for themselves or appropriated Native American cultures for their own, rather than Indian, purposes (Grinde and Johansen 1991, xviii).

That some utopists clearly looked to Native Americans for utopian inspiration is supported by the fact that a few utopian societies attempted to initiate contact with nearby tribes, which, in turn, were attracted to the spiritual qualities of such groups. Among the societies that sought Indian contact were the Shakers, who fashioned some of their more expressive modes of worship during a phase in their history called "Mother's Work" on Indian dances and ceremonies they had witnessed. Shaker documents attribute spiritual wisdom to Native Americans, especially those who recognized the divinity of Ann Lee, and record several contacts with various groups. Several Shakers visited a tribe of Shawnees at Greenville, Ohio, in 1807, for example. They were "kindly received," but no Indians "were gathered into the Shaker society" (Andrews 1963, 90).

European Americans soon had to concede that America was not utopia and that Christ was not going to make a second appearance to those who awaited him. At the same time, the Europeans' arrival had destroyed whatever hopes for utopia the Native Americans had for their land. Nevertheless, the utopian theme did not disappear from the American national identity. Instead it adapted itself. Rather than touting the United States as a paradise waiting to be discovered, more seasoned Europeans began to portray their new home as a potential paradise whose realization depended on human effort and hard work. Jonathan Edwards, for example, urged his followers to transform their pioneer millenarianism into a motivation for a progressive life on earth, not just in the hereafter.

Towns were named *New* York and *New* Haven not only to express nostalgia for settlers' roots but also to convey the promise of genuine novelty through human endeavor, of more beauty and success than the colonists had known in the exhausted urban centers of their pasts. Later still, in the nineteenth century, the Western frontier offered a utopian alternative to the sins and vices of the city, which by then had replaced Europe as a signifier of aristocracy, luxury, and vice-ridden culture. In more recent times, the notion of the frontier has been replaced by the myth of unrelenting progress and the cult of novelty and youth, which promises a return to lost innocence (Eliade 1966, 265–68).

As we have seen, echoes of the American utopian heritage reverberate today, despite the realities of unequal economic and social opportunity in the United States. The harsh realities of life for immigrants, despite their continued utopian optimism, strike many Americans as doubly disappointing precisely because of the utopian symbolism the United States still enjoys. America promises utopia, and its failure to realize that promise makes its sins seem much worse than bigger sins seem in other places. Where the promise is greatest, so too is the potential for disillusionment.

THE WESTERN UTOPIAN HERITAGE

The historical moment during which the American colonies were occupied by white Europeans undoubtedly contributed to the nation's utopian associations. By the seventeenth century, a collective Western utopian consciousness had been more than two thousand years in the making, starting with the depictions of New Jerusalem by Hebrew prophets, the utopian visions of Plato and Aristotle, and Christianity's vision of a heavenly kingdom, achievable only after death, which combined the Jewish land of milk and honey, Plato's vision of the Ideal realm of the Soul, and Isaiah's apocalyptic vision (Johnson 1968, 87–

90). Perhaps the clearest articulation of that Christian vision was St. Augustine's fifth-century (C.E.) *The City of God,* in which the struggle between human sinfulness and selfishness on the one hand and heavenly beatitude on the other is conceptualized as a contrast between two social organizations. Fallen Rome represented to Augustine the end of man's [*sic*] hope for utopia on earth, based on political and economic principles (ibid., 87–90). To replace Roman ideals, man must found the City of God in which the Christian love of God takes precedence over the love of self (Merton 1950, xii–xiii). Augustine's use of the social metaphor in portraying God's vision of perfection demonstrates the depth of the utopian impulse in the Western imagination.

While the Middle Ages produced some utopian texts by various Crusaders, as well as the work of Dante, the real flowering of the utopian literary form in Europe occurred during the Renaissance, from 1400 to 1700. Examples from that period include Sir Philip Sidney's *Arcadia,* Edmund Spenser's *The Faerie Queene,* Shakespeare's Forest of Arden in *As You Like It,* Francis Bacon's Platonic legend in *New Atlantis,* John Bunyan's restatement of New Jerusalem in *Pilgrim's Progress,* and John Milton's synthesis of classical, humanist, and Christian thought in *Paradise Lost* (Johnson 1968, 131–34).[2]

In 1516 Sir Thomas More published his *Utopia,* thereby coining the term that would ever afterward denote humanity's quest for ideal social conditions. More's term combines *eutopia,* meaning a good place, with *outopia,* meaning no place, and suggests that the perfect society, while imaginable, does not exist (Sullivan 1983, 32). Explicit utopianism was, therefore, originally a literary and philosophical genre rather than a practice. European settlement of America would change that, however, as social planners heeded the call of the abundant lands of the so-called New World and braved numerous hazards for the chance to effect their plans.

More's *Utopia* is a complex work that embodies both the template of utopian invention and its ironic possibilities. More ruminates on the benefits and hazards of a society predicated on "natural reason" rather than on the divine law to which he himself was deeply devoted. Therefore, recent scholarship has questioned the degree to which More took seriously his idealized society (Ackroyd 1998, 168)—although there is

2. Christine de Pisan's *The Book of the City of Ladies* (1404–5), though suggestively titled, is not really a utopian work, but rather a list of women's virtues and a defense against misogynist attacks on women by Jean de Meun and Matheolus in the thirteenth and fourteenth centuries. She was a champion of women, but she did not advocate structural social changes (Gottlieb 1997, 294). Her City was not a utopian vision.

little doubt that later utopians were quite serious in pursuing their own versions of such societies. More's Epicurean philosophical interests led him to associate life's material pleasures, such as food, clothing, and housing, with philosophical pleasures and justice (Surtz 1967, 390–91). In that tradition, pleasure is natural, involves no pain, and entails no loss of greater pleasure or social harm. More was also influenced by other philosophies, however, including that of Plato. Thus, his utopia is communistic and egalitarian, offering the best of life to all, not just the wealthy. In that tradition Utopians support marriage, euthanasia, sexual equality, and education (ibid.). But More's views were not constructed purely of "pagan" philosophical influences. So he may have taken these natural, pre-Christian pleasures just far enough to reveal their troubling consequences (Ackroyd 1998, 169). He seemed, for example, to distrust communism's ability to motivate people without the prospect of individual gain (Sullivan 1983, 32–33). And because he was a onetime monk, it is unlikely that More himself supported euthanasia.

By the eighteenth century, when white European Christians were eyeing North America as a utopian preserve, the world picture had changed. As they imagined their perfect societies, the Neoclassicists of the eighteenth century were responding to the Reformation, the Counter-Reformation, French and Swedish nationalistic wars, vicious commercial rivalries, and the Cromwell era, to name only a few horrors. Inevitably, they were more discouraged about human nature than their Renaissance forebears had been. Thus, instead of ideological abstractions, such thinkers stressed *institutions* as curbs on the foolishness and selfishness of mankind: "Instead of hoping for perfection, they settled for workable improvements" (Johnson 1968, 192). The writings of Hobbes (*Leviathan,* 1651), Swift (*Gulliver's Travels,* 1726), Voltaire (*Candide,* 1759), and Samuel Johnson (*Rasselas, Prince of Abyssinia,* 1759) represented such views, as did the philosophies of both the American and French Revolutions, which promised to replace tyrannies with working utopian systems composed of ideal institutions and laws (ibid., 220–21).

AMERICAN UTOPIAN THOUGHT AND PRACTICE

By the nineteenth century, when the majority of American experimental utopian communities emerged and when utopian literature flourished in the United States, a more Romantic view prevailed, although an emphasis on human institutions continued to replace visions of a faraway or heavenly home. Even such religious groups as the Mormons and the Mennonites believed that God's blessing could be earned through earthly pursuits, such as living and working together and sharing both goods and faith (Johnson 1968, 220–21). The increasing importance of science in the nineteenth century influenced utopian visions in many forms, from Marx's economic determinism to the Darwinist visions of Edward Bellamy (*Looking Backward*, 1888) and (somewhat later) Charlotte Perkins Gilman (*Herland*, 1915), in which a perfected—more highly evolved—human race was credited with creating perfected, more highly evolved societies.

The century also produced a few utopian resisters to ideas of collectivity and the benefits of technology and science, however. Among them was Henry David Thoreau, who considered the truly free individual, rather than any imaginable form of social organization, as the premise of a genuine utopia (Johnson 1968, 267–71). Thoreau's version of an American utopia was based on individual liberty to "'pursue such a mode of life as may enable you to do without [goods and services], and where the state does not endeavour to compel you to sustain the slavery, and war, and other superfluous expenses which directly or indirectly result from the use of such things'" (quoted in Frye 1966, 47).

Among the most influential of the nineteenth-century literary utopias was Edward Bellamy's *Looking Backward, 2000–1887*, published in 1888. Bellamy's vision exemplifies the utopian novel as social commentary, with a focus on the shortcomings of the present age as seen through the more intelligent perceptual and analytical powers of people in the future. The novel identifies communism as the catalyst for human improvement and credits a change in mind-set, the realization that rethinking the necessities of food, clothing, and shelter as a collective rather than an individual issue would remove the anxiety that had attended their procurement in all previous ages. "Ceasing to be predatory in their habits, [human beings] became coworkers, and found in fraternity, at once, the science of wealth and happiness," Bellamy proclaimed ([1888] 1968, 236). From the perspective of a more communal age, all previous eras, especially the nineteenth-century present, are revealed as cesspools of poverty, selfishness, class stratification, immorality, greed, and antisocial brutality, all of which have resulted from "the old social and industrial system, which taught [men] to view their natural prey in their fellow-men, and find their gain in the loss of others" (ibid., 231).

Thus, the novel reinforces a theme becoming typical of utopianism in its era: human barbarity should be attributed not to the essential evils of human nature or to original sin but to unfavorable environments. Bellamy compared the stunted humanity of the nineteenth century to a rosebush trying to grow in a bog and producing, therefore, only a few sickly buds. What else could men [*sic*] do, in conditions comparable to those in the Black Hole of Calcutta, but scramble for material goods at the expense of their fellows ([1888] 1968, 233, 238)?

Bellamy was among those utopian writers who believed that a scientific approach to human society would produce the best results (Shklar 1966, 108). Many experimental communities reflected similar scientific views, which did not replace but, rather, complemented their religious interests. Indeed, religious concerns often inspired scientific experiment, as they did for the Shakers, who perceived a seamless compatibility between their spiritual mission and their invention of dozens of technical devices, including machines for turning broom handles, printing bags and labels, cutting leather, basket making, and washing clothes (Andrews 1963, 113). Once established, such groups frequently redefined their religious mission in quasi-Enlightenment terms, as an obligation to comprehend God's intentions for humankind, to use the God-given tools of reason and experimentation, and to apply human understanding in a social order.

The Amanans, for example, came to America for religious reasons, inspired by Christian Metz's 1842 divine revelation that the United States should be the new home for his German group (Nordhoff [1875] 1966, 25). That spiritual beginning in Ebenezer, New York, led eventually to the manufacture of Amana freezers and microwave ovens. Women utopian writers of the nineteenth century, who tended to focus less on public policy and technology than men writers of the same era, also applied reason and supposedly scientific principles to the task of designing social systems for the fulfillment of human potential—an aspect of God's supposed plan that women were so often denied. That no female Thoreau emerged may reflect women's greater commitment to communitarian than to individualistic utopian visions (Kessler 1984, 6–7).

Many Americans shared the view, proffered by the newly forming social sciences, that microcosmic communities could be a viable approach to social change in a newly, and somewhat brutally, industrialized America. The plethora of experimental communities in nineteenth-century America can be explained, in part, by the widespread acceptance of that idea. Such communities appeared to address the country's labor and land settlement problems. Those utopian hopes dimmed considerably by the last quarter of the century, although the Great Depression of the 1930s revived them somewhat in the form of New Deal policies for cooperative land resettlement (Holloway 1966, vii, x).

Not all Americans welcomed utopists, of course. Even relatively popular groups had detractors, some of whom expressed their opposition to new forms of race relations, sexual practices, or leadership (especially female leadership) with violence. Early Shakers, for example, were beaten and jailed for their loyalty to a female leader and for their conscientious objection to military service. Such beatings probably hastened the premature death of Ann Lee in 1784. Yet, for the Shakers, resistance only strengthened resolve. Believers responded to attacks and protest by forming stable communities to replace their earlier, loosely organized society (Nordhoff [1875] 1966, 128; Andrews 1963, 49–52).

Variations on the utopian theme among nineteenth-century communities were seemingly endless and remarkably diverse in ideology, if not in population, which was limited primarily to whites of European descent. Despite some ideological similarities, including a preference for communal ownership, cleanliness, humane values, charity, good health, long life, and fairly comfortable living standards, American utopists enacted a wide range of family forms, sexual and reproductive practices, work rules, financial arrangements, educational schemes, diets, farming techniques, interracial relationships, and even gender roles in the quest for the perfect society to ensure whatever version of human happiness or God's grace the particular group had in mind.[3]

Some, like the Shakers, the Rappites (or Harmonists), the Sanctifi-

3. The literature on American utopian communities is vast. It is not possible to describe the hundreds of communities here or even to give detailed descriptions of those used as examples. This chapter's survey can only suggest the variety and concerns of American utopists. The common characteristics listed in this sentence come from John Nordhoff's 1874 study of ten communal societies: the Amana Society, the Harmonists at Economy, the Separatists of Zoar, the Shakers, the Oneida and Wallingford Perfectionists, the Aurora and Bethel Communes, the Icarians, the Bishop Hill Colony, the Cedar Vale Commune, and the Social Freedom Community (Nordhoff [1875] 1966, 400–404). They represent only a sample of the century's experimental forms and ideals.

cationists (or Woman's Commonwealth), and the Koreshans, identified celibacy as the path to God's grace as well as to sexual equality. Others, like the Oneidans, preferred controlled but nonmonogamous sexual relations and reproduction. Having seen no evidence of conventional marriage in heaven, Oneida's founder, John Humphrey Noyes, saw no reason to include marriage in his postmillennial heaven on earth. Instead, he encouraged "complex marriage" in which all men and women were married to one another but promiscuity was discouraged and reproduction was tightly regulated for eugenic purposes by the community's governing body (Baker 1980, 62; Kanter 1972, 12–13). Zoarites, Aurorans, Icarians, and most Fourierists (including those at Brook Farm) remained committed to the idea of the nuclear family. Indeed, the Icarians forbade celibacy (Nordhoff [1875] 1966, 388). Some groups never resolved the family/sex question. For example, Bronson Alcott, Transcendentalist co-founder of Fruitlands in Massachusetts, could not decide whether to become celibate or to remain an active husband and father of four daughters, including Louisa May, then age ten. Bronson was pressured by the community's chief economic supporter, Charles Lane, to adopt celibacy and create a "consociate family" at Fruitlands, in an effort to defray the social costs of exclusive and selfish nuclear family bonds. Although Fruitlands dissolved within one year (1843–44) and Bronson thereafter recognized the utopian potential of private family life, he continued to be haunted by the concept of a consociate family (Muncy 1973, 90–92).

Most nineteenth-century communities were by necessity agrarian in design and practice. Exceptions included the Oneidans and Amanans, who depended for their economic support in large part on manufactured items, such as silk thread, wool fabric, and, eventually, silverware. The Sanctificationists, an all-female celibate society, were also an exception. Boardinghouses and hotels provided their economic base. Any generalization about production, however, obscures the variety of activities in which utopists engaged for their own subsistence, some of which became sources of income. The Shakers were agrarian, but they also sold boxes, cloaks, and furniture originally made for their own use. Other communities produced farm implements, preserves, dried herbs, baskets, and other items that they sold to outsiders as well (Nordhoff [1875] 1966, 390).

A few communities were dedicated to very narrow ideals or principles. The Adventist Millerite community in Groton, Massachusetts, for example, which took its name from founder William Miller, lasted only one year because the prophecy on which it was based—the end of the world between the equinoxes of 1843 and 1844—did not materialize (Horgan 1982, 78). Another one-year experiment, which lasted only from 1860 to 1861, was the Harmonial Vegetarian Society of Arkansas. Its adherents—ten men and seven women—advocated free love and anarchy, as well as strict vegetarianism. The group's ideological menu did not suit their neighbors very well. In 1861, a mob attacked their leader, J. E. Spencer, and forced him to flee for his life. The community finally succumbed to the Civil War, which brought Confederate soldiers to the community's house and outbuildings (Muncy 1973, 206).

Most communities had very large visions, however, in their quest for social perfection, including basic concepts of work, marriage, reproduction, and even social justice. In a few cases, those agendas attracted ex-slaves or free blacks to white utopian societies, although their experiences in such communities were mostly discouraging. For example, freewoman Rebecca Jackson, a seamstress from Philadelphia, moved to the Watervliet Shaker community in 1847, hoping that the society would be a mechanism for evangelizing urban blacks. Jackson became discouraged about the Shakers' apparent focus only on their own survival. Although she was permitted to establish an "outfamily" among Philadelphia African Americans, there was no enthusiasm among the Shaker leadership either for the social reform Jackson envisioned or for the individualized female spiritual leadership she sought (Brewer 1993, 140).

Isabella Van Wagener, known to history as Sojourner Truth, also tried life in utopian societies with somewhat negative results. Her first experience, in The Kingdom, ended in disaster after she was falsely accused of the murder of the group's founder, Elijah Pierson, and relieved of most of her savings and possessions. After The Kingdom fiasco, Van Wagener tried an Owenite-Fourierist community in Massachusetts, the Northampton Association of Education and Industry. Although Northampton tried to live up to its promise of sexual and racial equality, as The Kingdom did not, the group's economic structure, which emulated a stock company, was not adequate to sustain the community.

Van Wagener left the association before its collapse. In 1856, she tried Harmonia, a spiritualist Quaker seminary and community near Battle Creek, Michigan. Harmonia had connections with the antislavery movement, but by the time of her association with the community (whether or not she was a full-fledged member is unclear), the renamed Truth had begun traveling and speaking for abolition and women's rights and, therefore, had little interest in a permanent home. When she moved from Harmonia, she did not seek another community for herself, but she was instrumental in creating the Freedmen's Village in Arlington, Virginia, for escapees from the southern states after the Emancipation Proclamation in 1863. She also advocated dedicating public lands in the West for use by former slaves; at one point, she even supported establishing a "Negro State" (Chmielewski 1993, 30–32).

GENDER AND THE AMERICAN UTOPIA

Many utopian communities recognized that gender equity was a major social problem and dedicated themselves to some version of female emancipation, although rarely to suffrage, since their goal was typically social isolation rather than political participation. Charles Fourier, for example, whose ideas about organizing work around human passions led to the founding of twenty-two independent, mostly unsuccessful phalanxes in Europe, Latin America, and the United States, wrote in 1841 that "'the extension of women's rights is the common foundation of all social progress.'"[4] Other utopian social designs promoted women's education, dignity, and full partnership in the operation of a community. Clothing reform and sensitivity to the prevailing sexism of nineteenth-century life gave hope to women who joined such utopian communities (Kesten 1993, 94).

But despite their rhetoric and good intentions, few experimental communities successfully enacted gender equity. Indeed, the ironic utopian present focus frequently further enshrined the conventional sexual division of labor and promoted time-honored sexual stereotypes in such communities, just as it limited utopists' ability to enact racial justice. Thus, most gender reforms in utopian communities were more symbolic than genuine (Kesten 1993, 98–100). Few women held leadership positions in mixed-sex societies, and very few communities were established by women in their own behalf.

An example of utopia's mixed success with effecting gender justice is New Harmony, which was founded by Robert Owen in 1825 in part to promote women's economic independence through education,

---

4. Quoted in Gottlieb. According to certain French dictionaries, Charles Fourier was the first to use the term "feminism" (Gottlieb 1997, 275).

egalitarian marriages, and sensible clothing. Owen supported simple divorce procedures and eschewed what he called irrational religion, which he regarded as a key source of women's subordination. But Owen's vision was restricted by the blinders of his era. Regarding women as morally superior to men, like most of his mainstream peers, Owen tended to see them as delicate and not quite human. Thus, even though he understood women's historical disadvantages and sought to overcome them, Owen nevertheless concluded that they were unfit to govern society equally with men (Kolmerten 1990, 71–76). The fact that Owen's son, Robert Dale Owen, became an effective advocate for women's rights in the Indiana Legislature, working for married women's property rights and liberalized divorce laws, illustrates a ripple effect from at least a few utopian attempts at significant social reform. That his efforts succeeded only after New Harmony folded, however, suggests that the small experiments were, at best, catalysts for gradual social change (Holloway 1951, 114).

Gender reforms in some communities, such as Oneida, actually increased women's subordination to men because female empowerment was equated solely with liberal sexual practices that men typically controlled. Indeed, the failure of sexual emancipation efforts like Oneidan complex marriage and Mormon polygamy to achieve gender equity may help explain why women utopists were more likely than men to join celibate communities. Celibacy actually proved to be a much stronger equalizing force between the sexes than any other form of sexual experimentation in utopian communities (Kitch 1989b, 125–59). The many broken promises to women in the utopian movement with regard to gender equity may well have caused its collapse at the end of the nineteenth century (Kesten 1993, 112).

Communities that were more successful at promoting women's equality and status include Brook Farm and the Shakers. At Brook Farm, gender stereotyping of work roles decreased over the community's brief, six-year history. A number of single women joined and took full advantage of the rich educational and cultural environment provided by its school and by such visitors as Margaret Fuller and Lydia Maria Child. The absence of any religious influence was perhaps the key to sexual equality at Brook Farm (Freibert 1993, 76–77). The Shakers retained traditional sex roles, but they managed to achieve at least symbolic gender equity through their requirement that both sexes be represented at all levels of community governance, a practice that reflected the bisexual nature of God and of Christ, of whom the community founder, Ann Lee, was the second incarnation in female form. In addition, despite work roles that mimicked conventional sex-role divisions, most nondomestic tasks involved equal efforts by both sexes. The Shaker version of role complementarity, producing equal respect for men and women, functioned better than its mainstream counterpart in nineteenth-century America. In addition, celibate Shaker women were generally considered morally superior to celibate Shaker men, which gave the women a kind of spiritual edge in Shaker communities.[5]

There were also a few exceptional groups, founded by women in their own behalf, in which women's leadership promoted gender justice. Among them were two very different communities—Nashoba and the Woman's Commonwealth. Frances Wright's Nashoba, founded in 1825 in Tennessee, had dual liberatory purposes: the emancipation of slaves as well as women through the elimination of private property, class distinctions, nuclear families, and religion. Wright's experiment ended in controversy in 1829, probably because its neighbors suspected the community of promoting free love between the races (Holloway 1951, 115).

The Sanctificationists' community, eventually known as the Woman's Commonwealth, promoted women's emancipation by freeing them from marriage through celibacy, thereby freeing them from the restrictive laws regulating married women's economic activities in nineteenth-century Texas. Started in Belton, Texas, in the 1870s by Martha McWhirter, the Commonwealth had religious origins, primarily in the Methodist Church. But the success of the community of about twenty-five women, over an active period of more than thirty years, probably had more to do with McWhirter's business acumen than with either the group's support of women's rights or its spiritual commitment. Indeed, it worked the other way around. The women's economic success at running hotels, boardinghouses, and a commercial laundry motivated the Sanctificationists to support women's property and voting rights (Kitch 1993, 43–45, 153–54, 333–38). A third female-founded community, the Shakers, defined women's emancipation via the principle of gender complementarity.

Gender issues were more prevalent on the literary than on the experimental side of nineteenth-century utopianism, especially among American fiction writers, many of whom were women (as we shall see in more detail in chapter 2). Depending on who is counting, between

---

5. For more details on the working of the Shakers' system of role complementarity, as well as Shaker women's spiritual "edge" in status within the group, see Kitch 1989b.

10 percent and 50 percent of utopian works published by American women during the century can be considered feminist.[6] Among them are Mary Griffith's *Three Hundred Years Hence* (1836), Elizabeth Corbett's "My Visit to Utopia" (1869), Marie Stevens Case Howland's *Papa's Own Girl* (1874), and Lois Nichols Waisbrooker's *A Sex Revolution* (1894) (Kessler 1984, viii; Lewes 1995, 18). Few African Americans of either sex wrote utopian novels during the same period, probably because lingering racism, even after the abolition of slavery, kept their imaginations focused on survival in the here-and-now.[7]

Ideas driving the literary utopias of the period were less religiously based than those that motivated founders of experimental communities. Literary utopias typically lacked political analysis and depicted the future's emergence from the past as a moral rather than a realistic or political process, although it sometimes involved violence. As in the communities, however, the literature emphasized the pragmatic and expressed faith that institutions can change human beings for the better and that transformed humans can create better societies.

THE MODERN AMERICAN UTOPIA

After a fifty-year lull, experimental utopian communities made a dramatic comeback in the late twentieth century. The modern communal impulse peaked (but did not disappear) in the late 1960s and early 1970s, when possibly as many as two or three thousand communities, including lesbian separatist feminist collectives, few larger than thirty people, sprang up across the United States. Some of them were religiously inspired, such as The Family, Apple Tree Acres, Messiah's World Crusade, and the Brotherhood of the Spirit. More recent communities have included environmental groups, such as The Community in Basin Farm (started in 1989), and feminist communities, such as Chester Creek House (restricted to lesbians in 1981), Blue Moon (started in the early 1980s), Hei Wa House (founded in 1985), and Acorn (founded in 1993) (Fellowship for Intentional Community 1996, passim). Findhorn, a Scottish community, became popular

---

6. Carol Farley Kessler (1984) claims that 42 percent of 150 utopian works by women can be considered feminist. Darby Lewes (1995) claims that 10 percent of ninety-five such works are feminist.

7. One such rare utopian novel was Lillian B. Jones's *Five Generations Hence* (1916), which envisioned utopia in Africa in five generations. It will be discussed in more detail in chapter 2. Most often, instead of imagining new worlds, African Americans dreamed and sang of Canaan, by which they meant Canada.

with Americans in the 1980s. Modern communes differ from their nineteenth-century utopian predecessors in many ways: they involve fewer visions of social reconstruction, less hope for the future, and fewer people, and they often entail a nostalgic look backward to simpler, less complicated times rather than an excited look forward. But there are also surprising similarities in theme across the centuries: dissatisfaction with capitalism, interest in enacting religious precepts, concern for social justice for women and minorities, and temperance (though the modern object tends to be drugs rather than alcohol), in addition to other themes (Kanter 1972, 165–67). For reasons we shall consider in more detail in chapter 2, feminist utopian fiction has also flourished since the 1970s.

Utopianism's enduring popularity has withstood intense criticism, including proclamations of its imminent demise, like those by scholars Judith Shklar and Frank Manuel, as well as attacks by twentieth-century dystopian literature. It has even borne accusations about its dehumanizing tendencies, such as those leveled against B. F. Skinner's 1948 *Walden Two* (the fictional inspiration for Twin Oaks and Walden Three), which critics accuse of creating pleasing but conformist people (Johnson 1968, 296). Political theorists of the Frankfurt School have argued for keeping a utopian spirit alive to inspire alternative societies that go beyond normative models. Otherwise, they claim, "we will never develop the political will to transform society" (Shklar 1994, 56). And of course, many feminists have continued to welcome utopias and utopianism.

Utopianism has even found its way into postmodern theory, which on its face seems antithetical to the typically homogeneous, unified visions of classical or ideological utopias. Yet, some theorists have identified postmodernism's multiplicity and diversity as itself a utopian state. Tobin Siebers, for example, has characterized the postmodernist attention to parts rather than wholes, to desire rather than politics, and to pastiche rather than design as a "heterotopia," a celebration of the irrepressibility of heterogeneity and unreconciled conflict (1994, 7). If utopia fulfills human desires, Siebers reasons, why can it not fulfill the postmodern desire for contradiction, diversity, and playful juxtapositions?

Thus, while some would consider Los Angeles the epitome of a failed utopia, postmodernist Aaron Betsky thinks it still has utopian possibilities. True, "L.A." is no longer the fulfillment of a Jeffersonian dream of a gentleman farmer in a California bungalow, picking oranges from his own backyard tree. But the city's centerlessness, sprawl, and ethnic divisions and conflicts signify different human desires on which careful planning could capitalize: Betsky proposes a transportation system linking the city's parts like "connective tissue." The linkages would "allow Los Angeles to realize its rhizomatic nature as a sprawl" and create a utopia of decentralization and invisible networks (Betsky 1994, 96–118). To be a postmodern utopia, Los Angeles must be allowed to develop according to its own logic (Siebers 1994, 29).

"WE ARE ENCOUNTERING ROUGH REALITIES": FROM UTOPIA TO UTOPIANISM

At first glance, the dizzying array of utopian literary visions, philosophies, and experimental communities surveyed so far suggests little to fear from a monolith called utopianism.[8] It is difficult to imagine a single theme underlying a cacophony of utopian voices over the centuries, which have touted as ideals everything from vegetarianism to complex marriage, totalitarian governments to anarchy, ascetic simplicity to the "connective tissue" of modern transportation. Indeed, taken as a compendium of details about ways to improve the human condition, no consistent composite picture of utopian design emerges. Yet, despite the diversity of social schemes and dreams gathered under the utopian umbrella, there *are* certain consistencies in theme, analytical form, attitude, and effect, and there is, arguably, a set of attitudes we can identify as *utopianism.*

Some theorists have suggested that one cohesive characteristic of utopianism is its relationship to deep psychological motivations that produce a "utopian impulse" in all human beings. Regardless of its specific object, that impulse reflects hard-wired human dissatisfaction with the status quo and ability to remember the past, ruminate upon the present, and project the future. Such a utopian impulse gives humanity an illusion of control over its destiny. Psychoanalytic theory attributes the impulse to buried unconscious memories or desires. Freud explained it as the manifestation of a persistent memory of a perfect time—probably in the womb—when all desires were ful-

8. The subheading is a quotation from John Allen, a member of the Brook Farm Association for Industry and Education, a one-year variant on the Brook Farm theme, which lasted from 1844 to 1845. Allen and his associate, John Orvis, barnstormed New England to raise funds for the Association, and they were shocked to find a resistant audience who did not accept that changing society was as simple as the Brook Farm movement claimed (Kesten 1993, 272).

filled and life was free from worry. Jung attributed the utopian impulse to the "collective unconscious," an expression of archetypal myths of perfection, such as the Garden of Eden or the Golden Age (Johnson 1968, xii–xiii). Postmodernists attribute it to perpetually unfulfilled and inexplicable human desire, which demands multiple and heterogeneous responses based on irreconcilable differences (Siebers 1994, 38).

If there is such a utopian impulse, it reflects utopianism's most positive side—its power to fight despair and unhappiness, however defined, while promoting positive values, however defined. Unshackled from original sin by the eighteenth century, utopianism has provided a plausible theory of a plastic rather than a predetermined human nature (Walsh 1962, 70). Utopianism leads us to believe that societies can be good, that they can and should be harmonious, unified, and peaceful. From utopianism we learn to attribute war and injustice to a poor environment rather than to human nature, and to counteract such evils with environmental change. A Thoreau excepted, utopianism valorizes group life and human perfectibility. It imagines that better societies or social organizations, even if they are antiorganizations, will produce better people, and that individuals will be happy if society is good and arranged to promote happiness (Kanter 1972, 33–34; Walsh 1962, 71). For many of us, such aspects of utopianism are very appealing.

Also appealing is utopianism's capacity to critique existing societies, governments, and cultural mores in compelling ways. Bellamy denounced greed; the Shakers opposed slavery; the Oneidans criticized religious intolerance and supported religious diversity, even including Judaism (Nordhoff [1875] 1966, 270). By the same token, the utopian impulse led many utopian thinkers, especially after 1800, to decry divisive sectarianism and denounce the oppression of women. Many attacked the evils of alcohol consumption, drug and tobacco use, and irresponsible sex. Indeed, through such critiques, utopians have often been ahead of their time.

Despite such attractions, however, there are other, more troubling aspects of the utopian impulse—of utopianism as a worldview and an approach to social change—that cannot be ignored. One especially troubling aspect of utopianism is its "present focus," which, as we have seen, is the underside of its talent for social critique. While resisting the present, utopianism often remains, firmly and paradoxically, attached to it. The failed promises of many utopian communities to women provide a stunning illustration. Thus, while communities touted sexual equality, they often perpetuated the conventions of their own era in their treatment of actual women, as in the maddening sexual stereotyping in various community newspapers, such as Hopedale's *Mammoth* and the Fourierist *Phalanx* (Kesten 1993, 104–5). Women were typically relegated to domestic work in most communities, despite rhetoric about shared labor or gender equality.

At Bronson Alcott's Fruitlands, for example, members were forbidden to use animals for work or food, but male members of the community thought nothing of working poor Abigail Alcott to the bone. She was one of the few people at Fruitlands who were practical enough to engage in subsistence work rather than merely in Transcendental philosophical discussions. "My duties have been arduous," she wrote, longing to return to her previous life, "but my satisfaction small" (Kesten 1993, 99). When Abigail's health began to suffer from her endless chores, Charles Lane, community founder, observed (in a letter to Henry David Thoreau) that the community needed more *women,* since "far too much labor devolved on Mrs. Alcott" (Muncy 1973, 91; Horgan 1982, 80). Although Lane was certainly correct in thinking that Mrs. Alcott was overworked, his proposed solution was definitely restricted by his cultural blinders.

Experiments with traditional sex or reproductive roles usually resulted in worse conditions for women than those they had left behind in mainstream society. Oneidan "complex marriage" destroyed women's traditional wifely and maternal roles, for example, but it only exacerbated their identification as sex objects required to defer to men. Oneidan girls had only limited access to education; no girls from the community attended college or received formal instruction after age twelve (Klee-Hartzell 1993, 198). In short, to an extent almost unthinkable in mainstream life in the United States, women's activities were defined entirely by their sexual and reproductive roles.

The Shakers provide another, less dramatic example. Although the tradition of gender hierarchy was challenged by the community's egalitarian governance practices, that goal did not eliminate the convention of female domestic service. Shaker women were still expected to serve men's domestic needs. Thus, each Sister was assigned to make a particular Brother's bed, do his laundry, and sew on his buttons (Andrews 1963, 123, 181).

The New Harmony community also attempted to liberate women from conventional roles, but its notion of liberation was severely limited by the nineteenth-century context within which it was defined.

Owenite women, even more than Oneidan women, were understood as egalitarian partners in a New Moral World, and they shared work assignments in many community industries. Yet, they were still expected to spend their "free time" doing traditional female chores, and they were responsible for their own family's home, food, and clothing. One group member, Sara Pears, expressed dismay that "perfect equality" at New Harmony actually meant sharing kitchen work equally among *all women* (Kolmerten 1993, 39–43).

Such instances of utopian present focus where women were concerned reveal how easily hidden assumptions and preconceptions can distort even the best-intentioned plans for social reform. The disappointment and occasional despair expressed by utopist women also exemplify the hazards hidden in hyperbolic utopian expectations.

UTOPIAN FAILURES

One test of utopianism is its poor success rate. Indeed, one synonym for "utopian" could be "short-lived." American utopian societies founded from 1780 to 1860 survived an average of only four years. Many lasted for even fewer, including Nashoba, New Harmony, and Fruitlands. Only the rare community endured for even a generation. Among the prominent exceptions are Amana and the Shakers. Amana survived for ninety years, and the Shakers endure to this day as the only American utopian community to have survived in any form for more than two hundred years after its founding. Also unique is its membership size. During the peak years of the mid-nineteenth century, there were six thousand Shakers living in a score of villages (Kanter 1972, 63, 246; Kesten 1993, 301–2).

Recently founded communities have shared the more typical fate, dissolving in just a few years. Some have ended very dramatically, suggesting the inadequacy of most utopian foundations for sustaining communal practice. One example is the mass suicide by nine hundred members of Jim Jones's Peoples [*sic*] Temple, in Guyana, in 1978. Another is the conflagration that ended the Branch Davidian Ranch in Waco, Texas, in 1993.[9]

Before assessing the reasons for the collapse of these groups, we should note the similarities between their utopian origins and those of

9. Lest we think such incidents are behind us, let us recall the cyanide-laced Kool Aid suicides of the followers of Heaven's Gate in Rancho Santa Fe, California, in 1997.

many attractive utopian experiments of the nineteenth century. Like their predecessors, the modern groups' inspiration was religious; they believed they had identified the ultimate "good" of human society; their members were willing to sacrifice all previous relationships—including those with their governments and families—for the good of the community. Such utopian principles link them to the Shakers, who renounced their families of origin and declined to vote or serve in the armed forces, as well as to dozens of other groups. Though fairly gregarious, the Shakers were advised to keep to themselves by their leaders, such as Hervey Elkins, who wrote in 1853 that Believers should not visit with "the world's people, even their own relations . . . unless there exist a prospect of making converts, or of gathering some one into the fold" (quoted in Nordhoff [1875] 1966, 177). Jones's followers also renounced family ties and resisted government interference, which is why they emigrated to the jungles of South America. The Branch Davidians sought self-sufficiency by growing their own food, making their own clothes, defending themselves, and maintaining group privacy.

On paper at least, the Peoples Temple can even be seen as exemplary of progressive nineteenth-century utopianism. In the tradition of Frances Wright, founder of Nashoba, Jim Jones was a professed antiracist who dedicated his ministry, first in California and Indiana and then in Guyana, to establishing a racially integrated Paradise. Seventy percent of those who followed Jones to the jungles of South America were black; many of them were elderly and supportive of Marcus Garvey's old Back to Africa movement of the 1920s. Jim Jones had been a champion of integration since the 1950s, when he established his Peoples Temple in Indianapolis, opened a soup kitchen that served three thousand meals a month, and provided clothes and other necessities to the poor. Consistent with the religious philosophy of the Woman's Commonwealth, Jones's congregations were ecumenical. Like the Shakers, the Oneidans, and scores of other utopian thinkers, Jones believed in achieving his communal goals by breaking up family units, owning everything—including children—in common, and legislating and regulating believers' sexual behavior (Wright 1993, 66–70).

What do the tragic endings of these communities say about utopianism? Some would argue that David Koresh and Jones were simply extremists and that moderation in their leadership styles and behaviors would have saved Jonestown and the Davidian Ranch. Perhaps their obsessiveness or madness could not be curbed, even by the huge group at Jonestown. Perhaps their followers were simply stupid or drugged. Perhaps a violent confrontation with the outside world was inevitable, since both groups were also apocalyptic. Such beliefs drive groups into a defensive, survivalist lifestyle in which any resistance by outsiders only reinforces millenarian predictions that history itself will conclude in the group's confrontation with the evil forces arrayed against them (Barkun 1993, 597). To a millenarian, death can seem like salvation.[10] Others would argue that outsiders provoked the trage-dies, that the F.B.I. precipitated the conflagration in Waco, and that Representative Ryan of the United States Congress and members of the press, who visited and met their deaths at the Jonestown colony just before the end, led Jones over the brink. Perhaps.

Yet, the failures of those two communities also echo other failed experiments and visions, and suggest a potentially dangerous core in utopianism itself. Clearly, Koresh and Jones were obsessed with their visions and abusive of their power. While preaching sexual control, for example, Jim Jones was sexually frenetic himself, although only with white partners (so much for racial integration). His followers excused his promiscuity as a reflection of his enormous psychic gifts (Wright 1993, 72). David Koresh apparently fornicated with nearly every fe-male in sight, including children, instituted a concubine system called the House of David among his followers, and married more than one underage girl (Berry 1993, 55). But hypocrisy and excess are not unique to the Koreshes and Joneses among utopian leaders. Nor are the isolationism, separatism, reliance on charismatic leaders, inade-quate systems of checks and balances on individual or elite group power, or exaggerated faith in one's own good intentions, evident in these two suicidal/violent utopias, unique to these leaders or commu-nities. Utopianism must be held accountable if it does not provide restraining mechanisms to prevent its tenets from becoming poison punch or fire bombs.

Utopianism can also provoke disaster because it depends on mod-els and plans that rarely encompass the complexities of human needs and behavior. When utopian models categorize, divide, and oppose ideas and people to fit their worldview, they inevitably overlook im-portant connections among those same ideas and people. By the same token, when utopian models ignore or rationalize contradictions and

10. Apocalyptic groups also existed in the nineteenth century. The Millerites provide an example. But many utopian societies of the period, including the New Harmonists and the Shakers, declared themselves postmillenarians; that is, they thought the apoca-lypse had already occurred and that they were living in a new age after the millennium.

conflicts within their views or romanticize their goals, they can miss the problems most in need of solution. For example, the postmodernist "heterotopia" relies upon a vision of balance among diverse ethnic and racial groups that underestimates the hatred, misunderstanding, and deadly competition for scarce resources underlying diversity in American life.

OTHER HAZARDS

Not all of utopianism's flaws have produced such dramatic disasters as those that ended the Peoples Temple and the Davidian Ranch, but all utopias have the potential to produce unintended consequences and disappointment. For example, utopian thought tends to ignore the lesson of the Jemez that good and evil, division and unity, often co-exist across a fine line, sometimes as two sides of the same event, impulse, emotion, or act. As a result, utopianism tends to underestimate the degree to which social evils can be the unintended consequence of social benevolence (or vice versa), as well as the degree to which good must be calculated along a continuum of benefits and harm: When does providing for the general welfare become big, intrusive government? When does compassion for weakness facilitate dysfunction? When does one person's freedom become another's oppression? When, for example, does the utopian separatist become a dangerous isolationist? By the same token, utopianism may overestimate the human capacity to anticipate all the consequences of even the most generous impulses or positive social values.

Despite utopianism's inability to foresee all consequences, utopian thought may endeavor to predict the future by drawing prescriptive social maps that transform the game of life—with its twists, turns, surprises, and unknowns—into a kind of ritual, whose outcomes can be anticipated and controlled. Ironically, such maps, coupled with the typical utopian "discourse of perfection," actually become apolitical, in that they reject conflict, as in race relations, and ignore the processes by which it might be resolved. The utopian desire to control outcomes typically excludes strategies of peaceful opposition and dissent, measured negotiation, and persistent political pressure (Bleich 1989, 24; Walsh 1962, 60). Few utopias contain opposition parties, let alone protesters.

Indeed, more common in historical or fictional utopian communities is banishment of people who will not or cannot conform to the group. The Shakers, for example, thought members who criticized their way of life had low motives, and they expected such critics to leave if they could not "gradually work in with us" (Nordhoff [1875] 1966, 159). The Icarians punished transgressions of the "principles, laws and regulations of the Community" by "public censure, by deprivation of civil rights, or by the exclusion of the transgressors" (Hinds 1973, 73). In general, utopianism assumes that disagreement reflects the error of the dissident rather than flaws in the utopian vision.

Utopianism also frequently relies on charismatic leaders and pays little attention to the democratic succession of leadership. John Humphrey Noyes, founder and leader of the Oneida Community, provides an example. Noyes's leadership role included the initiation of all the community's virgins into sexual intercourse shortly after their first menses, to prepare them for complex marriage. One young woman, Jessica Catherine Kinsley, reported that she found the community's emphasis on—indeed, insistence on—sex strange, mysterious, and incomprehensible, since other community values supported a sense of innocence among the young. But there was no question of resisting Noyes's prerogative, for she had also been taught to regard the leader as "almost *divine*" (Klee-Hartzell 1993, 197).

In truth, the survival of many communities depended on the survival of a particular leader. For example, the prosperity of the Sanctificationists coincided precisely with the lifetime of Martha McWhirter, despite her (unusual) attempt to arrange for leadership after her death. Even literary utopias frequently assume the eternal benevolence of leaders, so they rarely include mechanisms for the transfer of power from founders to subsequent generations. They also ignore history's lesson that leaders convinced of their own selflessness and altruism can sometimes do more damage than less-inspired rulers (Walsh 1962, 61).

Transfers of power are rarely discussed in utopian literature or theory, and in utopian experimental communities such transfers have seldom been democratic. Indeed, violence and/or the dissolution of the community have sometimes resulted when leadership has changed. For example, when some members of the Icarian community lost faith in founder Etienne Cabet, primarily because of his advancing age and decreasing mental powers, the ensuing struggle, though peaceful, lasted a year and resulted in a schism in the group. Afterward, only a small band remained with Cabet at Nauvoo, Illinois, and he died in 1856 a broken man (Hinds 1973, 66).

Even utopian systems specifying the process of election have not necessarily restrained the powers of an absolute leader. In the best cases, as among the Zoar Separatists, an Ohio community that lasted from 1817 to 1898, community rules required periodic elections and specified terms of office for leaders and group administrators. But even in such cases, without a body of law to refer to, elected leaders could attain unlimited power, with no check on their decisions about the common good (Nordhoff [1875] 1966, 107; Kanter 1972, 246). The Shakers were one of the few groups to endure (more than) long enough to produce adequate rules to check and direct the power of their leaders. By 1845, previously oral community rules were written down and disseminated to Shaker societies. They included hundreds of specific directions about clothing, worship, language, food, and even the painting of buildings. They also included a description of the duties of the ministry at New Lebanon, of elders, deacons, and trustees (Andrews 1963, 243–89).

More typically in both literary and experimental utopias, however, the concepts of government and law are minimized, or even rejected, and decisions are made by direct participation and consensus, with little attention to the fate of dissenters except the possibility of exile. If elections occur, they tend to be indirect and without accountability. As a result, most experimental or literary utopias offer few safeguards against tyranny (Walsh 1962, 61, 170).

Sustaining members' interest in communal life has also been problematic among utopian communities. Even the Shakers had difficulty remaining vital and viable for successive generations. Signs of discontent among the younger Shaker members, especially of the Western communities, were evident as early as the 1820s. Although some Shakers, primarily two eldresses, argued for a wider application of Shaker doctrine "to meet the spirit of the time," it was already too late. Membership decline was by then foreordained (Andrews 1963, 225–36). Most of the second generation of Woman's Commonwealth members, primarily the daughters of the first, remained in the community only while their mothers were alive. Their duty done, they left to marry or to seek other occupations. The inability to anticipate change is an ironic defect in a worldview presumably dedicated to preparing for the future.

Another hazardous feature of utopianism is its reluctance to test its own foundational principles. Although many nineteenth-century utopists considered themselves to be engaged in social "experiments" and put great stock in the new positivist social science emerging at the time, very little scientific experimentation occurred. Communities rarely researched alternatives to their founding precepts, or developed testable hypotheses, or created mechanisms for modifying the course of their experiments if they proved unsuccessful. Utopian optimism about human perfectibility, for example, was not typically tested against the lessons of history that power corrupts, or that people often do not know what will make them happy, or that good intentions do not always produce good results, or that people often tire of their own happiness (Walsh 1962, 71).

Additional failings of utopianism have been explored in dystopian literature. From Jonathan Swift's *Gulliver's Travels* (1726) to Margaret Atwood's *The Handmaid's Tale* (1985), writers have seen the underside of utopian promises, including the totalitarian shadow lurking behind them. Many dystopian novels, including H. G. Wells's *The Time Machine* (1895), Aldous Huxley's *Brave New World* (1932), and George Orwell's *1984* (1949), have been inspired by the same Marxism that also inspired some utopian visionaries. To Wells and Huxley, however, Marxism was a utopian philosophy gone awry. (Indeed, nothing has done more to dampen the American utopian propensity than the rise—and eventual fall—of Soviet Communism.) Wells also saw the negative potential of technology to empower unharnessed leaders, who could become brutes and destroy intelligence, virtue, initiative, and progress (Johnson 1968, 267–68).

William Golding (*Lord of the Flies*, 1954) depicted the underside of utopian assumptions of innocence, especially when confronted with the prospect of absolute power (Johnson 1968, 270–71). Having seen several nineteenth-century wishes come true, including the rise in importance of technology, some twentieth-century thinkers became convinced that optimistic utopian visions were a mistake, that human goodness did not always prevail, that people's characters and their inventions are generally both good and bad, and that the plasticity of human nature allows for both moral and immoral behavior.

What is more, dystopian writers like Orwell (*1984*) understood that the shaping of human beings for allegedly positive purposes can create automatons, people brainwashed to enact certain behaviors without commitment to any underlying values. Orwell stressed the need for free choice in the creation of genuine social or individual good. Similarly, dystopian writers have explored the dangers of shaping individuals entirely to social norms, no matter how virtuous those norms may seem. Their work suggests how little we know about the relationship between individual (eccentric, unpredictable) happiness and social organization. It exposes the limits of social planning, which might inadvertently destroy an invisible, internal social logic (Walsh 1962, 166–71).

Dystopian visions raise important issues: perhaps accidental societies are better at accommodating humanity's incidental rationality than planned ones could ever be; perhaps successful societies are ones in which competing forces are perpetually balanced and negotiated; perhaps happiness results from alternating highs and lows, rather than from predictable positive experiences (Walsh 1962, 166–71).

Even when utopianism addresses such issues directly, however, other flaws in utopian thinking can present additional problems. Postmodern heterotopists have accommodated life's accidental and irrational qualities, but, as we have seen, their vision suffers from a present focus that may obscure other compelling logics (or ill-logics). Their "found logic" of multiplicity and disorder is not simply discovered but also shaped by selection of specific qualities to emphasize over others. It overlooks, for example, the interconnections and patterns that also characterize contemporary society. Thus, despite their rejection of a "grand narrative" to explain the present or to shape the future, in order to "utopianize" heterotopists have had to embrace a grand narrative, even if it is a narrative that rejects grand narratives (Siebers 1994, 8). Non-plans are still plans.

UTOPIANISM BEYOND UTOPIA

Most important for the purposes of *Higher Ground* are the qualities of thought that accompany the utopian impulse or the utopian approach to social change. Indeed, the case against utopianism in feminist thought and theory, even in the face of the many benefits for feminism that utopianism seems to contain, concerns primarily its implicit forms rather than its explicit designs for social organization.

Among the qualities of utopian thought that limit the scope of feminist theory is its tendency to concretize ideas, to transform ambiguity and contingency into absolutes (Tillich 1966, 306–7). Because of that tendency, utopianism typically creates separate categories for ideas, people, and objects that disregard their connections. Therefore, fanaticism and fundamentalism are close relatives of utopianism, as they exaggerate utopianism's need for exclusivity. Because one either belongs or does not belong in utopia, people become overdetermined by the criteria established for membership in or exclusion from the utopian vision. (Heterotopia would also suffer from this fate: could a modernist or a romantic survive in heterotopia?) To the Shakers, there were two kinds of people in the world: celibates and generatives. To Jim Jones, everyone was either a friend or a foe of the Peoples Temple. There were no hybrids, no critical friends or friendly critics. Having assigned labels, utopian thinkers may never again consider their contingency or arbitrariness. Utopian thinkers may not account for the role of metaphor in label construction or in the terminology of their belief systems. They may mistake the figurative, symbolic quality of language for the literal.

In addition, the founding ideas of utopian thought tend to become fixed and to remain unexamined, even if utopists themselves are diligently self-critical about their own adherence to those founding principles. Thus, as we have seen, few utopian experimenters analyzed the possible unintended consequences of their fundamental worldview. At Oneida, for example, which was famous for its members' self-criticism, the community's reproductive system that resulted in "stirpiculture" babies was not subject to critique; the community's male leaders emphasized the presumed genetic benefits of group practices and gave little thought to their effects on the community's young women. Such habits of utopian thought overlook the causal relationships that exist among all elements of a system and ignore the fact that any changes in a system involve many related changes, often with unintended results (Richards 1980, 33). Without such analysis, the massive social overhauls typical of utopian schemes can become dangerously unpredictable and uncontrollable.

That conclusion points to utopianism's sometimes tragic irony: its present focus. Our own assumptions that modern people have surely outgrown that utopian flaw illustrate it as well as the examples we have seen throughout the history of utopian thought and experimentation. Through the benefits of hindsight we can identify, say, Charles Lane's blind spot about sex roles in his analysis of Abigail Alcott's excessive workload at Fruitlands. We are less able to see modern utopian pitfalls, however, as in Aaron Betsky's heterotopian vision of Los Angeles.

A related flaw is utopianism's appeal to self-interest. Just as my desire for the kitchenless house emerged when I had small children, more women of childbearing age joined the celibate Shaker societies than did men or women of any other age group or social circumstance.[11] Added to utopianism's present focus, its accommodation of self-interest heightens its potential for parochialism and creates the false impression that analyzing a problem is tantamount to solving it, when, in fact, understanding what is wrong does not automatically reveal what is right (Richards 1980, 38).

Finally, utopianism entails certain epistemological implications through its particular approaches to the acquisition and validation of knowledge. We shall consider more of these implications in chapter 3. For now, we can note the ways that utopian thought can depend on an epistemological loop, in which ideas build on particular, often insufficiently examined or limited premises. At its most extreme, this problem generates *coherentism,* a system in which beliefs are justified by their relationship to other held beliefs and knowledge claims rather than by their relationship to evidence or anything that can pass for "truth" (Duran 1991, 13). Although such systems may present an internal logic and may be valid, they can and often do lead to errors and falsehood. Indeed, coherent systems have no particular relationship to truth, because the premises on which they are based can be either true or false, valid or invalid, sound or unsound. Our fervent belief in them does not guarantee their validity (ibid., 30–32).

When constructed on erroneous premises, coherent conceptual systems can lead to disastrous mistakes. Hans Christian Andersen's "The Emperor's New Clothes" is a classic example of an invalid closed conceptual system. Having swallowed the fraudulent tailors' claim that their cloth would be invisible to anyone unintelligent or unsuited for his or her job, the townspeople, nobles, and king all claimed to be able to see it. That there was no cloth to see was difficult to establish, since no one wished to reveal him- or herself as unsuitable or otherwise unintelligent. Astrology is another example of a closed conceptual system. It depends on an initial faith in the influence of stars and planets on human life, a belief that prevents believers in astrology from noticing how generalized horoscopes are and how adaptable to a wide variety of circumstances.

Utopianism often involves closed conceptual systems built on false premises that are poorly or completely untested. For example, the first

---

11. Shaker women outnumbered men in all age groups. Indeed, the proportion of women among the Shakers never dropped below 56 percent. But in the childbearing age group of twenty to forty-four, women outnumbered men two to one. See D'Ann Campbell, "Women's Life in Utopia: The Shaker Experiment in Sexual Equality Reappraised—1810–1860," *New England Quarterly* 51 (March 1978): 29n.

man to call himself Koresh, Cyrus Teed, hypothesized in the 1880s that the Earth is really the interior of a hollow sphere (Kitch 1989a, 98–99).[12] Teed, a physician/alchemist, founded a group called Koreshan Unity in Chicago and moved the group to Florida in order to test that proposition. His "experiments" consisted of lining up poles along a beach and proclaiming that their uphill march to the horizon proved the accuracy of his theory. He took into account no factors other than his hollow-sphere theory when he conducted such tests, including the possibility that land can rise in spots even on a globe. His followers, accepting Teed's premise, offered no challenges to the methods of his "science."

Even valid first principles, when unexamined, can undermine their adherents' best intentions. The commitment of the founders of the Woman's Commonwealth to celibacy offers an example. When that commitment was made, celibacy was a rational, even clever response to a world in which married women had no economic rights, marriage was essentially a sexual-economic bargain, and divorce was difficult to obtain. The women's newfound celibacy drove husbands to the divorce court and freed Commonwealth women to own property and conduct business. But as the daughters of those founders grew up, celibacy made less sense. Conditions had changed. After 1899, when the group moved from Texas to Washington, D.C., the daughters saw fewer restrictions on married women's property rights as well as more educational and employment opportunities for women than their mothers had seen in Texas thirty years earlier. Thus, the younger generation of members rightly questioned their mothers' principles. Despite their upbringing in the community since childhood, many daughters eventually chose to pursue economic independence in the context of heterosexual romance and marriage. Their mothers' solution no longer answered the daughters' questions (Kitch 1993, 54–55, 110–11, 224–25, 235).

For the Shakers, the communal ownership of property and pacifism were also useful first principles that supported the group's attractiveness and, thus, its survival. As time passed, however, those precepts became liabilities as they began to discourage men, who were eager to fight in World War I and reluctant to relinquish their possessions to a community, from becoming Shakers. Because the society was

12. There is some evidence that David Koresh, of the Davidian Ranch, knew about Teed (who took the name Koresh because it was the Persian translation of his first name, Cyrus) and his community, Koreshan Unity. What else David extracted from his predecessor's theory, which included celibacy, is hard to tell.

committed to a dual-sex organization, the precipitous decline in male membership after World War I threatened its very existence. Yet, regardless of the threat to its survival, community leaders were not inclined to reexamine the group's founding precepts. Instead, in the 1920s, the elders decided to close membership in the society altogether.[13] Steadfast adherence to principle is often a virtue, of course, but if and when it compromises survival, then reexamination of principle in light of changing circumstances may be in order. Accommodating change can also be a virtue.

Further distorting utopianism's typically closed conceptual frame, even when first principles are valid and enduring, is its unwillingness to acknowledge its own relationship to other ideas and modes of thought. Very few ideas spring full-blown from the brains of a single thinker or a single group. To the extent that utopianism isolates its own innovations, it distorts the reality of multiple influences and misses opportunities to enrich itself through interaction with compatible people and ideas. The distortion produced by ideological isolation is becoming increasingly familiar to all Americans as we recognize that cross-fertilization among the ideas and beliefs of Native Americans, African Americans, Asian Americans, and other groups who populate the United States is a logic that cannot be denied, except in the interest of promoting a utopian view of one group or another as "real Americans," superior to others. A post-utopian view recognizes the interdependence of thought and invention, as it also acknowledges the continuum of positive and negative consequences for any and all achievements.

APPROACHING REALISM

Utopianism's alternative—realism—contrasts with these conceptual pitfalls in various ways, as we shall continue to explore throughout *Higher Ground*. In many disciplines, realism entails subjecting ideas,

---

13. Although the general explanation for the demise of Shakerism is the group's commitment to celibacy, living Shakers protest that cause as vehemently as did their nineteenth-century predecessors, who argued that belief systems do not survive because parents pass them along to their children, but rather because succeeding generations adhere to them voluntarily. That belief prompted the Shaker policy prohibiting membership before the age of twenty-one, the age of rational consent, even among children raised in the community. Using the same logic, modern Shakers—all women—have argued that Shakerism ran afoul of the popularity of World War I among American men as well as of the creeping materialism that followed the war. (Interview with Sister Bertha, Canterbury, New Hampshire, June, 1983).

values, or rules to analytical processes that recognize changes over time. Debates over realism have demonstrated the close interconnection of apparent oppositions or dualities. Existentialist Paul Tillich has expressed such a realistic view of utopianism itself. For Tillich, utopianism is both true and untrue, fruitful and unfruitful. Its truth for Tillich lies in its expression of humanity's inner aim and essence, the *telos* of human existence. Its untruth lies in its assumption of an unalienated humanity, which overlooks the inevitable "finitude and estrangement of man" from his essential being, which is ultimately unattainable. Likewise, Tillich finds utopian thinking fruitful, insofar as it opens up possibilities and provides "anticipatory inventiveness," but unfruitful insofar as it describes "impossibilities as real possibilities" and becomes wishful thinking, a self-defeating unrealism (1966, 296, 299–300).

As Tillich's analysis suggests, realism can reflect utopianism's desires. Realism can be an agent for social change, but it typically starts from different premises than utopianism. Realism also seeks truth, but usually through probing and complicating its variations rather than by defending a fixed position. Realism entails validating knowledge, but it usually involves questioning rather than possessing it.

Realism is more cognizant of ambiguity and contingency than utopianism tends to be. Realism enters the analysis when the arbitrary and symbolic nature of language is being explored, thereby revealing the mutability and fluidity of categories and their labels. Realism recognizes that human knowledge and depictions of truth may not constitute all knowledge and truth. Realism considers the limits to establishing truth once and for all.

Realism rarely engages in prediction, as utopianism sometimes does. Since it recognizes the unknowable, it leads us toward the visionaries whose prophecies unnerve us or disturb the familiar rather than toward those who reinforce our preconceptions.

Based on the history and uses of the term, which we will explore more fully in chapter 5, realism seems to have much to offer the task of feminist theorizing. It provides an alternative to utopianism that explores ideas' unintended consequences by probing for their traitorous propensities and recognizes that even the grandest of ideas may contain the seeds of their own destruction. Realism represents an alternative that seeks the fine line between the best and worst attributes of even our most cherished precepts.

Realism also allows us to consider the benefits of salvaging the best of *what is* even as we seek novelty, of drawing no hasty conclusions about *what ought to be* based only on knowing—or claiming to know—what is wrong with the present. Realism leads us to disavow the discourse of perfection and attend to the task of justifying feminist knowledge claims. It encourages us to consider balancing apparently oppositional concerns rather than casting our lot too hastily with one or the other.

Many feminist thinkers have taken realistic rather than utopian approaches to the problems of sexism, gender roles, women's diversity, the linguistic construction of gender, and numerous other topics that concern feminist thought and theory. In part III we will explore the anatomy of their realistic thinking. Before we do that, however, we have more utopian ground to cover—feminist utopian fiction and contemporary feminist experimental communities, in chapter 2, and utopian feminist thought and theory, in chapters 3 and 4 in part II.

T W O   *Feminist Utopias*

Feminism is a form of fantasy.
—Susan Gubar, "Feminism and Utopia"

*Feminism, today, is the most utopian project around. . . . [It requires] a sense
of the potential for a different and better society, which our activity can create.*
—Daphne Patai, "Beyond Defensiveness: Feminist Research Strategies"

Without utopianism, feminism will grind to a halt.
—Lucy Sargisson, *Contemporary Feminist Utopianism*

*Dear Conference Registrant: We ask those who are coming to the [1995 Na-
tional Women's Studies Association] conference not to wear perfumes, not to
use nail polish remover, and not to smoke. . . . Many of our members are
very allergic to the chemicals in make-up, most soaps and detergents, deo-
dorants, as well as in perfumes themselves—and tobacco smoke of all kinds
makes them really sick.*
—1995 N.W.S.A. Conference Announcement, University of Oklahoma

Contemporary American feminist thought resonates with utopian
voices. Both Daphne Patai and Susan Gubar have emphasized
feminism's need to imagine entirely new worlds. Lucy Sargisson has
even linked feminism's very survival to utopianism. More common is
a subtler connection between feminism and utopianism, such as that
evoked by the 1995 National Women's Studies Association (N.W.S.A.)
conference announcement, which implies the possibility of an ideal,
controlled space and time that is completely free of offensive substances for the presumed benefit of all.

Utopianism is compatible with feminism because it reinforces feminists' claim that society, rather than nature, determines social roles and human worth. Both feminism and utopianism also embrace, even depend on, the need for large-scale social change. Utopianism has often been invoked to support specific changes that would benefit women, such as reproductive reform, and, like feminism, it has offered hope to people who have been ignored or oppressed.

Despite that compatibility, however, even feminist utopianists have sometimes felt themselves betrayed by the almost automatic connection of feminist and utopian thought. Gubar and Patai are good examples. Gubar modified her definition of feminism as fantasy in the very essay in which she formulated it. She immediately recognized that the feminist utopias produced by such fantasy might be so harmonious that someone suffering from the "imp of the perverse" (quoting Edgar Allen Poe) would "[long] for somewhere of intolerance, discord, egotism, violence, individualism, and—most of all—adventure." She blamed utopian feminism for focusing too much on differences between men and women and for perpetrating a kind of hypocrisy. She noted that, even as they seek the free play of the female imagination, feminist utopias generally establish a kind of orthodoxy that distrusts anything not "certifiably feminist" (1986, 80–83).

We have already seen what became of Daphne Patai's utopian approach to feminism. In 1983, she called feminism a utopian project and claimed that "everyone involved in feminism is animated by [a utopian] vision: the protest against injustice implies a vision of justice; the satire of the present implies . . . a positive pole against which the present defects show up more clearly" (1983, 150). By 1994, however, when she co-authored *Professing Feminism,* her mind and voice had changed. Instead of utopian visions, she was writing "Cautionary Tales from the Strange World of Women's Studies." Her utopian dreams for feminism had become nightmares.

Sargisson remains an unreconstructed supporter of utopianism as the fruition of feminism, but even her support is qualified. What she embraces is a redefinition of utopianism according to recent feminist utopian novels that reflect postmodern feminist values, such as multiplicity and open-endedness (1996, 20–21). She admits that there have been less desirable feminist utopian visions that express "desire for full presence (perfect society)" and "represent the end of play forever." She finds such utopias static and universalizing (ibid., 108, 20). Thus, her enthusiasm for utopianism's role in feminism both discounts its historical influence on the quality of feminist thought, which is the focus of this book, and ignores the potential of utopianism to disillusion its adherents, as it did Patai.

Indeed, Patai's disappointment in women's studies students and classes is a predictable, if unintended, consequence of her utopian expectations for the field as a pure and sophisticated pursuit of knowledge, free of error and deception. Such expectations inevitably exaggerated her negative judgment of women's studies students, whose immaturity and shallow thinking would only have confirmed more realistic expectations of undergraduate students. Without utopianism, it is easier to remember that clear thinking can and must be taught, that prejudices often interfere with the learning process, and that oversimplification goes with the undergraduate territory. Many fields besides women's studies must develop strategies for dealing with such problems.

The implicit utopianism of the 1995 N.W.S.A. conference notice more closely resembles the form that has shaped many feminist agendas. By expressing the desire for a completely scent-free environment for the annual conference, the notice fosters expectations of perfection and harmony. Such expectations reflect N.W.S.A.'s long history of conflicting constituencies demanding equal accommodation by the organization in everything from the content of the conference to representation on the Governing Council. The organization's profile has changed dramatically since 1995, but at that time conference planners clearly saw a duty to accommodate allergic reactions as well as identity differences.[1]

The announcement reflects the shortcomings of such expectations and attempts at accommodation. Utopias may require a discourse of harmony and perfection, but why does feminism? Expecting a world

1. I have been working since 1997, as part of a group of Program Administrators and members of the Governing Council in N.W.S.A., to effect some changes in the organization. It will soon be a more professional organization that pays more attention to curricular and scholarly matters than to questions of identity. However, the group's history does contain examples of utopianism based on identity categories as well as the failures of such utopian dreams, including the dramatic 1990 N.W.S.A. Conference at Akron, Ohio. At that meeting, a complicated personnel issue, involving an African American woman employee in the N.W.S.A. national office, led to protests that nearly brought down the entire organization. The situation was utopian on both sides: N.W.S.A. leaders believed that every conflict could be negotiated, mediated, or discussed away and assumed everyone's goodwill in a common cause; those supporting the terminated employee and disrupting the conference held utopian views of race that assigned good and evil to behavior and motivations primarily on the basis of race. Indeed, so strong were those associations that women of color on the organization's side of the issue were, like Anita Hill, considered white by the protesters because they did not behave as women of color were supposed to behave. For details, see Patsy Schweickart, 1990.

without conflict, especially among equally legitimate but competing claims, is a recipe for disappointment, since such a world can hardly exist. Despite N.W.S.A. members' best intentions, for example, eliminating all scents and chemicals from their persons is nearly impossible in today's world. Some chemicals are necessary for treating medical conditions. Some members might be allergic to products without scent. Some necessary products are always scented.

Further, adopting utopia's historical preference for uniform values nullifies one of N.W.S.A.'s primary duties, to provide a forum for discussion and debate about feminism and women's lives, both of which entail challenges, contradictions, complexities, and conflicting needs that should be at the heart of the conference. Identifying and proscribing conflicts prior to such discussion forecloses debate and does little to eliminate the realities against which idealized visions always struggle. Indeed, the admonition to "just say no" to such complexities is little more than a utopian magic wand. What we need instead are reasoned guidelines for the fair evaluation of needs, desires, and ideas for considerate behavior.

Another disturbing aspect of the utopian 1995 announcement is its intimation that certain personal habits (or aversions)—being allergic to perfume, for example—could be criteria for N.W.S.A. membership, as they were for Shakerism or Oneida perfectionism. Those who are not allergic to "most soaps and detergents," as "many members" are, might wonder about their qualifications for the organization. Perhaps N.W.S.A. prefers members with such allergies. Thus, through utopian attempts at accommodation, the organization might have inadvertently promoted an image of exclusiveness rather than the sense of inclusiveness that it sought to promote.[2]

Through such effects, utopianism sets up feminist thinking for certain self-defeating consequences. It promotes inflated expectations, exclusive mentalities, and disillusionment. Its presumption that a par-

2. Because there was no overt evidence of the ill-effects of utopianism at the 1995 N.W.S.A. conference, I think it does no harm to N.W.S.A. to analyze its conference announcement from that year. Actually, the 1995 conference was very successful, although I would not attribute its success to the atmospheric warning. In fact, the warning went pretty much unheeded: people wore scents, and clusters of smokers huddled around the entrances of every building in which sessions were held. I would also note, however, that a harried staff of volunteers at the conference was made even more harried by certain demands for personal accommodation by attendees, so a spirit of utopianism was still alive at the conference. It is partly because such demands had become common at N.W.S.A. meetings that I believe the organization needs to continue its efforts to dispel inflated expectations that accompany utopian feminist worldviews and contribute to both unreasonable demands and inevitable disappointment.

ticular right course of action, attitude, or behavior has already been determined often short-circuits inquiry. Instead of preconceptions, feminist thought needs strategies for self-reflexive analysis and debate that take into account diverse human needs and situations in changing contexts.

"UTOPIAN THINKING IS CRUCIAL TO FEMINISM": THE FEMINIST-UTOPIAN LITERARY CONNECTION

Despite such hazards of utopian thought and despite the doubts some feminist writers have expressed or demonstrated about utopianism, a close connection between feminist and utopian thought persists among American feminists.[3] Perhaps the most explicit manifestation of that connection is the large body of American feminist utopian literature that has been produced over the last 150 years. That impressive canon has helped to persuade many feminist thinkers to accept Frances Bartkowski's view of feminist theory as "fundamentally utopian in that [it declares] that which is not-yet as the basis for a feminist practice, textual, political, or otherwise" (1989, 12). Many such thinkers question how feminism could *not* be utopian, since its assumption of gender equality, which has never existed, must be imagined in order to be discussed (Mellor 1982, 243–44). And what better way to express feminism's fundamental utopianism than in fictional visions that provide "alternative *vicarious* experience, spur[ring] us as readers to reevaluate and act upon our own world," thereby breaking the bonds of the existing order (Kessler 1984a, 5–6)? What better way than in fictional visions to explore the mutual concern of feminism and utopianism with three important questions: What exists? What is good? What is possible? Feminism says that sexism exists, that it is bad, and that an alternative nonsexist society is possible (Kiser and Baker 1984, 29). Feminist utopian fiction typically explores concrete models of that alternative society.

Some feminist scholars have even embraced utopian fictional visions as the vanguard of feminist thinking. Marleen Barr and Nicholas Smith, for example, claim that "to conceive of utopia . . . is from the outset to reconstruct human culture," which is what feminism is designed to do (1983, 1). "Feminist fabulation," as Barr calls utopian fiction, "tells a different, nonpatriarchal story about women" upon which we can build new realities (1990, 31). To Frances Bartkowski feminist

3. The subheading quotation comes from Frances Bartkowski (1989), 12.

utopias demonstrate "demanding revolutionary transformation" that reshapes desire, anger, and despair into the contours of hope. The fiction is an important site of radical feminist theorizing "that . . . demands a long, close look, for it is the 'place ideology is coiled: in narrative structure.'" Bartkowski also credits feminist utopian visions with taking our imaginations "beyond the pairs, oppositions, dualities, and polarities that we know and live and tell from along the faultlines of gender" (1989, 10, 14, 3).

Many scholars credit feminist utopian fictional visions with recovering a real, pre-state egalitarian past (Baruch 1984, xiii). Even more credit such visions with allowing us to "interrogate the present" (Bartkowski 1989, 11). "Utopia registers our fantasies of the future," writes Jean Pfaelzer; "these fantasies embody our relationship to the realities of the present" (1990, 199). The "imaginative models" in utopian fiction can help us evaluate and replace the destructive models in the real and present world, according to Dorothy Berkson (1990, 113). Such models, claims Lucy Sargisson, can challenge and transgress various aspects of the social order, including the concept of order itself, linear time, stable truth, and reality, as well as gender stereotypes, social codes, and the nuclear family (1996, 201). "Without utopian thinking," writes Drucilla Cornell, "feminism is inevitably ensnared in the system of gender identity that devalues the feminine" (1991, 169).

As we briefly explore the utopian fictional heritage of feminist thought, however, we must also remember the underside of utopianism. As feminism's most explicit connection with utopianism, it is probable that feminist utopian fiction embodies both the best and the worst of that connection: inspirational characters and scenarios as well as conceptual flaws and limitations.[4]

THE FICTIONAL HERITAGE

Scores of fictional texts, dating back to European works produced as early as the seventeenth century, offer for readers' delectation and

---

4. The category "feminist utopian fiction" is not a precise one. I define it as a subspecies of fantasy fiction, which also includes elaborate and nonhuman fabulations as well as science fiction, among other genres. This chapter focuses upon fiction created by women with specific reference to the conditions of women's lives, particularly in some kind of ideal state or future time. The term "feminist" has been applied to much of the fiction after the fact of its creation. It reflects the usage of the fiction by feminists attempting to establish its meaning and value in modern times. The analysis that follows

rumination a wide and occasionally wild range of possibilities for social arrangements and designs that encourage and support female power, identity, and independence. They constitute the canon of feminist utopian fiction. A selected survey of that canon, with emphasis on the American texts of the nineteenth and twentieth centuries, reveals both its appeal and its sometimes paradoxical dangers for feminist thought and theory.

The European Foundation

At the beginning of the twentieth century, when Charlotte Perkins Gilman published her now classic *Herland,* there had already been at least a two-hundred-year history of fictional visions of ideal all-female or arguably feminist societies. Among the earliest writers of feminist utopian fiction were seventeenth-century French *précieux* authors, who envisioned sanctuaries in which educated women enjoyed without male interference a life of intellectual, aesthetic, and sensual pleasure.[5] One example of this genre is Marie-Catherine D'Aulnoy's "L'isle de la félicité." Written in 1690, this work depicts a world apart and safe from intrusions by men at a time when such immunity from male influence and dominance was rare for women. The island's exquisite landscape and luxurious accommodations evoke the image of Versailles, which in its own day symbolized the pursuit of intellectual and sensual pleasure. As in *Herland,* the tranquility of the island is disrupted when a male intruder, a Russian prince, wanders onto it, and as in the Gilman novel, one of the islanders falls in love with him. The couple live together happily for three hundred years (longevity being a function of "innocent and tranquil pleasures") before the prince notices that he has "done nothing that could put his name among the ranks of heroes." His "feminization" on the island suddenly seems threatening to him, just as it does to Terry Nicholson, Gilman's most "macho" visitor to Herland. The prince leaves the island and meets his death, as Time catches up with him (Capasso 1994, 44–47).

Another example of a European, all-female utopian vision, *Millennium Hall,* was created by British writer Sarah Robinson Scott in 1762.

---

is necessarily brief and incomplete. Only certain aspects of the fictional works can be mentioned, and many others will necessarily go unnoted.

5. Although there were male *précieux,* the movement appealed primarily to women. Its goals included aesthetic and moral reform, specifically the purification of language and manners and the appreciation of the arts. The most prized relationship among its adherents was friendship. The salon was the focal point of the movement, and many of its writers were great hostesses of the period. (See Ruth Carver Capasso 1994, 35–36).

Scott's novel depicts a utopian community in which women pursue their own spiritual and intellectual interests without the threat of male power and violence. The model of female friendship in the novel is the idealized mother-daughter relationship, which forms the basis of a functional home and, by extension, a successful community. The founders of the community are independently wealthy, so various issues of industry and economy are not addressed, as they would be in another 150 years in *Herland*. The question of female sexuality is considered, however, albeit in a somewhat veiled manner, as it is not in the later novel. The chief symbol of that sexuality is a community of dwarfs, giants, and other "monsters" whom the women of Millenium Hall maintain and protect behind a sturdy fence on their property. The "monsters" have been ogled and commodified by an insensitive public, just as women who rejected the norms of heterosexual life were often vilified or pitied in eighteenth-century Europe. The enclosure of the "monsters" represents their protection from danger and abuse, just as celibacy represents sexual freedom for the ladies of Millenium Hall (Dunne 1994, 65–71).

American Fiction, Nineteenth and Early Twentieth Centuries

By the nineteenth century, American women writers were contributing enthusiastically to the utopian literary canon. Anticipating Gilman's maleless society by more than thirty years was Mary E. Bradley Lane's *Mizora: A Prophecy,* which was published serially in the *Cincinnati Commercial* in 1880–81. Most of Lane's uniformly blonde heroines do not even know that men have ever existed, but an outside visitor learns that they had vanished from Mizora more than two thousand years earlier (the exact time period of "manlessness" that Gilman specified for Herland). Mizoran women had first wrested power from men, then eliminated crime and war, improved the state of morality, and expanded opportunities for women's education. Eventually men became superfluous to the society's government and social structures. Therefore, they disappeared (talk about magic wands!). Like Gilman's Herlanders, Mizoran women discovered that mothers are the "only important part of all life" and that reproduction without men is not only possible, it actually improves the human species (Lane [1880–81] 1984, 124–35).

Such manless (or man-free) societies are a staple of feminist utopian fiction, but they are not the only model in the genre for achieving female freedom, independence, and power. Between about 1840 and 1920, a prolific period for feminist utopian novel production in the

United States, marriage reform rivaled the popularity of male extinction in fictional utopias. Indeed, the majority of the fifty-five feminist novels from that period, as identified by Carol Farley Kessler, focused on the unfairness of marriage to women and the inadequacy of the traditional family for children. But the improved society they imagined remained co-ed.

Reflecting the challenge of societal assumptions by the women's suffrage campaign, feminist utopian fiction of the period, especially after 1869, often portrayed women not as vengeful revolutionaries but as social reformers seeking a sexually integrated society through the implementation of enlightened social programs (Lewes 1995, 44). Mary Griffith's *Three Hundred Years Hence,* published in 1836, is an early example of this model. Having gained political power sometime after 1836, women in Griffith's novel transformed society in three hundred years. They first eliminated war and established a reverence for religion. Then they concentrated on reforming the insurance industry and modifying building codes to prevent fires. Their most visionary reforms sound tame or even counterproductive of their goals by today's standards: a concrete-lined water system, trains that could travel at thirty miles per hour, inheritance rights for wives, and the guarantee of sewing jobs or vocational training for poor girls. The reformers did not propose to eliminate men or marriage, however (Griffith [1836] 1984, 42–45).

Several writers of the period, including Charlotte Perkins Gilman, identified women's economic self-sufficiency and support of children as essential to utopia. For example, Jane Sophia Appleton imagined, in her 1848 "Sequel to 'The Vision of Bangor in the Twentieth Century,'" a twentieth-century society in which women who provide their own food and clothing through their own labor are "not obliged to enter the marriage state, as a harbor against poverty." Following the socialist model of Charles Fourier, such women take their place alongside men and receive just compensation for their work. Men provide for their own domestic needs because women have forsworn household labor as "an occupation which brought so much social degradation and wear and tear of body and clothes!" (Appleton [1848] 1984, 56–57).

Gilman's belief in the perfectibility of the human race through deliberate social engineering was anticipated by Marie Stevens Case Howland's *Papa's Own Girl* (1874). Like Appleton before her and Gilman after her, Howland was influenced by Fourierists, whose communities she visited in France and Mexico. She actually lived in a

Mexican Fourierist cooperative community from 1888 to 1893 and took her inspiration for utopian fiction from a visit to Jean Godin's Familistère in the 1860s (Kessler 1984b, 95). In *Papa's Own Girl,* Howland depicts the dream of a Social Palace system, in which balanced lives, enriched by work, exercise, amusement, social converse, education, and love, are guaranteed to men and women. Howland explains that "this spirit is based on the sentiment of equality, the recognition of human rights everywhere," as well as on respect for workers ([1874] 1984, 102–3). Feminist sentiments are expressed in the novel, including support for women's economic independence and marital freedom, but its greatest advocates for such views are men.

In addition to sharing in such features, Gilman's own work, including *A Woman's Utopia* (1907) and its revision, *Moving the Mountain* (1910), as well as *Herland,* involves the physical redesign of living spaces. Thus, public nurseries, communal kitchens, and woman-centered apartment houses replace the private home, and professionalized household services relieve the domestic drudgery of individual women. Gilman's other reforms include meaningful, paid work for women and the curtailment of men's prerogatives (Kolmerten 1994, 110–11).

The society depicted in *Moving the Mountain* exemplifies Gilman's utopian values. Tobacco, alcohol, prostitutes, and hunting have all been eliminated. Married women keep their jobs and their birth names, which they pass on to their daughters. The novel emphasizes the importance of economic activity to women's liberation. The male narrator, having just been rescued after thirty years in Tibet, is told that the vast changes he sees in the society of 1940 are due in large part to women's having awakened to their potential as economic producers. In about 1912, women flexed their economic muscles, toned by their experience as wives, mothers, and consumers, and started businesses to sell healthful food and to provide household workers. "We were so used to the criminal waste of individual housekeeping," the visitor is told, "that it never occurred to us to estimate the amount of profit there really was in the business" (Gilman [1910] 1980, 185). Gilman did not address issues of class, however, or consider at whose expense middle-class women's profit would be made.

Many turn-of-the-century works, such as Alice Ilgenfritz Jones and Ellen Merchant's *Unveiling a Parallel* (1893) and Lois Waisbrooker's *A Sex Revolution* (1894), shared Gilman's emphasis, evident in *Herland,* on the primacy of motherly love and maternal values. Waisbrooker's

character, Lovella (whose name means "spirit of motherhood") determines that the "power of mother love . . . shall take the place of brute
force" in society (Kolmerten 1994, 113). Such sentiments reappear in
the culture of Gilman's *Herland,* which is predicated on the values of
childrearing. In Herland, motherhood is not just an instinct, it is
rather an art and a science that only the most gifted practice directly
by caring for and educating children. Other Herlanders do work that
indirectly promotes children's growth and well-being, such as producing food, tending the forests, and building houses.

Many other novels of the period also promote the idea of nontraditional work for women. In Anna Adolph's *Arqtiq* (1899) and
M. Louise Moore's *Al Modad* (1892), women fly planes. In Eloise O.
Richberg's *Reinstern* (1900), women farm. They run for public office
in Helen Winslow's *A Woman for Mayor* (1909) and engage in physical
labor in Martha Bensley Bruère's *Mildred Carver, USA* (1919). In such
novels, work not only provides personal satisfaction and communal
benefit, it contributes to individual development and even enhances
the quality of male-female relationships (Kolmerten 1994, 116).

In contrast to the American focus on marriage and family, British
writers of feminist utopian fiction during the nineteenth and early
twentieth centuries concentrated on legal and political reform. Motherhood was never the foundation of a new British utopian state, as it
clearly was in American novels. British utopias tended to be urban,
mixed-sex, and futuristic, rather than hidden societies in remote locations, an idea that better matched the American landscape and
utopian heritage. The changes envisioned by British writers are gradual and reformist rather than revolutionary, even though they often
involve scientific and technological as well as political advances, and
frequently reflect the authors' socialist sympathies (Albinski 1990, 51;
Lewes 1995, 62–67).

The Doldrums

The decades between 1920 and 1960 were a relatively "dry" period for
feminist utopian fiction. Kessler found only six feminist utopias out of
the twenty-seven utopian novels published by women during those
years. Three of the six focus on heterosexual relationships as the central feature of a woman's life, a much narrower female universe than
that envisioned in earlier works (1984a, 14). After World War II, several women with androgynous names—Andre Norton, Leigh Brack-
ett, Marion Zimmer Bradley, and J. Hunter Holly—wrote novels for

the science fiction market (Donawerth and Kolmerten 1994, 10). Their emphasis on macho male heroes undoubtedly reflects the disdain of the Freudian age for female protagonists who deviate from domestic and conventionally feminine identities.

An exception for the period is a novella by Isak Dinesen, "Babette's Feast," published in 1953. It recounts the tale of a remarkably gifted chef, Babette, who is also a fugitive revolutionary from the civil strife in Paris in the 1870s. Babette comes to live with relatives in Berlevaag, a small village in Norway. Her relatives are members of a harsh, strife-ridden Puritan commune that has lost its sense of communal harmony and pleasure. Babette's cooking, especially the spectacular feast she prepares with money she wins in the lottery, brings joy back into the Norwegians' post-utopian lives. Dinesen's idea of utopia is subtle, even skeptical of the utopian ideal, depicting utopia as a state of mind rather than a place. (Its like would not reappear in the literature for more than twenty years.) In Dinesen's story "it is precisely when [the Norwegian Puritans] cease to renounce the pleasures of this world and accept them as, at the very least, an inevitable part of the ways in which community holds together, that they come closest to realizing the utopia they long for. Babette knows, but won't preach, that the aesthetic experience at its most disciplined, inspired reaches is not in any limited sense 'of this world'" (Goodwin 1990, 14).

The Late Twentieth Century in American Fiction

After 1960, the publication of feminist utopian fiction blossomed. Kessler discovered forty-two works she considered feminist that were published between 1960 and 1983, and her survey omitted scores published since. According to Kessler, about one-third of the works she studied from that period promote communitarian values. The societies they describe involve commonly held property and collective responsibility for food, clothing, childrearing, education, medical care, travel, and recreation. Work roles, especially domestic work roles, are not assigned by sex. Families are not nuclear and generally involve more than the usual number of parents. At the same time, the society guarantees perfect safety, especially from rape or assault. Despite the communal focus, the novels provide for privacy and autarchy (self-governance). Typically, the society meets people's needs (at least the ones they identify) but also requires that all of its members be committed to meeting the needs of others (Kessler 1984a, 17–18).

Kiser and Baker characterize the novels produced in this period by their insistence that "an inhumane, impersonal, atomized public" sphere cannot be maintained separately from "a supposedly humane and personal private sphere [that invents] a humane and connected whole." The best way to create a genuinely connected whole, according to the novels, is through communities that function as extended families. Such works also support the notion that women develop their individual identities in the context of relationships and that their personal growth is nurtured by connection with others rather than by competitive, individualistic striving (which is the way men presumably develop). Because of their socialization for a noncompetitive world, women in these novels need little financial reward as a motivation for work (Kiser and Baker 1984, 31–32).

The characteristics that Kiser and Baker identify are evident in Thea Plym Alexander's *2150 A.D.* (1971) and Marge Piercy's *Woman on the Edge of Time* (1975). Alexander's novel portrays the family as a social model that eliminates competition and, therefore, the need for government or regulation (Sargent 1983, 21–22). Piercy's text contrasts the brutality, individualism, materialism, classism, racism, sexism, and competitiveness of contemporary America with a future time in which small, egalitarian communities thrive on a model of cooperative, decentralized local governments and deregulated familial relationships. The future society, Mattapoisett, enforces no restrictive sex roles or even fixed gender identities. People relate as individuals in fluid and negotiated, rather than legislated, relationships. All identities, including gender, racial, and ethnic ones, are primarily matters of choice. (The novel thereby eliminates the female gender identity that presumably bred its nurturing, humane qualities in the first place.) Maternity, supposedly a key source of positive communal values, is no longer solely a female value or experience. Babies are created outside the womb, and men take hormones that enable them to breastfeed the infants they then help to raise. Each child has three "mothers," male and/or female, to nurture him/her ("per" in the novel). Although the society is predicated on communality, however, everyone (except children) lives alone, and individuals have much autonomy and control over their lives.

Taking a different tack from other critics, Darby Lewes sees a remarkable similarity between women's utopian novels of the 1960s and 1970s and those of the 1860s and 1870s, since both periods were characterized by the traumas of a brutal war and "a heady climate of civil libertarianism." In both periods, women engaged in intense political activism—abolition in the nineteenth century and anti–Vietnam War and civil-rights work in the twentieth—only to be reminded of their political inferiority after the battles were won. Utopian literature provided an outlet for the alternative of unselfish relationships, sisterhood, and gentle partnership models that might have changed the political landscape but seemed so improbable in real life (Lewes 1995, 120). Lewes pairs Suzy McKee Charnas's *Motherlines* with Mary E. Bradley Lane's *Mizora* as one example of the connection.

Other critics characterize feminist novels of the post-1960 period by their portrayal of nature as a pattern to which human activities should conform, rather than as something to be controlled. Among this group are Piercy's *Woman on the Edge of Time,* as well as Dorothy Bryant's *The Kin of Ata Are Waiting for You* (1978) and Sally Gearhart's *The Wanderground* (1979). Women in such fiction are associated with nature in a positive way. Nature is identified as the source of social life, as well as of a form of spirituality that replaces conventional, externally imposed religion (Kiser and Baker 1984, 33; Kessler 1984a, 17–18).

Yet another critic, Frances Bartkowski, divides novels of the period into two categories: warrior utopias ("a dynamic utopia of potential and process") and maternal utopias (utopias "of projection and planning where all is in place"). Monique Wittig's *Les Guérillères* (1969), *The Wanderground,* and Joanna Russ's *The Female Man* (1975) fit the first category. (Supporting Bartkowski's categorization, some of Russ's characters settle conflicts through duels.) *Woman on the Edge of Time* and *The Weave of Women* (1978) by Esther Broner fit the second (Bartkowski 1989, 59). *The Wanderground* and *Les Guérillères* are also lesbian separatist versions of the all-female community, although Gearhart's women tolerate certain men, called "gentles," who have fled, like the women, an increasingly repressive, patriarchal, and dysfunctional City.

Broner's novel asserts maternal values by beginning with the birth of a baby girl, whose Hebrew name, Hava, means "Eve." The baby's birth marks a new beginning for a collection of independent women who reproduce in the usual way, but at their own discretion and without the support or permission of men. The novel is set in Israel in the 1970s, and its dystopian foil is contemporary Israeli political and religious life. The women of the novel construct a modest utopia within existing Israeli society by exploiting ruptures in its patriarchal law, especially religious law. The novel also plays on the biblical heritage of Judaism by, among other things, defining the ten commandments of women, which include *not* breaking hearts, or stealing "attention, time, affection, or memory," or replacing a woman friend with a man (Bartkowski 1989, 112, 125).

Other critics define yet other categories for organizing modern feminist utopian fiction, categories that rearrange specific texts, fill in explanatory gaps, and emphasize a range of themes and notions of women's futures. In addition to the works already named, "classics" of the period include at least the following additional texts: Ursula Le Guin's *The Left Hand of Darkness* (1969) and *The Dispossessed* (1974); Mary Staton's *From the Legend of Biel* (1975); Suzy McKee Charnas's *Motherlines* (1978); Doris Lessing's *Canopus in Argus* series, including *The Memoirs of a Survivor* (1975), *Shikasta* (1979), *The Marriages between Zones Three, Four, and Five* (1980), and *The Sirian Experiments* (1981);[6] Suzette Elgin's *Native Tongue* series (I in 1984, II in 1987; III in 1994); Katherine V. Forrest's *Daughters of a Coral Dawn* (1984); Joan Slonczewski's *A Door into Ocean* (1986); and Pamela Sargent's *The Shore of Women* (1986).

THE RETREAT FROM UTOPIA

The appeal of this rich and inventive fiction is evident. It portrays innovative gender relations and social practices that valorize women. It inspires optimism about the possibilities of social planning and design. The novels offer consolation for the repeated frustration of feminist political goals in real life. They also offer escape from such realities and the chance to consider alternatives. They may even open up new conceptual spaces in which positions of binary opposition are disrupted and replaced (Sargisson 1996, 109). Indeed, the utopian subject position suits women's own social marginalization in gender-polarized and hierarchical societies that often view women as outsiders in their own lands (Lewes 1995, 11–16).

Furthermore, some of utopia's visions have even been realized, albeit without the advent of utopia or increased reverence for women: many women keep their own birth names and pass them along to their daughters; laws and customs regulating marriage and divorce have been reformed; we have a five-day work week; technology has arrived to "improve" our lives; there is more gender equality than there used to be; women have made some inroads into previously all-male professions; the sexes are not as distinct from one another as they once

6. As we shall see, Lessing's and Le Guin's novels straddle utopian/non-utopian tendencies and themes.

were; and many domestic services have been professionalized. Gender roles are even "bending."

Utopian portrayals can be especially compelling for those who face impossible role expectations, violent and oppressive personal relationships, overt sex discrimination in the workplace, and/or unfair practices in a variety of settings. Perhaps that is why lesbian vampire utopian fiction has emerged as a recent subgenre, as illustrated by Jewelle Gomez's *The Gilda Stories* (1991). Some of the fiction is also uplifting in its valorization of women's experiences as mothers and social reformers, by recognizing their unsung (and generally unrewarded) contributions to the well-being of their families, communities, and nations. Many plots minimize men's automatic power and prerogatives, or eliminate men altogether, and redefine the social good according to values women allegedly prefer or embody.

Such a list of qualities seems, at first glance, to constitute a veritable compendium of feminist principles. Why shouldn't this fiction stand as a primary resource for feminist thinking about the problems it addresses? Why shouldn't today's feminist thinkers and planners work to establish the solutions and designs contained in the utopian novels and stories?

Moreover, critic Lucy Sargisson claims that correct readings of feminist utopian fiction make it even more compelling for contemporary feminist thought. She explains that interpreting utopian fiction only in terms of its contents reveals only its shallowest attributes— transparent ideal societies that address narrow human deficiencies and pertain to the modern state (1996, 15–16). From such a content-based approach, she admits, utopias do look static, as if politics have come to a screeching halt (ibid., 19). If we approach utopian fiction from the perspective of its function, however, we find many works that are transformative, "ironic and satirical rather than perfection-seeking" (ibid., 42), in the tradition of Thomas More. Among such works are the novels of Angela Carter, including *The Passion of New Eve* ([1977] 1982), a utopian/dystopian satire that "escapes the finality of utopias of perfection." Like other texts in this new genre, Carter's novel is speculative; it ridicules the universals of the past and "create[s] new conceptual spaces in which radically different ways of being can be imagined" (ibid., 20–21). Such novels exploit their fictitiousness, and flaunt the fact that they are feigned and deceptive. They should be read as falsehoods, pretenses, shams (ibid., 43).

Sargisson is clearly correct that some contemporary feminist utopian fiction has gone beyond the conventions of utopian thinking.[7] Indeed, some recent writers of feminist speculative or fantasy novels have overtly retreated from traditional utopianism, refusing to portray feminist values in traditional utopian terms. They have rejected utopianism's rigid categorizations and moral certitude. Instead, they have created more ambiguous fictional forms, inserted skeptical characters into their work, and opened rather than closed their novels' conceptual frames, seeking subtler approaches and embracing feminist diversity.

The fictional retreat from utopian feminism blossomed in the mid-1980s, but it was prefigured in earlier works. Ursula Le Guin subtitled her 1974 *The Dispossessed,* for example, *An Ambiguous Utopia.* Although the novel pursues utopian approaches to social change, feminism within the novel, symbolized by the utopian planet Gethen, is characterized as imperfect and complex. Despite their society's lack of gender roles, fixed sexual identity, rape, or war—all issues associated with feminist goals—Gethenians are still subject to betrayals, suicide, assassinations, and raiding parties (Peel 1990, 39–41). Even Wittig and Piercy punctured the veneer of their utopian worlds by exploring their characters' unconscious minds and allowing them to question certain social roles that characterize their utopias. Such moments undermine the novels' utopian visions, which are otherwise promoted in the works. Similar moments can be found in the fiction of Russ, Charnas, Bryant, Broner, Gearhart, and Sargent (Jones 1990, 119). Charnas's *Motherlines* takes on the feminist utopian concept of sisterhood, for example, by portraying the women's "tribes" in the novel as jealous and contentious. The novel describes its protagonist, Alldera, as disappointed on that score: she "had wanted the women to be perfect, and they were not" (Barr 1983, 62).

Skepticism about utopian forms of feminism increased after the publication of Zoe Fairbairn's *Benefits* in 1979. Set in England in a future that looks a lot like the present United States, the novel begins with the suspension of all social programs, except for a baby bonus to mothers who do not work outside the home. That remaining benefit has the unintended effect of undermining the nuclear family, as women learn they can live without men. The government then corrects its mistake by withdrawing the baby bonus from women who do

---

7. She is less correct, I believe, in her assertion that many nineteenth-century feminist utopian works can be read in this same way (Sargisson 1996, 20).

not live in traditional families. Eventually a worsening economy forces the government to reverse its values and to require that contraception be practiced by all but a few state-certified women (White 1983, 143). Through these convoluted but politically realistic events, the novel demonstrates the nasty turns that apparently feminist social reforms, such as government support for mothers and wages for housework, can take. It thereby undermines its readers' confidence that feminists can easily define the world we wish to inhabit. Fairbairn's novel paved the way for the ambivalence about feminist utopianism that blossomed in the 1980s in the works of such writers as Margaret Atwood, Doris Lessing, Ursula Le Guin, and Octavia Butler (Green 1994, 170).

The ironic political twists depicted in Fairbairn's novel foreshadowed Atwood's *The Handmaid's Tale,* which was published six years later. Atwood's work illustrates well the conjunction of utopian and dystopian worlds. Her fictional Gilead stands as a warning about the treachery of desire by demonstrating the hazards of fulfilled as well as unfulfilled wishes (Fitting 1990, 144). Offred, the novel's featured Handmaid, whose only role is to give birth to babies for one of the ruling Commanders of Gilead, understands well the pitfalls of feminist utopian desires. The child of a 1960s radical feminist, Offred remembers thinking about her mother, "She expected too much from me. . . . She expected me to vindicate her life for her, and the choices she'd made. I didn't want to live my life on her terms. I didn't want to be the model offspring, the incarnation of her ideas" (Atwood 1985, 157). Now living in someone's idea of utopia, but her (and our) idea of Hell, Offred also sees how feminists' desires for women's power, sisterhood, and state-supported maternity have been twisted by nightmare forces of social change. Having participated in a typical Gileadan group birthing, where a dozen Handmaids watch while one of their number delivers a baby to be raised by a Commander's barren wife, Offred thinks sardonically, "Mother. . . . Wherever you may be. Can you hear me? You wanted a women's culture. Well, now there is one" (ibid., 164). The pretense of giving women what they want—that is, fulfilling utopian dreams—has resulted in worse conditions in the novel than those that precipitated earlier feminist utopian yearnings.

The novel suggests not only that dreams and ideas can have unintended consequences but also that utopianism itself can obscure important dangers. Few feminists identified banking practices as a major issue in the 1960s, for example, although the issue of extending credit to women was important. Yet it was precisely what no one was noticing—the ways banks can control credit—that became key to women's eventual entrapment in Gilead.

The dystopian side of utopian feminism is also revealed in Doris Lessing's *Marriages between Zones Three, Four, and Five* (1980) and Ursula Le Guin's *Always Coming Home* (1985). Within the context of her utopian vision, Lessing subverts the virtues of utopian feminism by depicting Zone Three, which has all the earmarks of a feminist utopia, as a self-satisfied and complacent society that ignores the parts of reality that do not immediately concern it (White 1983, 138). In this series of novels, Lessing disparages utopian visions "where nobody is possessive or destructive or has bad taste in furniture" but where uniformity, self-centeredness, and a lack of imagination contribute to women's oppression without their realizing it. In Lessing's utopia, dangers for feminism include parochial stagnation and the weakness that results from a life free of adversity. The novel ends with a movement toward Zone Two, which is neither feminist nor patriarchal but rather a place where extreme difference transcends the dualities informing the other Zones (Peel 1990, 36–38).

Le Guin's novel *Always Coming Home* goes even further to express contempt for utopian thinking in general. Pandora, the voice of Le Guin in the novel, says, "I never did like smartass utopians. Always so much healthier and saner and sounder and fitter and kinder and tougher and wiser and righter than me and my family and friends. People who have the answers are boring, nice. Boring, boring, boring" (1985, 335). The novel's deconstructive form, in which some twenty-five discontinuous sections of narrative about the Kesh civilization, Kesh documents, and an appendix that explains their customs, dress, and language and even provides recipes, suggests that utopia is a process to be redefined continuously and chosen repeatedly over dystopian alternatives that might seem more exciting (Khanna 1990, 132–33; Fitting 1990, 152). The text is a catalyst to creativity and change, but in no fixed or predetermined direction. It signifies the tension between practical limitations and the power of utopian possibility (Khanna 1990, 139).

Such novels return us to Sargisson's argument that feminists have redefined utopianism to incorporate its own self-critique, thereby opening up more nuanced imaginative spaces in which feminists can envision social change. Once static, utopia is now fluid; once unitary, utopia is now multifaceted. "Progress, movement and the perpetuation of struggle take the place of finality in many (contemporary and historical) utopian texts" (1996, 20). Sargisson might agree with Donawerth and Kolmerten that the newer novels' challenge of absolutes, such as separatism, and questioning of public feminist discourse nicely complicate the standpoint of the feminist "we" (1994, 12).

I would make a different argument, however. The turning away from the utopian model and toward subtler theoretical approaches to future social visions strikes me as a rejection of utopianism and an admission of its limits and negative effects. When feminist fantasy fiction writers want to explore complex societies and contradictory truths, unidealized or undemonized individuals, multiple and conflicting worlds, they renounce the conventions of utopias and utopian thought. They disassociate themselves and their work from the historical definitions of utopianism, in recognition that utopianism limits and even undermines the quality of feminist thinking.

The limitations such post-utopianist writers fear include many we have already seen: the present focus that restricts the scope of utopian social solutions; the emphasis on specific practices that, no matter how appealing, de-emphasize the necessity for revisable processes to meet changing needs and conditions; the flattering of women's sexual, maternal, or peace-keeping characteristics, which inevitably confines and universalizes women's identities; the mistaking of problem reversal— such as installing women in nontraditional occupations—for problem solution, such as creating actual social and economic justice for women. That women now fly airplanes and head companies does not, in and of itself, address the complex conditions that disadvantage women. That married women routinely work has not eliminated women's economic dependence on men. The effects of job segregation on women's wages see to that. That women are no longer chained to their kitchens has created a new threat: fat and sugar addictions from the fast food that has replaced nutritious home cooking. Utopian details do not necessarily add up to utopia, as novels often imply they will. Nor does simply disrupting present sexist ideas and practices, a quality Sargisson admires in recent fiction, necessarily produce effective social change.

Utopian fiction's "present focus" can be summarized in Darby Lewes's metaphor of traveling to the future in "a house trailer and bringing along all the comfortable paraphernalia of home" (1995, 6–7). The writer's present condition and context provides a vocabulary for social design that rarely anticipates future realities. Thus, Mary Griffith could believe in 1836 that guaranteed sewing jobs for poor women would improve women's economic lives for the next three centuries. Likewise, British writer Margaret Cavendish, in *The Description of a New World, Called the Blazing-World* (1688), could overlook the influence of her aristocratic heritage and seventeenth-century worldview as she called for a benevolent dictatorship for the ideal future. As empress of a world that she creates according to her own lights, Cavendish's protagonist projects the consuming issues of her day—education, philosophy, and religion—as the consuming issues of all time (Khanna 1994, 20). Wearing their present blinders, *précieux* French novelists defined the ups and downs of heterosexual love as women's fundamental problem. As one heroine notes, "an innocent and completely pure love would be the sweetest thing in the world, if it could last" (Capasso 1994, 52–53). More to the point, pure love can be the sweetest goal in the world only to people for whom health, money, education, housing, food, and a dozen other material problems are under control, as they were in the writers' world.

Another aspect of the utopian present focus is its unwitting incorporation of prevailing gender stereotypes and conventions. For example, although startling for its time on some levels, Gilman's *Herland* also clearly reflects many nineteenth- and early twentieth-century conventions, such as "woman's sphere," "feminine nature," and the "eternal feminine." Herlanders' monosexuality can even be read as a valorization of female sexlessness, the virtues of which were implicit in late-Victorian sexual ethics (Bartkowski 1989, 26, 31). By the same token, romantic turn-of-the-century ideas about domestic womanhood led utopian fiction writer Helen Winslow, in *A Woman for Mayor* (1909), to abort Mayor Gertrude Van Deusen's political career on account of love. Gertrude does not seek re-election as mayor because an appropriate male candidate, her fiancé, appears on the scene. Even though Gertrude has previously disparaged a purely intimate, narrowly focused domestic life, the novel suggests that she lives happily ever after because "the loving heart of the woman was to stand alongside the strong desire of the man" (Kolmerten 1994, 118). Another sign of present focus in nineteenth- and early twentieth-century works are representations of the era's racist and anti-Semitic views, for which modern critics find themselves apologizing.[8]

Even novels that have argued for what Lewes calls *vatic* reform—a combination of women's rationalist or public/political power and their private/domestic power as a moral force—often synthesize existing gender ideologies. While shocking to some of their contemporary

---

8. For example, see Kessler on Mary E. Bradley Lane's *Mizora* (1984, 117).

readers, novels in that category, such as Marie Howland's *Papa's Own Girl* (1874) and Alice Ilgenfritz Jones and Ella Merchant's *Unveiling a Parallel* (1893), adhered closely to the moral orthodoxy of their day. Even the rebellious women in those novels who shun marriage or own businesses remain "womanly women who champion domestic values" as they insert themselves into the forbidden public arena (Lewes 1995, 93–106).

Confining contemporary influences are also evident in Lillian B. Jones's *Five Generations Hence* (1916), possibly the first utopian novel by an African American woman. Jones's novel envisions a utopian society for American blacks in Africa, which she imagines will be completed after the work of five generations. The society's chief architect, Grace Noble, cannot pursue her dream in Africa, however, because her husband's job keeps the couple in Texas. Grace claims that she is entirely happy with the marriage and motherhood that confine her and delay her utopia until the next generation, though she does note that she hopes to raise her daughters with different values: on the model of her independent, single missionary friend, Violet Grey (Kolmerten 1994, 120). Thus, even though she is aware of the stifling effect on her creative vision of her era's conventions of femininity, Jones nevertheless allows them to postpone her heroine's utopian dreams.

Because we probably share them, the blinders impeding the view of modern writers are harder to detect. Indeed, we might be tempted to assume that literary works produced in the present transcend such a present focus and achieve true visionary insight. Such an assumption would merely utopianize the present, by characterizing today's writers as necessarily better, smarter, more progressive, and less confined by their preconceptions than yesterday's. How do we know how the fragmented, conflicted, and multiple realities of today's most apparently progressive feminist novels will seem to readers in one hundred years?

To assert our generation's perspicacity is also to discount the value of history, as many utopian fictional works do by predicating social change on the decimation of a previous civilization and the renunciation of the past. For example, Wittig's *Les Guérillères* utilizes only the present tense and asserts the importance of "the now in which history must be written." "The women warriors learn the 'ancient texts' of history the better to overthrow them" (Bartkowski 1989, 39, 42). Many novels imply that history has little of value to teach and that the future, which belongs primarily to the young, requires a completely fresh start.

We can see inklings of the utopian present focus in the way that some recent novels have rapidly become dated. Already the novels of the 1970s and 1980s seem practically passé, with their emphasis on small-scale, communal, use-value–based societies predicated on maternal values. Today's readers smugly criticize Piercy's *Woman on the Edge of Time*, for example, because of its slightly old-fashioned "flower child" tone. Indeed, critic Michelle Green calls the inhabitants of Piercy's Mattapoisett "too gentle to be believed" (Donawerth and Kolmerten 1994, 170). To readers in the post-petri dish generation, the citizens of Mattapoisett may also seem overly enamored of reproductive technology. By the same token, after a decade or more of watching women in power, today's readers might find such separatist novels as *The Wanderground* or *The Female Man* politically naïve. We can no longer be sure that all the "good guys" in the world are female.

More recent utopian novels that stress individual psychology as the primary route to social change, emphasize interpersonal communication and self-revelation, and promote a kind of spiritual dimension may also soon be dated by those particular stamps of the 1980s (and 1990s). Joan Slonczewski's *A Door into Ocean* offers an example. The novel explores many 1980s feminist values, such as gender-bending sexuality, female solidarity, and feminine altruism and attention to emotions, but its utopianism defines it as a period piece of popular psychology. The Sharers from Shora, for instance, express their individuality by categorizing their personalities—Merwen the Impatient One, Usha the Inconsiderate, and Spinel the Impulsive One. Although slightly royal in tone, that act of self-definition both reflects the decade's fascination with psychological taxonomy and, ironically, reifies the characters' roles, identities, and loyalties, thereby replicating the rigidities that the flowing feminist ocean society is presumably designed to replace.

Indeed, their attempt to project into the future brings many utopian fictional works into the shaky realm of World Fairs and weather forecasting. In utopias, as in all forms of prediction, defining current problems is only one part of the challenge. Even more difficult is anticipating the chaos introduced into any system by the passage of time. Unanticipated paradigm shifts and climatic forces, technological advances or disruptions, multiplying variables that interact with one another, and unpredictable historical events that change social and individual (even feminist) values are as important considerations as are today's or yesterday's dynamics. Also problematic is the difficulty of accepting or even hearing the most accurate of forecasts. Sometimes the message is too overwhelming to take, as in the case of global warming. Sometimes the accuracy upsets popular wisdom, as seers from Cassandra to Winston Churchill have discovered. How do we know that fictional works which reinforce comfortable feminist values are not drowning out more important but less appealing voices?

FROM UTOPIA TO THEORY, OR VICE VERSA?

Feminists sometimes claim that feminist utopian fiction promotes the development of feminist theoretical ideas. An example of that claim is Frances Bartkowski's assertion that "the refusal of hierarchy at the core of contemporary feminist theory arises from the knowledge that women have been spoken both for and about" in feminist utopian fiction (1989, 12). Many admirers of utopian fiction and experiments credit them with leading the way in social reform. In truth, however, it would be more accurate to make the opposite claim, that feminist utopias reflect not only the general gender ideologies of their day, as we have seen, but also its feminist thought. Indeed, even Sargisson recognizes that feminist utopian fiction reflects the increasing complexity and variety of feminist theory.

Kessler's division of American feminist utopian fiction into the three periods described above illustrates that point (1984a, 9). Feminist utopian novels flourished between the 1840s and 1920 because that was the time period of suffrage activism, as well as agitation by some feminists, including Elizabeth Cady Stanton, for liberal divorce laws, married women's property acts, and expanded economic roles for women. Few feminist utopian novels were produced between 1920 and 1960 because public feminist activity decreased during those years, based on the false assumption that the passage of the Nineteenth Amendment would lead naturally and logically to the larger goal of gender justice. At the same time, Freudian ideas of femininity became popular and limited public support for the kind of roles feminist utopian fiction typically portrays. As feminism resurfaced in the late 1960s, however, so did the publication of feminist utopian fiction, which reflected changing social attitudes about civil rights and women's liberation.

Coming from a slightly different perspective, Bartkowski herself makes the same case. She explains that "the periodization of utopian writing and thought . . . chart[s] certain moments or ruptures in Western social history—those times when utopian desires/projective longings are driven by both hope and fear, those times particularly marked by anticipation and anxiety." Thus, the last decades of the nineteenth century produced much utopian fiction. Reflecting changes in feminist thinking as well as thinking about feminism, twentieth-century feminist utopian fiction began to focus more on patriarchy than on capitalism, which was the evil of choice in the previous century (1989, 7–9). Following the same pattern, the thrust of feminist utopian fiction changed at the end of the twentieth century as feminist theory became more concerned with differences among women, with interlocking characteristics and life situations—such as race, class, and sexuality—and with postmodern theory.

Donawerth and Kolmerten extend this aspect of Bartkowski's argument by charting the close connection between a particular time period's ideas of women's liberation and the fictional utopian visions of the same period. Thus, in the seventeenth and eighteenth centuries in England and France, women writers of utopian fiction focused on education, the central issue in the contemporary debate about women's rights. They imagined cloisters, salons, schools, or country houses with large libraries in which women could enjoy intellectual pursuits unencumbered by male ridicule or by domestic duties and expectations (1994, 6). Seventeenth-century French *précieux* writers created fiction from their movement's focus on the role of aesthetic, moral, and linguistic reform in expanding women's social identities. Their fictional communities could hardly serve as models for widespread social change, however. Rather, the novels depicted utopian refuges for upper-class women whose lives resembled those of the authors (Capasso 1994, 35–50).

Nineteenth-century utopian fiction reflected not only romantic ideas about women and the sexual division of labor but also "the nineteenth-century goals of feminism to secure property rights, divorce, suffrage, and careers for women," according to Donawerth and Kolmerten. They agree with Kessler that marriage reform, along with a focus on paid work, education, suffrage, and cooperation characterize American novels during this period because those were the concerns of the century's feminists (1994, 7).

The contrast we have already seen between British and American utopian novels of the nineteenth century also reinforces the point: utopian themes reflect place as well as time. "Place" for British utopian writers became a high-tech future, as far removed as possible from domesticity and from the masculine, commercial British "frontier." "Place" for American utopian writers became a private retreat, an extension of feminine "frontier" values embedded in the nurturing moral high ground occupied by American pioneer women. Thus, the

British protagonist of the period is a public, political being, sometimes even a prime minister, who is focused on suffrage and socialist solutions to public problems and is disinterested in the family as a site of social change. In these ways she resembles British feminists of the period. Meanwhile, the American protagonist is a down-to-earth (even if urban) woman who exerts private moral strength that derives from her maternal nature, the embodiment of key (although not all) American feminist concerns (Albinski 1990, 51, 63; Lewes 1995, 62–68).

Even those writers whose works have become classics of the twentieth-century American feminist literary canon and whose utopian visions have become metaphors for feminist values—like Charlotte Perkins Gilman's *Herland* (for a mother-centered society), Ursula Le Guin's *Left Hand of Darkness* (for androgyny), and Marge Piercy's *Woman on the Edge of Time* (for gender-bending roles and personalities and for extrauterine birth)—actually reflect theoretical positions nascent or already established among feminist thinkers. Le Guin owes her views on androgyny to numerous theorists, including Plato and Carl Jung (Rhodes 1983, 110–15). Piercy did not invent the idea of gender-free motherhood. Feminist object-relations theorists such as Dorothy Dinnerstein and Nancy Chodorow, among others, were already exploring the importance of dual parenting to the elimination of misogyny. Gilman's own *Women and Economics* (1898) preceded and provided the foundation for her fiction's emphasis on the "natural" economic relationship between mothers and children. Such examples suggest that utopian fiction serves as a site for experimentation with emerging or established ideas through metaphorical systems rather than as a site of ideological invention. While the visions of utopian fiction have given life to abstract feminist notions, they exist in a parallel universe to theoretical works more often than they serve as inspiration for original theoretical constructions.

FEMINIST CRITICAL APPROACHES TO FEMINIST UTOPIAN FICTION

Given the realities of feminist theory's relationship to feminist utopian fiction that we have been mapping, an appropriate criticism of that fiction should recognize both its creativity and its limitations. Such criticism should provide balanced, analytical, and—well—critical readings of the fiction that has been so important to so many feminists. When we examine existing feminist criticism of feminist utopian fiction, however, a measured response is not what we typically encounter. Rather, the criticism has often displayed utopian characteristics of its own.

Many critics approach the novels from stances of idealization, boosterism, and optimism, among other utopian qualities. Lucy Sargisson intends, for example, to prove the utility of utopianism to feminist thought "through [its] journeys into uncharted and unfamiliar territory, and . . . [its] spaces in which visions of the good can be imagined" (1996, 5). Her intention resembles many similar critical goals. Carol Pearson set out in 1977 to prove that the novels she studied, which include Gilman's *Herland* and Piercy's *Woman on the Edge of Time,* do not romanticize children or impose racial distinctions. Thus she overlooked an equally compelling counterclaim that the novels' presentation of children is entirely romantic, since children in both novels are depicted as innately angelic and without flaws, other than those imposed by parents and society. Neither novel, of course, accounts for the possibility of genetically or physically induced behavioral disturbances. Further, Pearson's assertion that the novels are free of racial or ethnic distinctions ignores Gilman's disparaging remarks in *Herland* about Jews.

In addition, critics often seek within the novels the secrets of an elemental or quintessential feminism. Such an approach is also utopian, even fundamentalist, in its quest for a definitive and authentic feminist vision. Ironically, as we have seen, even the critical literature itself does not support such a project, since different critics frequently perceive different feminist essences in the fiction they survey.

A comparison of some critical observations about feminist utopian literature through the 1980s illustrates the point. Carol Pearson compares eight feminist works published from 1880 to 1975. She finds the following common feminist denominators: a focus on women's low status and low pay for their work; the primacy of motherhood; the absence of crime, due mainly to an absence of men; the lack of sex roles, if men are present; a lack of class structure or racial distinctions; love rather than money as a primary motivation for work; communal responsibility for child care; no romanticization of children; no sexual taboos (except against rape); no centralized government; a preference for small-scale social organizations; and the interconnection of self and world, as well as of humans and nature (1977, 58).

Frances Bartkowski analyzes ten novels published between 1915 and 1986 which she considers feminist. In them, she identifies the following common feminist characteristics: an emphasis on the power of speech and naming; communal social systems in which "the will to power is what arouses the greatest suspicion"; interest in power *to* rather than power *over;* government by consensus; and work, exchange, and family systems predicated on women's roles in reproduction (1989, 161–66).

Finally, Donawerth and Kolmerten study novels produced in a comparable period and find the following feminist themes: interest in cooperative sisterhoods or collectivism (instead of hierarchy); men's recruitment to "female" values or the establishment of a separate place for women; the creation of new myths central to women's identities; the elimination of binary oppositions; and a focus on women's lived experiences, especially motherhood. They claim that feminist utopian visions entail multiple worlds existing in relation rather than in opposition to one another (1994, 12–14).

There are a few overlaps in the critical interpretations. Motherhood, small-scale communities, and consensus forms of governance appear on all lists, for example, reflecting cultural or, in seventeenth- and eighteenth-century terms, evangelical, feminist interests in the inherent value of traditional female attitudes and behaviors—especially nurturing behavior and motherhood—and women's primarily moral and ethical power (Lewes 1995, 76–77). Even if these are accurate observations about the novels, however, the presence of those particular feminist values does not constitute a feminist essence. They certainly reflect positions that feminists have embraced, but they are not necessarily either essential to or comprehensive of feminism, which is immensely more diverse.

Of even more interest are the differences in the lists. Given the rather random selection of novels in the critical surveys, such differences are somewhat predictable. But the critics focus less on specific novels than on their symbolic value to feminism, without noticing how their own interests and the feminist politics of their own era shape both their selections and their interpretations. Thus, Pearson notices women's low wages in 1977, a time when equal or comparable pay was a primary feminist concern. Bartkowski emphasizes new forms of power in 1989, when that was a popular feminist topic. Her work followed by only a few years Marilyn French's *Beyond Power: On Women, Men, and Morals* (1985) and other works on feminine power. Donawerth and Kolmerten mention new myths of women's identities in the mid-1990s, when psychoanalytic and Jungian theories were the focus of much feminist theorizing.

Perhaps even more significant in these critical examples is what is not included. Few critics of the utopian canon analyze the value or accuracy of the novels' version of feminism, and few mention any oversights in the fiction. Thus, communal forms of government are noticed but not probed. Few critics consider whether suspicion of centralized government is a helpful feminist value or ask whether the woman-friendly, egalitarian, even maternal social policies utopia favors could develop or survive without a centralized government. By the same token, having noted the support for anarchy in some novels, few critics ask whether anarchism genuinely serves feminist interests or what feminist interests it might serve.

Such aspects of feminist utopian fiction should raise many questions, however. For example, we need to understand to what extent the traditions of utopianism itself, such as its distrust for strong government, rather than any essential feminist construction are responsible for the anarchism in such feminist works as Staton's *From the Legend of Biel*, Dorothy Bryant's *The Kin of Ata Are Waiting for You*, Thea Plym Alexander's *2150 A.D.*, Joanna Russ's *The Female Man*, and Suzy McKee Charnas's *Motherlines* (Sargent 1983, 3–9). By the same token, we need to understand to what extent the preference for personal over social relationships and the distrust of authority typical in such works negate feminist desires for communality, which often appear in the same works. Further, we need to explore how we can reconcile with feminism Elaine Baruch's observation that women prefer statelessness (or anarchy) because of their history of subordinating their own needs to those of others (1984, xii). We must consider whether a truly positive feminist value can be predicated on the tradition of women's self-abnegation.

Criticism of feminist utopian fiction should also explore the difficulty of addressing in the utopian context cultural, ethnic, and class differences among women, as well as ideological diversity or even conflict within feminism. For example, many feminists would dispute the value of Mary Staton's sentiment in *The Legend of Biel* that "we have said no to all systems good or bad, and to all who run systems, good or bad" (Sargent 1983, 19). Among them would be socialist or materialist feminists who support centralized economic control, and even liberal feminists who support women's equal participation in civic institutions. In addition, critics would do well to note that few feminist utopian novels portray democratic processes or depict the value of political debate. If such feminist variations are unwelcome in utopia, then we must begin to understand utopianism as supportive of only certain kinds of feminist views and not as the vanguard of feminism itself.

Criticism of feminist utopian fiction should also explore the variations and exceptions that do appear in the literary canon. For example, Margaret Cavendish's 1668 *Blazing-World* does incorporate dissent within utopia by providing for arguments (called Orations) among characters who have different approaches to women's participation in the public and private spheres. Darby Lewes characterizes the debates as reflecting rationalist/egalitarian models versus evangelical/moral models of feminism. The former base women's freedom and happiness on men, and the latter base those values on women's unique qualities, such as their freedom from political responsibility in the domestic sphere. Lewes also identifies works that reconcile the two positions in a *vatic* approach (1995, 74–77). The discussion of such exceptions and variations does not, however, dominate the critical canon, which frequently seems more determined to unify the fiction and to reveal particular feminist principles within it. Such an approach diminishes the importance and value of ideological diversity within feminist thought.

Balanced, analytical criticism of feminist utopian fictional works can, of course, celebrate the fiction while also revealing the limitations of utopian visions that discourage or omit the value of inquiry, exclude mechanisms for change, preclude debate, and overlook the need to negotiate legitimate but conflicting interests. A post-utopian critical perspective can promote methods for evaluating feminist ideas in the fiction and thereby avoid the temptation, now inflated by critical utopianism, to develop feminist values and approaches on the basis of insufficient information or analysis. Without such methods of evaluation, feminism becomes an impoverished foundation on which to build a society. Such post-utopian approaches to utopian fiction would ultimately enhance its value for feminist thought and theory by, for instance, assessing whether the recurrence of particular themes, such as communitarian socialism, means that their value has been proven in some way for feminist theory or simply that they conform to utopian expectations (Kessler 1984a, 8).[9]

Post-utopian criticism of Marge Piercy's *Woman on the Edge of Time*, might explore the deeper meanings of the novel's communal value system, especially as it conflicts with its parallel respect for rights to privacy: adults in Mattapoisett live alone, but the society depends on a

---

9. Kessler notes the predominance of communitarian socialism in the novels and the lack of influence by the other two types of feminism, but she does not explain the reason for it.

consensus model in which citizens achieve a collective sense of the common good. Decisions are made in groups that discuss issues until general agreement about their resolution is achieved. (In contrast, the Shakers built a sense of group affinity through communal—though single-sex—living arrangements.) The novel does recognize that the society's individualism can breed dissension by providing for conflict arbitration and resolution. But the only recourse in Mattapoisett when conflicts cannot be resolved is banishment or an imposed temporary invisibility (Piercy 1975, 211–14). (Rare crimes are punished by execution, after the second offense.) To conclude from this scenario simply that the novel supports communal values is to overlook its real challenge for feminist theory: how to reconcile values of individualism, privacy, and communality.

By the same token, post-utopian criticism would question the novel's assumption that harmony is an overriding feminist value, as demonstrated by its repeated critique of competition. In Mattapoisett, competition and friction are presumed to emanate from failed individual psychology, from "lack of rapport," as well as from the "patriarchal division of labor" (Piercy 1975, 211–14). Remove those irritants, the novel suggests, and harmony, justice, and equality will prevail. That scenario assumes but does not prove that competition is always bad and harmony is always good, either for feminism or for society at large. Post-utopian criticism could lead the way in a discussion of that issue.

Comparing the enactment of such presumed feminist values in various fictional works is another important post-utopian critical task. To discover the possible costs and benefits of achieving consensus on a large scale, for example, we can juxtapose Doris Lessing's utopian *oeuvre* to Piercy's novel. Lessing, too, imagines a world that is unified and communal; she wants people to achieve harmony among themselves and between themselves and animals. But the harmony she imagines implies conformity with an overall Order, based on an essential Necessity. Harmony can be achieved "only insofar as we are in harmony with the plan, the phases of our evolution," she writes. While Lessing doesn't promote dictatorial rule, she does envision a voluntary "internal perception of [the] validity" of Order and Necessity, which amounts to almost the same thing (White 1983, 135).

Lessing depicts an "inherent rightness" approach to government. She rejects politics altogether in the usual sense, not because of its history of patriarchal power plays or domination by males, as some writers do, but (perhaps ironically) because of its alleged emotionalism, a supposedly female/feminist value. Lessing considers politics "an essentially emotional enterprise, proceeding especially from pity and pride" and leading "to the unacceptable condition of some people running the lives of others" (White 1983, 134). Related forms of Lessing's ideas appear in several other feminist utopian works, among them those by Sarah Robinson Scott, Charlotte Perkins Gilman, and Mary Staton, as well as Piercy. What are the implications for feminist thought of such novels' association of feminist values with various kinds of unified orders, governed by single sets of values to which all right-thinking utopian citizens conform, albeit in a voluntary and/or intuitive (female) way? Do such scenarios also have dystopian connotations? Comprehensive post-utopian criticism of feminist utopian fiction should compare and evaluate such fictional forms of government, especially in light of the promotion of anarchy in other putatively feminist works.

THE TEST OF THE PUDDING

Post-utopian criticism would also compare women's actual experiences in utopian settings with fictional portrayals of the same or similar experiences. As we have seen, the historical record suggests that feminism has been hospitable to utopianism, but the reverse has not always been the case.

As we have seen, nineteenth-century American utopian experiments often failed to implement feminist reforms, even when they intended to. Recall the experiences of Abigail Alcott at Fruitlands and of Oneidan women discussed in chapter 1. Late twentieth-century communities, both in the United States and abroad, offer additional examples. In separate experiences in the mid-1980s at two communities, Twin Oaks in Virginia and Findhorn in Scotland, Batya Weinbaum and Arlene Sheer discovered that utopian practice, even when informed by the allegedly feminist values and social reforms typical of feminist utopian fiction, did not necessarily fulfill their feminist dreams.

Batya Weinbaum was confident she would find Twin Oaks a feminist utopia, because of its communal organization, which promoted economic equity for all and valued women's traditional labor. She noted, in short, that Twin Oaks is run "so [that] many of the structural requirements for the liberation of women are met." Nevertheless, Weinbaum was disappointed during her 1984 stay at Twin Oaks. Despite the community's efforts to eliminate gender prejudice in employment practices, to make "everyone feel at home throughout the entire workplace," to reevaluate the institution of motherhood so that pregnant women earn labor credits for their reproductive work, to share responsibility for childrearing, and to give priority to the so-called female values of nurturance and emotional expressiveness, Weinbaum still found a low level of "feminist consciousness." The primary reason was the inability of the community's structural changes either to meet or to obviate individual needs, even for those who had lived at Twin Oaks during its entire twenty-six-year history, and even though maternity—presumably women's most pressing need—was fully accommodated. Nevertheless, Weinbaum concluded, Twin Oaks' society did not fully address women's "different norms" (1984, 161–67).

Arlene Sheer began her ten-week stay at Findhorn, Scotland, in the early 1980s with similar expectations. Yet, Sheer's experience, which also disappointed her, illustrates even further the gap seldom bridged in utopian design between social structure and individual needs. Like Twin Oaks, Findhorn is organized to equalize work burdens and to eliminate gender-specific roles. But at Findhorn, work is also deemed a spiritual experience and a manifestation of love. Following Fourieristic guidelines, people choose work assignments as their spirits direct. In addition, much time is devoted to the sharing of emotional responses to everything and everyone in the (utopian) belief that airing feelings is tantamount to changing or controlling them. Despite her enjoyment of Findhorn, however, Sheer discovered that the structural changes and almost compulsive attention to relationships had little effect on two key psychological realities: older men, who were still considered sexually attractive, were not attracted to women of their own age; and older women were upset by their loss of sexual allure (1984, 147–52). Echoing the history of Oneida and the Woman's Commonwealth, the community's policies and practices did not sufficiently accommodate the psychological needs or counter the perhaps sexist socialization of individual members.

Added to women's experience in nineteenth-century communities, these relatively modern utopian experiences illustrate the tremendous challenge entailed in social design. Among other complexities, the problems that such designs attempt to address involve both individual and collective components. Purely collective or social solutions may or may not win individual hearts and minds. Moreover, artificially imposed social schemes can obscure without eliminating psychological and social dynamics, which tend to become exaggerated under suppression. Just as forty years of Communist rule masked the ethnic and religious conflicts of eastern Europe without destroying them, utopias can actually expand the needs they ignore.

Weinbaum's and Sheer's responses to their communal sojourns also demonstrate another effect of utopian expectations. As with the many critics who have analyzed feminist utopian fiction, Weinbaum's utopian mindset prevented her from interrogating her own definition of feminism as the recognition and pursuit of women's "different norms." Therefore, she pronounced unfeminist practices at Twin Oaks that others might have judged very differently. Sheer's utopian mindset also obscured her personal interest in Findhorn's practices and dynamics. She did not consider the impact of her own age—over fifty—on her assessment of the community's feminism, nor did she address concerns that a younger or older woman might have had.

POST-UTOPIAN CRITICISM

Although a comprehensive, post-utopian criticism of feminist utopian fiction has yet to be written, some critics have challenged the feminism of specific utopian visions and questioned utopia as a model for feminism. Darby Lewes, for example, has revealed that the utopian fictional genre, even when produced by women writers, is not necessarily suitable for portraying truly egalitarian societies or for challenging the natural hierarchy of the sexes. She identifies as feminist only one in ten of the ninety-five utopian novels written by women in the nineteenth century (1995, 18).

Among the critics questioning the feminist credentials of particular utopian fictional works is Jewell Parker Rhodes. Rhodes criticizes Ursula Le Guin's *Left Hand of Darkness* by arguing that its foundation in androgyny reinforces gender stereotypes and implies that neither sex is whole and self-contained but, rather, requires the other in order to be complete. Rhodes asks, "Isn't it perhaps more appropriately feminist and more realistic to suggest that one of the pre-conditions for utopian society is the belief that men and women, excluding physical differences, are equal . . . are not deficient, as androgyny implies, in their capacity for human response; rather, social conditioning modifies and restricts behavior to gender categories? Isn't it more feminist to assume that neither sex is predisposed to act out any set of gender-associated qualities?" (1983, 111, 115).

Hoda Zaki takes on the hidden conservatism of feminist utopias. Using Katherine V. Forrest's *Daughters of a Coral Dawn* as an exemplar, Zaki notes that beneath the typical feminist utopian pattern of small decentralized governments, a motherly leader, consensus decision making, organic unity among society members (all women, in this case), and the disappearance of political tension lie hereditary rights, appointed rather than elected officials, stifled debate, and personality cults. Cybele, the society in *Coral Dawn,* is an hereditary matriarchy, based on kinship, status, privilege, and a family-based ideology. Its political realities are "hidden under images of motherhood, sisterhood, kinship, sibling rivalry, and certain notions of the home." Even more distressing to Zaki is the novel's suggestion that political problems can be solved by individuals acting alone. She argues that such feminist notions of utopia represent a "retreat from the domain of oppositional activity and political discourse" (1984, 126–29).

The simplicity and inflexibility of most utopian visions disturb Sarah Goodwin because those qualities impugn the flexibility and complexity of feminism. She tempers her criticism, however, with appreciation for the way utopian visions identify "the capacity within the possible to change for the better" (1990, 2–4).

Jean Bethke Elshtain criticizes the ideological tendencies of utopian thinking itself. Elshtain argues that ideology actually destroys rather than promotes "the capacity for concrete thinking." She deplores "the utopianism of ideological certainties [which] flows from thought that is never a diagnosis of a real situation. . . . What may begin as a response to social conditions," Elshtain continues, "may become a self-reproducing artifact of its own drive toward systematization" (Goodwin 1990, 3). Equally incapacitating, according to Elshtain, are utopianism's universal narratives and subjects, ahistorical searches for the roots of all ways of life, defined endpoints, and epistemic privilege for women (1986, 16–17).

Ellen Peel finds utopianism anathema to feminism's real intent—a questioning, doubting, inquiring attitude about all settled convictions. The skeptic rather than the utopian thinker is more consistent with that intent, Peel explains. Utopianism fixes on and implements specific ideas from feminism, but skeptical feminism "directs suspicion not only toward patriarchy but also toward the pat answers of utopian feminism" (1990, 34–35).

Not all critiques of the fiction's value for feminist thinking are obvious. Some can be discovered by comparing critical analyses of the same literary works. For example, comparing Marleen Barr's and Sarah Goodwin's analyses of Isak Dinesen's "Babette's Feast" reveals a hidden disagreement between them about what, exactly, is feminist about the novella. Goodwin claims that the work's feminism resides in its subtlety, its attribution of utopia to a state of mind, covert and unconscious, rather than to overt attempts to create utopia, like those of the unhappy Norwegian Puritans. Goodwin therefore concludes that "a feminist utopianism might well look for its own realization partly in concealed moments, rather than in the less possibly real vision of a violent revolution or a pious experiment in communal life" (1990, 16).

Barr, on the other hand, finds feminism in the story's exploration of woman's inferior status as well as in its fantastic quality. To her, Babette is a "female alien" who slowly becomes integrated into the Puritan community. Her feminism is revealed in her nurturing behavior, cooking for others, and in her role as feminist fabulator, promoting an undervalued female art form—cooking—which, like quilts, is linked to the domestic female tradition. "Like the feast, feminist fabulation presents the possibility of new physical worlds and new mutual social respect" (1990, 24–25).

TOWARD HIGHER GROUND

Such dissenting voices provide the basis of a post-utopian critique of utopian feminist fiction, but a more cohesive effort would do even more to reveal the ways in which utopianism both molds and is molded by feminist ideas. That is, while the novels respond sometimes brilliantly to present conditions—by absorbing them, reflecting them, and critiquing them—they also impose the requirements of utopianism itself: categorizing people and ideas, emphasizing practices rather than processes, offering solutions rather than questions, promoting unified themes rather than competing values, exaggerating the effects of social design, and underestimating the lessons of history. To the extent that the fiction promises complete harmony and mutual understanding, it also breeds disillusionment.

A comprehensive post-utopian critical approach to feminist utopian fiction would examine the policies and practices in that fiction, asking in what ways they might be better or worse than the ones they replace. Such an approach would take into account the complexity and unpredictability of human beings, which render human nature inevitably ambiguous and the human response, even an individual's response, to social structures both positive and negative.

Higher Ground argues that the movement away from utopianism and toward realism produces a richer, and possibly more enduring, foundation for feminist thought. But rejecting utopianism as a metaphor for, or even a strong component of, feminist thinking also raises some additional questions. What, if not a realizable dream of social structures and practices, could feminism possibly be? How can feminist principles best be formulated and shared? What, if anything, do feminists have in common? Are there limits to the diversity of ideas that qualify as feminist? *Higher Ground* argues that the best approaches to those questions reside outside the parameters of utopian thinking. As the analysis proceeds, we shall explore other alternatives, rooted in realism, for the establishment of a principled yet flexible, dynamic, and complex framework for feminist thought.

11 UTOPIANISM IN FEMINIST THOUGHT AND THEORY

INTRODUCTION

Feminism is a movement that requires a vision of something else: a utopian perspective which inspires and informs the struggle against present oppression.
—Toril Moi, "Beauvoir's Utopia: The Politics of the Second Sex"

Beyond the canon of feminist utopian fiction lies a world of feminist essays, philosophical analyses, and political tracts in which utopia and utopian structures and expectations serve as powerful metaphors for feminist thought. As Toril Moi observes, such a utopian perspective makes a perfect foil for oppression in the existing world. Utopian voices beckon us to a new world in which feminist values are self-evident, women's insights are inevitably valuable, and the benefits of women's leadership are assumed. For some, the utopian connection seems unproblematic, even natural; they do not see in such appealing visions the hazards of utopianism as a framework for social change. As we have seen, however, the history of utopian thought should engender our caution. Even feminist thinkers must acknowledge the pitfalls of utopian approaches to social change.

That concern with the hazards of utopianism informs the next two chapters of *Higher Ground*. The first, chapter 3, "Detecting Utopianism," examines both explicit and implicit utopian habits in feminist thought, such as idealization and the exaggeration of social influences on human motivation and desire. In addition, chapter 3 explores certain epistemological flaws that frequently accompany utopian thought, including coherentism, foundationalism, confirmation bias, and the myth of the truth teller. Chapter 4, "Utopian Discourses," examines specific examples of utopian thinking in three categories of feminist thought and theory: the discourse of gender difference, the discourse of differences among women, and the discourse of linguistic construction. Among the utopian constructions that emerge from those discourses are gender dichotomy, identity politics, epistemic privilege, and gender-as-performance.

I recognize that an undertaking designed to represent feminist thought and theory may itself seem utopian, since the universe of texts that could be included is now so vast that no individual can hope to know, define, or even identify it all. I do not purport to represent that universe in full, however, nor do I claim to know it fully. Rather, I offer telling examples from texts published between the 1970s and 1999 in the three categories of discourse that form the analytical framework of this book. My selections reflect my knowledge of and involvement in feminist theory for the last twenty years.

In addition, throughout the analysis in both part II and part III, I have occasionally cited or referred to the work of a single theorist as both utopian and realistic. At first glance, that double usage might seem inconsistent, but it occurs for the simple reason that utopianism has not heretofore been recognized as an element of or an organizing principle for feminist theoretical work. Therefore, a particular theorist's body of work, or even a single essay, may well contain both utopian and realistic arguments or claims.

THREE *Detecting Utopianism*

*We, as women, have much to lose by giving up the utopian hope in the
"wholly other."*
—Seyla Benhabib, "Feminism and Postmodernism: An Uneasy
Alliance"

*What [besides matriarchy and separatism] could constitute a plausible femi-
nist utopia? One that might be achievable? One that wouldn't be totally
fantasy? Is there such a thing? . . . I think so. Let me restrict myself . . . to
these United States, with the stipulation that it is a model to be expanded
to the entire world, with whatever modifications each individual culture
required.*
—Suzette Haden Elgin, "Washing Utopian Dishes, Scrubbing
Utopian Floors"

*We separatists today feel that withdrawal of our energies from men is not
enough, it is only the first stage in our building of a female world. The second
stage is to engage in active confrontation of the patriarchy and its death culture, and to attempt to overthrow it by drastically facing the male problem
and solving it once and for all through the elimination of male control over
women.*
—Charoula, "Dyke Separatist Womanifesto"

Utopianism inflects contemporary feminist thought in various
ways. From the 1970s through the 1990s, many theorists have
explicitly invoked the name or processes of utopia in the formulation
of their feminist theoretical perspectives. From Charoula's "final solution" (1977) to Elgin's universal model (1992) to Benhabib's utopian
faith in the "wholly other" (1995), utopian perspectives have been

commonplace in feminist theorizing. Even theorists, like Benhabib, who recognize that utopianism has limits, often cling to the hope and promise it represents. Thus, while Benhabib appreciates that "postmodernism can teach us the theoretical and political traps of why utopias and foundational thinking can go wrong," she concludes that "it should not lead to a retreat from utopia altogether." Women need the utopian "wholly other"; feminism represents a "utopia of values," including ecology, nonmilitarism, and social unity (1995, 30). Benhabib's commitment to the utopian perspective in feminist thought echoes that of many other theorists. Among them are Paula Treichler, who laments that "no utopian pedagogical forms exist" (1994, 93), and Sandra Bem, who has a "vision of utopia in which gender polarization [and] androcentrism has been so completely dismantled that —except in narrowly biological contexts like reproduction—the distinction between male and female no longer organizes either the culture or the psyche" (1993, 192). Literary critic Toril Moi even warns that de-utopianizing feminism will de-politicize it (1993, 352).

Not all evocations of utopianism are quite so explicit, but much contemporary feminist thought and theory contains embedded utopian metaphors. That is, even though they refer to no specific historical community or literary work, and make no suggestion of a separate or ideal community or new social design, these metaphors reflect the patterns of thought underlying utopian literary and experimental movements. Such utopian metaphors include the equation of social change with utopian historical reversals, oppositional cultural practices, or Eden-like past or future visions (Lauret 1994, 156–57). Or they involve utopian assumptions that filter feminist thought: societies and human nature are perfectible; foundational ideas can be eternal and unambiguous; consistent happiness can be achieved; most problems can be defined and permanently solved; consensus can and must occur. Such a filter not only masks the inevitability—and benefits— of uncertainty and change, it can also inflate feminist expectations and lead to disappointment and disillusionment.

That utopianism and feminism have long been compatible, however, does not mean that they are or should be inseparable. After all, feminist theory is famous for denaturalizing familiar associations, as it has denaturalized women's nurturing roles and male dominance. Indeed, such disruptions of easy, apparently natural associations, rather than the provision of specific social visions, may constitute feminism's most enduring legacy.

Once an association seems natural and familiar, feminism should begin to investigate. And investigation reveals hazards. Elgin's utopianism, for example, leads to the imposition of a very United States–based analysis upon the wider world, with only minor variations. Charoula's utopianism leads her to exaggerate the male-female dichotomy in which women are figured as angelic and men as evil. Moi defines utopia as a politicizing force for feminism without explanation or justification, a common utopian tendency. By definition, utopian constructions typically resist validation and self-scrutiny. Thus, Moi does not explain why utopia is the only way for feminism to achieve a political identity. Benhabib does not explain how utopia relates to the "wholly other," or why women, who have so long been "othered," need such a thing. *Utopia* becomes a magic term used to bestow value on the concepts associated with it—ecology, nonmilitarism, identity, otherness, androgyny—while leaving those concepts, as well as utopianism itself, unexamined.

Underlying assumptions that gender or sexuality is always the primary salient feature of every human interaction reflect the utopian propensity to isolate behaviors and characteristics as the foundation of a utopian plan. The Shakers, for example, identified sexual activity and procreation (or the abjuration of same) as the foundation of all human thought, belief, behavior, and relationships. But imbuing a single act or characteristic with so much importance both distorts its meaning and obscures the significance of other characteristics.

Feminist theory that idealizes or romanticizes identity groups is also implicitly utopian. Not all lesbians are heroic, as Monique Wittig's *Les Guérillères* (1969) and certain lesbian separatist doctrines suggest. Not all mothers are infallibly wise, as some feminist utopian novels and certain feminist theories of female gender identity imply. While flattering, such characterizations set the stage for both external resistance to the hyperbole and internal dissent around unacknowledged diversity within the group.

Utopianism often leads feminist theorists to offer problem reversal as problem solution. Betty Friedan's proposals in *The Feminine Mystique* (1963) exemplify that process by suggesting that middle-class women's problem (mind-numbing, full-time housewifery) could be solved by inverting their world (exciting full-time careers for all women). But problems may or may not suggest their solutions, may or may not reveal the heart of the matter that really needs solving, may or may not be as universal or timeless as they seem. We have seen Friedan making that discovery for herself. In *The Second Stage* she found herself addressing the consequences of the "feminine mystique" by reversing it, evoking instead the "feminist mystique." Thus, she called for a "second stage" of feminism to undo the first. Ironically, however, she had to admit that the problem she was now reversing was one she had helped to create herself, by defining feminism in 1960s as opposed rather than connected to women's roles in the family (228). That definition was itself a utopian reversal.

Feminist pedagogy has been especially susceptible to utopian thinking. When students demand a classroom that is "a safe space" for women, for example, they imply a utopian desire for learning to occur without offense. But can it? If a "safe space" promotes misinformation or unexamined conclusions, even in the name of protecting feelings, then it interferes with learning and perpetuates ignorance. Often the "safe space" means a separatist space without men, a familiar construction in utopian novels. But is that configuration useful or necessary? In Sally Gearhart's *The Wanderground*, separatism seems necessary because men and women are defined as hopelessly divided, "no longer of the same species" (1979, 115). Thus, the only solution to the declared war between the sexes is complete separation. Utopia may need such distinct categories, such divisions between sexualized notions of good and evil, but why does feminism?

Also utopian are works on feminist pedagogy that make hyperbolic claims for the outcomes of women's studies instruction. For example, Carolyn Shrewsbury described in 1993 a "liberatory classroom," in which we "get beyond our sexism and racism and classism and homophobia and other destructive hatreds and . . . work together to enhance our knowledge; engaged with the community, with traditional organizations, and with movements for social change" (8). Her utopianism prevented Shrewsbury from considering whether a classroom can or should really accomplish all that. But, as Daphne Patai's disillusionment with women's studies suggests, once such utopian expectations have been raised for them, women's studies classrooms are very liable to disappoint. Utopianism also prevented Shrewsbury from considering whether a classroom should be a site for activism rather than one for defining and discussing the "-isms" she identifies for constructing and evaluating strategies for social change. If classrooms become the agents for predetermined acts of reform, then where will the evaluation and scrutiny of such acts occur?

Utopian social goals and hyperbolic expectations in women's studies pedagogy have sometimes completely replaced concern with learning goals and performance standards, producing disastrous results. Such strategies are utopian in a number of ways. They exaggerate the plasticity of human beings and the impact that small groups—like a single class—can have on the larger world. They also appropriate goals from one domain to another without careful thought, without asking, for example, to what extent classrooms should function like democracies and/or activist organizations. Women's studies professors Susan Stanford Friedman and Barbara Omolade have both documented their difficulties with such utopian approaches to pedagogy, which emphasize student empowerment and social change and overlook the realities of learning, teaching, and evaluation.

As a follower of theorists Herbert Kohl and Jerry Farber, Friedman approached her early teaching assignment with a distaste for authority. In her view, Kohl and Farber had discredited the use of authority in the classroom, devalued a teacher's training and experience, condemned learners' roles of powerlessness and vulnerability, and conceptualized the classroom as a site of social change. Friedman therefore wanted to create a classroom that empowered students and, by extension, reformed the society that had disempowered them in the first place. So, she de-emphasized her own authority to design and structure her courses and to evaluate students and emphasized students' power to control their learning experiences. The result was anything but utopia. Not only did her techniques do little to alter an unjust society, they also actually undermined the students' capacity for social agency by depriving them of her knowledge as well as the opportunity to challenge their own ideas and to develop methods for precise and rigorous thought. Her approach also inadvertently fueled cultural stereotypes about women as all-forgiving nurturers whose approval is unconditional (Friedman 1985, 203–8).

Omolade's initial vision of a nonhierarchical classroom was similarly utopian. Her premise was a utopian reversal; if the concept of hierarchy had created racism, sexism, and economic injustice, then absolute equality would create their opposite. Like Friedman's, however, Omolade's utopian pedagogical techniques backfired. Her desire to develop a sisterly relationship with her primarily nontraditional black women students and to make them feel like equal contributors to the learning environment resulted in the students' disappointment. They really wanted her to teach them, "not just to be sisterly and befriend or rant politics at them." Her equation of equality with sameness actually deprived Omolade's students of the benefits of *her* educational background and therefore her *unequal* contribution to the classroom. Only when she abandoned her utopian perspective did she recognize that her ability to challenge her students and to make rigorous academic demands on them would do more to overcome their power-lessness than would her utopian ideals (1993, 32, 37).

Similar utopian goals can also affect feminist organizations and create equally negative results. Again I turn to the National Women's Studies Association, whose utopian conference announcement we have already dissected. The organization's original charter, now revised, described its mission to support "all feminists involved in [feminist education] at every educational level and . . . setting." That mission, utopian in its scope, led to years of disappointment because, in reality, N.W.S.A.'s membership consisted primarily of college faculty involved in academic women's studies (Leidner 1991, 269). To compensate for that lack of diversity, the organization began to adopt governance policies designed to increase the group's membership in the preferred directions, including more racial and ethnic minorities and more K-12 teachers and community-based educators. Those policies resulted in the overrepresentation of certain groups, relative to their numbers, in the organization's decision-making process. That policy benefited the organization by encouraging a variety of perspectives and accommodating groups who were underrepresented, but it also created difficulties. It emphasized the very factors (individuals' sexuality or race, for example) that promoted irreconcilable difference and conflict, rather than factors (such as ideas) that could be negotiated and discussed. Second, it raised the expectations of underrepresented groups that they would find satisfaction in the organization despite their small numbers (ibid., 278, 287–88). Those expectations were difficult to fulfill.

N.W.S.A.'s desire to increase and diversify its membership was not in and of itself a utopian goal, of course. It was the overemphasis on that goal, especially in the face of its unlikelihood, that became utopian and risked making the organization dysfunctional for the existing membership, which made its existence possible (Leidner 1991, 278–79). Such a utopian gaze over the heads of current members suggested to them that they were less interesting to N.W.S.A. than those it had not yet attracted.[1] Without utopian lenses, N.W.S.A. and other feminist organizations would be in a better position to acknowledge their actual political base (Leidner 1993, 21), to "focus on realistic yet limited goals," to show "respect and care for the real people and programs that gain and lose whenever resource decisions are made,"

---

1. Changes in the N.W.S.A. constitution in 1999 went a long way toward solving these utopian issues about membership.

and to resist "the sort of idealism that allows virtue to trump respect" (Leidner 1994, 105).

Some feminist organizations have also approached the concepts of power and competition via utopian thinking which assumes that women do not desire power or feel competitive. Such approaches not only idealize women's presumed qualities in utopian ways, they also reinforce women's historical powerlessness, which was once mistaken for femininity. A more realistic view anticipates and takes into account the competitive feelings that emerge, even for women, when resources are scarce or once-denied rewards become possible (Keller and Moglen 1987, 23).

In an effort to achieve a utopian world without power struggles or competition, feminist groups have sometimes disparaged concepts of structure and leadership in the belief that structures themselves create oppression. In some instances, the utopian instinct for reversal has led groups to seek the opposite—structurelessness—as the remedy for such oppression. Jo Freeman is one feminist activist who discovered the hidden forms of oppression within that version of problem reversal. She observed in the 1970s how easily structurelessness in feminist groups became "a smokescreen for the strong or the lucky to establish unquestioned hegemony over others" because "it did not prevent the formation of informal structures, but only formal ones" (Freeman [1972] 1973, 152). Furthermore, Freeman found that structureless groups were mostly "politically inefficacious, exclusive and discriminatory against those women who are not or cannot be tied into the friendship networks . . . who do not fit into what already exists because of class, race, occupation, education, parental or marital status, or personality [and who, therefore] will inevitably be discouraged from trying to participate" (ibid., 162). Hardly utopia.

A truly lamentable by-product of utopian approaches to feminist organizations has been *trashing,* that is personal attacks by feminists on other feminists for their failure to live up to some, often unstated, feminist ideal. I have witnessed mild forms of trashing, and it is not a pretty sight. A woman will be speaking in a roomful of people she has reason to see as her colleagues and supporters. Suddenly, someone in the audience will stand up and tell her that she has violated a standard so crucial that she can no longer be trusted, or considered a member of this group, or worthy of her office. Often the first speaker will be joined by another or several others until the target of the trashing feels completely betrayed and humiliated. Trashing is typically directed at the most utopian of feminists, those who seek appreciation and assume that they will get it from the people they've worked hard to serve (Gage 1993, 16). Trashing is a cynical exploitation of human sincerity as well as of utopian discourses of perfection and hyperbolic expectations.

Underlying trashing, as well as other forms of feminist utopian thinking, is often the quest for feminist purity in thought and action. Such a quest implies that feminism, like sinlessness for the Shakers, can best be found within a narrow set of specified virtues. Feminist purity obviates the broad base of feminism and substitutes a feminist rule book, with heroes and villains, for a feminist toolbox. Motivating the quest for purity is often a fear of co-optation, the belief that feminists might compromise the essence of their beliefs (whatever those are) through certain specified actions or collaborations. Accompanying it are fears of flexibility, fears that make feminism into an absolute rather than a dynamic process.

Some feminist thinkers enact the quest for purity by developing an aversion to everything associated with patriarchy—"the manifestation and institutionalization of male dominance over women and children in the family and the extension of male dominance over women in society in general" (Lerner 1986, 239). While probably justified on some counts, that aversion can easily become exaggerated, since almost everything that exists is associated with patriarchy in some way. But when such an aversion leads to a kind of feminist purity that requires distance from all existing power structures and a priori negative judgments about existing modes of organization, it can backfire. Thus, some feminist purists might accuse a women's studies faculty of being co-opted by patriarchy in their desire to become a department, since departments were not a feminist invention and have even inflicted harm on women. But such a response risks sacrificing the benefits of existing structures in the name of resistance. How do we know that the goals of women's studies will be compromised when units become departments?

Robin Leidner, who has studied the issue of co-optation, found no evidence that "departures from feminist purity" would produce it. Leidner concludes, rather, that "it would be more useful for practitioners to consider carefully the kinds of outcomes that various strategies of engagement could produce than to hold each other to standards of feminist virtue that treat all engagement with mainstream institutions as co-optive" (1993, 23).

A similar quest for feminist purity is evident in the response of some feminist theorists toward others of differing views. For example, a recent anthology, *Radically Speaking: Feminism Reclaimed* (Bell and Klein 1996), which purports simply to describe conflicts between radical and postmodern feminist theorists, actually sets up a utopian dichotomy. On one side are postmodernists, called "po-mos" in the book, who have abandoned pure feminism. They are the enemies— one of the "Bad Guys of Backlash"—who cause feminism's troubles. On the other side are radicals, "righteous sisters" who have remained true to pure feminism. Although utopia needs a "we" and a "they," why does feminism? Wouldn't it be better, as Elayne Rapping suggests, to frame disagreements among feminists with the recognition that they "involve serious disagreement about how best to build a world in which women—all women—will . . . have the opportunity to thrive and prosper" (1996, 9–10)? Purity may be necessary in utopia, but why allow it to replace listening, learning, and negotiating in the formulation of feminist thought and theory?

UTOPIAN THEORIZING ABOUT FEMINIST THEORY

In truth, feminist thought and theory is a many-splendored thing. Some feminist theorists analyze women's subordination, describe women's experience, seek women's freedom, equal opportunity, and self-determination, and demand improvement in the material condition of women's lives (Gordon 1991, 105). Others focus more on the cultural representation of gender in advertising, art, film, and literature than on economics and politics. Still others synthesize those analyses. Some feminist thinkers predicate everything on the notion of equality, while others challenge equality as the mere normalization of men's rights and roles. Many tout self-determination as the key feminist goal, while others consider self-determination a white, middle-class value with little relevance to the community-focused worlds of African American or Third World women.

Indeed, feminism's varied and sometimes contentious history may help explain the attraction of utopianism, which seems to offer harmony among the myriad positions that have characterized feminist thought and theory over the years. But is harmony the highest goal? Doesn't the quest for harmony itself indicate a utopian mind-set in its automatic distrust of conflict, dialectic, and debate? How do we know that feminism is better off with a unified rather than a cacophonous voice? How do we know that internal dissension is not feminism's greatest strength?

If contention *is* feminism's strong suit, then we are strong indeed.

Feminist theorists have offered many, sometimes mutually exclusive, explanations of women's oppression: how and why women have been denied fundamental personhood, social, economic, and political rights; how and why women have not been able to promote their own best interests; how and why women have been thrust into oppressive loyalties, roles, jobs, symbolic and real positions, relationships, and/or political status. Various theories have also explored what the labels "woman" and "women" mean or whether they mean anything at all, how gender and power relate to one another in existing social structures, how issues of race, class, sexuality, age, and other markers of difference are intertwined with sex to construct women's diverse experiences, opportunities, and oppressions. Different theories have also suggested numerous, sometimes contradictory means of liberation from such gender-based experiences and oppressions.

In addition, the term *feminism* itself has had variable meanings over time. It has denoted (and still denotes) everything from the assertion of women's basic personhood, to the promotion of their equal social, economic, and political rights, to the representation of their interests (Richards 1980, 2), to the expression of their difference (from men) and unique strengths, to "women's release from unreal and oppressive loyalties" (McDowell 1990, 110).

Many taxonomies of feminist theory have acknowledged this plethora of feminist theoretical perspectives and definitions. In the 1980s, for example, Alison Jaggar (1983) and Josephine Donovan (1985) identified radical, liberal, Marxist, socialist, and cultural or "gender" feminism, the last referring to a belief in women's innate virtues and a desire to elevate those virtues to dominance in the wider society.[2] Rosemarie Tong's 1989 *Feminist Thought* omitted gender feminism, but included mothering and sexuality in the category of radical feminism and added existentialist, psychoanalytic, and postmodern feminism to the categories on Donovan's and Jaggar's lists. In 1994, Ann Ferguson surveyed the same universe in yet a different way: through specific issues, such as pornography, lesbian sexuality, separatism, and patriarchy (208). Tong has published a second edition of her text (1998) that modifies her original categories and adds multicultural and global feminism as well as ecofeminism to the list.

Nevertheless, despite the recognition of feminist variety among these different "theorists of theory," utopianism frequently lurks be-

2. Alison Jaggar, *Feminist Politics and Human Nature* (1983); Josephine Donovan, *Feminist Theory* (1985).

neath their patient explanations of feminism's vast diversity. For example, Donovan, Jaggar, Tong, and Ferguson all express utopian hopes for the eventual unity of feminist theory, or they plot trajectories toward the one *true* feminism, or they project a time or place (Eden?) when current controversies will be resolved. Tong, echoing the sentiments of Alison Jaggar, selected socialist feminism as the best of the theories in the 1989 version of her text. She regarded socialist feminism as the most abstract of the theories, the least beholden to existing social conditions and realities, and, therefore, the most objective (1989, 236). Tong's choice is utopian both because it identifies an ideal or ultimate version of feminism and because it suggests (as many utopian societies have done) that the fact of isolation from the "real" world produces value and virtue. Indeed, socialist feminism's greatest (utopian) qualification for Tong's first prize was its distance from the real circumstances of women's lives!

That she changed her mind ten years later illustrates the present focus of utopian schemes for social change. Tong admitted in the 1998 version of her book that she had earlier failed to notice the extent to which socialist feminism overlooks issues that she herself overlooked a decade earlier, such as racism, colonialism, and what she calls naturism. Having become more aware, in 1998 she found ecofeminism "the most inclusive form of feminism" for addressing those issues (278). Her point, that both she and feminism had changed, is precisely *the* point; when we force ourselves to select ultimate solutions rather than to engage in open-ended processes of analysis, we risk imposing dangerous limitations on our conclusions.

Utopianism also convinces many theorists that novelty in feminist analysis is necessarily an improvement on the past. For example, Judith Grant, in tracing the "development" of feminism, considers feminist liberalism passé primarily because of its association with the so-called first wave of feminism in the nineteenth century (1993, 2). Such notions become even more utopian when they seek to replace the past with its opposite or inverted image (Jameson 1985, 203). Utopianism also infuses the discourse of feminist theorizing that assumes rather than explores its own core values. For example, Ann Ferguson not only awaits feminism's "global analytic," an implicitly utopian vision of a grand unified theory, but she also assumes that the meanings of the analytical categories she chooses for that analytic —race, gender, capitalism, imperialism, and heterosexism—are self-evident and static (1994, 208). But assuming consensus about such important and complex terms, like presuming consensus on scented soap, eclipses debate on the foundations of feminist thought. It also presumes that feminism works best when it supplies unified answers and presents a single face, that there are no wrinkles in the fabric that connects us.

THEN WHAT IS FEMINISM?

Skeptics might well wonder whether all of this variety compromises the very meaning of feminism. What about the need to seek feminist common ground? Shouldn't we be comparing and judging the quality of feminist theories? Yes, I think we should. But seeking common ground and invoking standards are not necessarily utopian activities, unless they require that someone must be wrong, or insist that differences in ideas necessarily imply opposition, or accept as transparent all labels applied to various ideas or identities, or see feminism as an absolute or a set of universal and eternal rules, or consider debate and contention signs of weakness. It is utopianism, not feminism, that urges us to see a progressive trajectory of feminist wisdom through time or to believe that modern views are necessarily better than all those from the past. In reality, the past has value and progress can be treacherous, as well as vice versa. Perhaps feminism should be indeterminate. Perhaps feminism is best understood as a shared element of differing or even oppositional values, such as personal fulfillment and communal responsibility. Feminism can inhere, for example, in both the desire to have a child and the need to resist what Adrienne Rich calls the institution of motherhood.

Utopian theorist Joan Reif would not agree. She wonders what is so bad about a feminist utopian metaphor that allows theorists to "dream of more auspicious times and better places," or to work, write, and act as if their dreams can be fulfilled. Maybe nothing, as long as we recognize such dreaming for what it is. But Reif continues: utopian dreaming allows some feminist thinkers to turn "if only" into "what if" and "wishful" thinking into "will-ful" thinking. For them, utopia means subversion, the best way to dismantle "some of the most cherished institutions of the patriarchal society we inhabit—the family, the desire for social change, church, law and state." For them, utopian visions serve as myths that reformulate fundamental feelings and social emotions into symbolic discourse that heals the wounds of real society (Reif 1991, 8, 10, 3, 16, 21, 8). If feminism has therefore been the air in everybody's balloon, Reif implies, mightn't realism be an unwelcome pin?

Such evocations of utopianism can give realists pause, until we remember that dreams, disruptions, symbolic discourse, and myths are simply dreams, disruptions, symbolic discourse, and myths. They can point to desires, values, and acts of rebellion, but they are not tantamount to social-change strategies. In fact, as we have seen, they can lead us to acts that prevent meaningful social change. Abandoning utopian perspectives does not imply abandoning dreams, refusing to imagine a better world, accepting things as they are, going along to get along. Feminist theory can promote change, can help to combat sexism, racism, homophobia, and related social injustices. It can be optimistic. It can advance very different conditions for the oppressed *without being utopian*. In fact, as I hope to demonstrate, it will do those things better if it abandons utopianism.

THE CONSEQUENCES OF UTOPIANISM FOR FEMINIST THOUGHT

My resolve to seek post-utopian approaches to feminist thought and theory is reaffirmed when I consider perhaps the most dangerous consequence of utopianism—its effect on critical thinking. By avoiding counterarguments and ducking hard questions, utopian feminist thought distorts epistemological issues at the very heart of feminist thinking. Clearly, such a consequence is not unique to feminism. Any system of thought can be derailed by utopianism, even utopian thought itself (as we have seen). Equally clearly, reality can also disappoint. Realistic plans can produce unintended consequences and create all kinds of mischief. But utopianism increases the risk of such effects as well as of disappointment, because its beliefs and assumptions discourage many of the safeguards, such as critical thinking, that mitigate such risks.

Critical thinking is one of those terms that arouses the utopian hackles of feminist purists. It suggests capitulation to so-called masculinist values that feminists are supposed to deplore (reason, logic, linear thought) and seems to disparage alleged feminine and/or feminist approaches to knowledge (intuition, emotion, experience). Yet, that purist urge to distance everything feminist from everything known in patriarchy is utopian at its heart. It assumes that critical thinking must be the opposite of feminist epistemology or women's ways of knowing, a dichotomy that overlooks the interdependence and interconnection of thought and feeling, emotion and reason. In post-utopian analyses, intuition, belief, and opinion are elements of reason, and vice versa.

We test our beliefs; we intuit the course of action that we also reason our way toward. Our passions contain judgments.

Without utopian dichotomies, reason and critical thinking can serve feminist thought. Even more important, reason and its manifestation, critical thinking, support the ethics of feminism, the moral obligation to construct feminist judgments, opinions, and theories carefully in recognition of their serious consequences for individual lives and for society. Reason is a powerful tool for overcoming the stereotypes and prejudice that feminists intend to combat. Perhaps most important, critical thinking is our best weapon against fanaticism in ourselves and others.

Despite a certain reflex against reason as a patriarchal concept, most feminist objections to reason have actually been more opposed to the conventional *politics* of truth, logic, and reason than to reason itself. When women are defined as knowing subjects who determine the objects of their own knowing, and when knowledge is self-reflexive and scrutinizes and reveals its own processes, feminists acknowledge that reason can serve feminist purposes (Grosz 1993, 207–9). Without utopianism, feminism's compatibility with critical thinking becomes increasingly apparent. Critical thinking guards against biases, unexamined beliefs, inappropriate literalism, and other characteristics that prevent "constructive skepticism" about precepts and foreclose self-reflective evaluation of our own positions (Mullen 1995, 4; Paul 1990, 136).

It is utopianism, then, rather than feminism per se that has influenced some feminists to resist the idea of critical thinking, to define a worldview and defend it from "outsiders," to resist reevaluating first principles and practices from within. Utopianism encourages feminist *foundational thinking;* that is, identifying privileged sources or texts as self-evident or otherwise unimpeachable and, therefore, exempt from continuous scrutiny (Mullen 1995, 73–74). Such thinking pushes feminism dangerously close to the territory of religion.

If we imagine feminism in terms of foundational knowledge—a strong building constructed on stout footings—then we obscure the complex values issues of feminism that require continuous debate on the basis of observation and emotional responses, as well as deduction and logically developed criteria. Rather than buildings, the best feminist analyses are more like circles of rope, in which no one strand runs the entire length, yet the construction is strong, with each strand connected at many points to the whole (Mullen 1995, 105–6, 72–73).

Furthermore, foundational thinking can start us down the slippery slope to *coherentism,* which we have already discussed. Coherentism limits thinking to what an individual's particular knowledge or language community will allow. Knowledge communities are powerful, since even our sensory functions are affected by the words and opinions of other people. Confronting the principles within one's own community—even among feminists—can therefore be more difficult than confronting those from outside. The very criteria for validity are limited by that community's levels and standards of tolerance (Nelson 1990, 276–98). And adherence to community standards of validity can subject all thought to the weakness of those standards. Suppose the whole community has a prejudice or makes a conceptual error, as in "The Emperor's New Clothes"? Farther down the coherentism slope lies *confirmation bias,* in which foundational thinkers turn a deaf ear to anything except the reasoning supporting their own views (Mullen 1995, 54).

Foundational thinking can ultimately lead to *fanatical closure,* in which all explorations and questioning of beliefs are prohibited— sometimes on pain of death or torture. The nine-year *fatwa* against Salmon Rushdie for his novel *The Satanic Verses* is a chilling example of fanatical closure in the modern world. The Peoples Temple and the Branch Davidians, among other utopian communities, essentially mandated fanatical closure and required its practice as evidence of members' commitment. Ironically, however, such closure often signifies the weakness rather than the strength of a belief, since strong beliefs can withstand rigorous scrutiny (Mullen 1995, 16).

Foundational thinking further encourages its adherents to believe that their good ideas will get better when taken to their logical extremes. In reality, good ideas can turn bad with extension. As Susan Griffin has observed, it is the way of all ideas, especially as they become ideologies, to turn on themselves in some way: "One begins as a socialist, arguing that matter comes before spirit. One wins a revolution and vanquishes the enemy. But then one discovers the enemy is not yet dead. She is a poet whose words are vaguely unsettling. Who doubts. And then there are the prisons again, the police again, the old terror again." Ideologies may suppress or preclude certain feelings and observations, Griffin writes: "Suppose, for instance, one feels a love for the enemy, or . . . anger and hatred toward another of the same oppressed group? Suppose a woman hates a woman? These emotions are defined as 'incorrect.' And they become hidden. Thus, I become blind toward my own anger and fear. . . . In this way . . . each new ideology creates its own forbidden, subterranean world of reality" (1982, 166,

170). Like a rope, knowledge becomes stronger when its strands are appropriately limited in length.

Foundational thinking also promotes the *myth of the truth teller* (Mullen 1995, 83–87). In utopian communities, the charismatic leader often becomes the truth teller whose words are valued and accepted on the strength of his or her role. Feminists have historically avoided identifying official truth tellers, indeed even rejecting spokespersons in a utopian reversal of this very fallacy. But in recent years, that taboo itself has been reversed, as writings by representatives of particular groups—certain popular writers, for example, or those from particularly oppressed classes—have been granted sometimes automatic credence and status on the basis of their words' rhetorical effect. Thus, membership in a group rather than valid arguments determines credibility. By the same token, certain truth communities have sometimes been pitted against one another—such as women of color against white women, or women in general against "dead white males"—on the basis of group membership alone rather than on a careful assessment of their thinking.

Feminist thought and theory will benefit from avoiding such fallacies and pitfalls. Rather than loyal adherence to predetermined and unexamined precepts, post-utopian feminist thought must form a healthy ironic distance from its own cherished opinions and convictions. Such critical thinking helps to avoid the boomerang, so common in utopian social schemes, of recreating the very conditions the group rejects or countering flawed thought with more flawed thought. Critical feminist thinking must include mechanisms for monitoring its own arguments. Through such *mastered irony* the passions of feminism can avoid becoming fanaticism (Mullen 1995, 38). ("Mastered" is a gendered term, but let us not foreclose its usefulness on that account.)

Critical thinking will also rescue feminist thought from utopian literalism, a tendency to emphasize the representational aspect of language and to overlook its generative aspect. That is, utopians often accept their own labels for groups and ideas as transparent descriptors and overlook their function as metaphors, which both *represent* "how things are" and *create* "how things are" (Black 1979, 41).

Thus, utopian terms can become like "mantras" repeated almost ritualistically until their subtlety and symbolic qualities fade. Recognizing the generative quality of language, we must wonder to what extent Sally Gearhart's division of men into (only) two groups—rapists and gentles—contributed to the nightmare social scenario in *The Wanderground* from which her women characters had to flee. Among feminists, terms such as *patriarchy, difference, identity, experience,* and *essentialism* often become the terms of the debate rather than terms to be debated. The consequences of that slippage can be seen in the treatment by some feminists of theorist Carol Gilligan, whose *The Different Voice* (1982) explored alleged distinctions between male and female moral development. Once her work was accused of essentialism, however—that is, of promoting a presumed female essence—some feminist theorists rejected it altogether, in a kind of fanatical closure. Such wholesale disdain for ideas can create new hazards, though. Gilligan's critics, for example, embarked on what Jane Roland Martin calls the "slippery slope of infinite particularism," which eliminates even helpful or accurate generalizations (1994, 639).

Assertions of cause and effect can be yet another hazardous zone in utopian thought. All claims of causation are difficult to justify, but utopian analyses are especially liable to mistake correlations or temporal sequences for causation. The latter is known as the *post hoc* fallacy (*post hoc ergo propter hoc*). Utopian analyses are typically predicated on general causal claims that justify the utopian vision, social organization, or solution. For example, the Shakers observed that sex correlates with a corrupt world. Does that mean that sex causes the corruption? The Shakers said yes. Most people would disagree or at least see the interaction of sexual conduct with other causal factors. By the same token, as we have seen, some feminists identify patriarchy as the cause of all that oppresses women. Patriarchy is as ubiquitous as sex, perhaps even more so, but is ubiquity causation? That patriarchy correlates with almost everything that exists may not mean it can, therefore, be blamed for everything. After all, accepting patriarchy as a general causal claim for all misery in the world, on the grounds of its ubiquity, might also require accepting patriarchy as a causal claim for all the joy in the world on the same grounds. By the same token, the ubiquity of feminism in the world might also, someday, lead to its use as a similar causal claim, open to any and all interpretations. Better that we have strict scrutiny of causal claims, avoid the easy assignment of blame, and seek a complex understanding of such encompassing terms.

True causation involves not just correlation, but also satisfying what logicians call counterfactual conditions. That is, two events or conditions must first correlate in more cases than they do not, and then causation depends on demonstrating that, all other things being equal (the *ceteris paribus* condition), the correlation would not exist without the alleged causal factor (Mullen 1995, 181–84). Those are stringent standards indeed. Without them we can speculate about causation, but we must do so recognizing the difficulty of making definitive causal claims.

Utopianism often asserts causation without meeting those criteria. For example, celibate utopians believed they had demonstrated that sexual activity causes human corruption because they had created "uncorrupt" celibate societies. Yet, did they really prove their claim? In their separatist societies, all other things (social conditions) were not equal. Their communities so restricted members' behavior, even beyond sexual behavior, that the social conditions within them bore little relation to conditions in the outside world. Likewise, modern feminist separatist societies—real or fictional—prove little about patriarchy's causal role in the "real world." In a separatist society, many conditions, besides excluding men, are different from those on the outside. As we shall see, such communities demonstrate many things, but they do not necessarily prove patriarchy's full responsibility for women's disharmonious relationships or feelings of competition with one another.

Other epistemological consequences will become apparent as we proceed through part II. Suffice it to say for the moment that the idealization, demonization, classification, and absolutism of utopian thinking, among other characteristics, have negative implications for the quality of feminist thought constructed under its influence. Being alert to those implications can make us better creators and consumers of feminist theory, less subject to informal fallacies and less affected by *rhetorical goals and effect* than by the *epistemic goals* of arguments and ideas (Mullen 1995, 44).

Such awareness means inquiring into the claims of feminist thought and theory in new ways and recognizing that even our cherished ideas have limits; that the good can lead us to the bad; that definitions, categories, and claims of causation are tentative; and that neither the past, present, nor future deserves a particularly privileged place in our imaginations. Because utopianism has gone unrecognized as a core element of feminist theorizing, those and other utopian qualities, along with their epistemological consequences, have come home to roost repeatedly, like irritating chickens, throughout the course of feminist intellectual history.

FOUR   *Utopian Discourses*

Perhaps the best way to illustrate the influence of utopian thinking on feminist thought and theory is to consider the way it works in specific texts. For that purpose, I have grouped examples of feminist theory into three categories: the discourse of gender differences, the discourse of differences among women, and the discourse of linguistic construction. We shall return to these categories in part III as we explore post-utopian feminist thought and theory.

THE DISCOURSE OF GENDER DIFFERENCE: "THE PERFECT FEMALE ORDER"

Animals, vegetables and minerals are all dual—male and female.
—Shaker Elder Frederick W. Evans, *Two Orders: Shakerism and Republicanism*

Our sons will be characterologically damaged by patriarchy no matter what we do. . . . It doesn't matter how hard we try to teach our sons another way of being men, they will in some way still be monsters.
—Sonia Johnson, "Rearing Nice Sons Can't Change the World"

I am thankful that one of my children is male, since that helps to keep me honest. Every line I write shrieks there are no easy solutions.
—Audre Lorde, "Man Child: A Black Lesbian Feminist's Response"

Pointing out that feminist theorizing in the 1960s and 1970s started from the premise of sexual dichotomy, which figures men and women as distinct from one another in some fundamental ways, is almost too obvious to bear repeating.[1] Yet, recognizing that premise is essential to understanding how the idea of sexual dichotomy became as real in feminist discourse as it has been in society at large.[2] The recognition that "most women are speaking Urdu and most men are speaking Pali," as Gloria Steinem wrote in 1972, led feminists like Steinem to validate women's independent existence and to assert their rights of self-determination (Steinem [1972] 1983, 114).

Thus, the feminist discourse of gender difference began for some women with the simple desire not to "feel strange by myself or with a group of women in public" and "to discover I have sisters" (Steinem [1972] 1983, 118). For lesbian activist Cheryl Clark it began with a desire to topple male prerogative, which allowed "men at all levels of privilege, of all classes and colors . . . to act out legalistically, moralistically, and violently when they cannot colonize women, when they cannot circumscribe our sexual, productive, reproductive, creative prerogatives and energies" ([1979] 1983, 128). And it resulted for many in a discourse of gender difference that internalized basic distinctions between the sexes and then reversed the conventional hierarchy between them. Instead of cartoonlike feminine characterizations, this discourse created a self-defined, positive, powerful, moral, exemplary womanhood. Instead of pawns in men's games, women in this discourse stood together in sisterhood on behalf of women's own interests.

That positive spin on womanhood, that reversal of derogatory, sexist assumptions which has been so inspirational can, however, easily slide into utopian territory. It is not necessarily utopian to observe and explore women's contributions or to assert women's own definitions of womanhood. Nor is it necessarily utopian to generalize on the basis of evidence about a group of women, or about specific women and men in specific settings, or about the interaction of gender with other identity categories and power relations (Cameron 1998, 947). But it may be utopian to move beyond justified generalizations about gender

---

1. In my analysis of this discourse, I will be using the terms *sex* and *gender* interchangeably, since contemporary theorists have undermined distinctions between their definitions based on the biological aspects of the first and the social determination of the second. Both terms connote the influence of genes and hormones as well as of social mores and practices.

2. The subtitle for this section comes from the "Dyke Separatist Womanifesto." The full text is: "Man managed to destroy the perfect female order, and subjected women to slavery by assuming control of our reproductive system as well as of all our activities having to do with the production, maintenance, and furtherance of life and life's functions" (Charoula 1977, 1).

characteristics, to assume gender difference a priori, and to declare all women inherently powerful, moral, and exemplary. And, like many utopian constructs, such depictions of gender dualism can reinforce the very discriminatory visions of the sexes, which characterize women instrumentally, as mothers, or housewives, or sex objects, or help-mates, that oppress women in the first place. Indeed, they can even promote what we might describe as male utopian fantasies. By the same token, turning the tables, putting women on top where they were once on the bottom, is a utopian reversal that risks ignoring or over-looking the real causes of sexism, which may be sex distinction itself. Touting female virtue or superiority does not address that problem.

The discourse of gender difference that roots feminism in the as-sumption of gender difference on the one hand and in the inherent vir-tues of womanhood on the other is venerable indeed. As we have seen, feminist utopian fiction of the last three hundred years is replete with such visions. Nineteenth-century American feminist writers and ac-tivists, such as Maria Stewart, Carrie Chapman Catt, Anna J. Cooper, and Alice Paul, also saw "a world divided between a male principle of aggression and a female one of nurturance" and celebrated women's innate pacifism, virtue, and chastity (Gordon 1991, 97). Many such feminists believed that motherhood was women's defining experience, an idea that utopian fiction writers like Charlotte Perkins Gilman and Suzy McKee Charnas turned into the basis of entire fictional societies. They identified motherhood as the demonstration project for wom-en's nurturing nature and skills, which extended far beyond child care. Even Elizabeth Cady Stanton, whose writing emphasized equal-ity rather than gender difference, asserted distinctions between the de-structive, stern, selfish, warlike, violent, acquisitive "male element" and the female element, which was its opposite (ibid.). Indeed, in Stanton's case, as for many who followed her, gender was a metaphor for difference.

Despite some scathing denouncements of essentialism like those we have seen, utopian approaches to gender difference have remained attractive to many feminists, implicitly or explicitly. Carol Gilligan's work illustrates an explicit variety of such utopian discourse in its de-scription of women's "distinct moral language" and morality of re-sponsibility and care, in contrast to a male-defined morality of abstract justice. Gilligan pays minimal attention to differences among women or to the effects on her results of her a priori desire to discover such a female morality (1982, 73). (She might, of course, have been right de-spite those utopian flaws in her research methodology. Utopianism does not *guarantee* error.) Other examples include the work of theorists such as Mary Daly, Shulamith Firestone, Susan Griffin, Marilyn Frye, Luce Irigaray, Juliet Mitchell, Dorothy Dinnerstein, Nancy Chodorow, and Sara Ruddick, as well as a cadre of separatist writers such as Julia Penelope, Andrea Dworkin, Sonia Johnson, and Sarah Hoagland, and linguists such as Barrie Thorne and Nancy Henley. Each in her way has described or prescribed a salutary female practice or culture or articulated the virtues of a female personality or nature.[3]

Assumptions of sisterhood—what Robin Morgan calls "'an exhilarating assertion of the category *woman* as a central prism through which to perceive human experience'"—have followed from the feminist emphasis on gender difference. Feminism was supposed to create "'an alliance of women everywhere based in the commonality of women and in opposition to the patriarchal societies within which women live'" (quoted in Friedman 1995, 8). This strain of gender difference in feminist thought endured throughout the 1980s as feminist theory routinely romanticized women's ways of knowing, being, and valuing (Ferguson 1994, 205).

The point here is not to object to this discourse and the way in which it has articulated women's presumed strengths and special qualities, but rather to avoid donning utopian lenses that obscure the damage it can also inflict. One form of that damage has been the false universalization of all women into a single category, which we will address in detail in the next section of this chapter. Another is the irony of reinforcing male dominance by assuming or asserting male-female dif-

---

3. Examples of relevant texts by these authors include: Cheris Kramer, Barrie Thorne, and Nancy Henley, 1978, "Perspectives on Language and Communication," *Signs* 3(3): 638–51; Nancy Chodorow, 1978, *The Reproduction of Mothering: Psychoanalysis and the Sociology of Gender* (Berkeley: University of California Press); Mary Daly, 1978, *Gyn/Ecology: The Metaethics of Radical Feminism* (Boston: Beacon); Dorothy Dinnerstein, 1976, *The Mermaid and the Minotaur: Sexual Arrangements and Human Malaise* (New York: Harper and Row); Andrea Dworkin, 1981, *Men Possessing Women* (New York: Putnam) and, 1988, *Letters from a War Zone: Writings 1976–1989* (New York: Dutton); Shulamith Firestone, 1971, *The Dialectic of Sex: The Case for Feminist Revolution* (New York: Bantam Books); Carol Gilligan, 1982, *In a Different Voice: Psychological Theory and Women's Development* (Cambridge: Harvard University Press); Susan Griffin, 1981, *Pornography and Silence: Culture's Revenge against Nature* (New York: Harper and Row); Sarah Hoagland, 1988, *Lesbian Ethics: Toward New Value* (Palo Alto, Calif.: Institute of Lesbian Studies); Sarah Hoagland and Julia Penelope, eds., 1988, *For Lesbians Only: A Separatist Anthology* (London: Onlywomen); Luce Irigaray, 1985, *This Sex Which Is Not One*, trans. Catherine Porter with Carolyn Burke (Ithaca, N.Y.: Cornell University Press); Juliet Mitchell, 1975, *Psychoanalysis and Feminism* (New York: Vintage); Sara Ruddick, 1989, *Maternal Thinking: Toward a Politics of Peace* (Boston: Beacon).

ference, since, historically, most such assertions have served that purpose (Uchida 1992, 547). That is why it is so tempting to reverse them in feminist theory. Less obvious are the consequences of hyperbole and idealization, of overemphasizing sex as opposed to all other human characteristics, and of leaving the world dichotomized, just as we found it, and possibly no better off.

Difference without Feminism

In assessing the value of the feminist discourse of gender difference, we should examine sex-distinction literature beyond feminist borders, where gender-difference literature enjoys immense popularity. That literature reveals how gender-distinction analyses, while supporting feminist arguments on the one hand, can be used to support misogynist, antifeminist arguments on the other. Camille Paglia's celebration of gender difference is a case in point. Paglia extols woman's distinctive qualities as a sign of her innate mystery and glamour, of her "cave of archaic darkness." But the price Paglia exacts for dwelling in that cave is a female intelligence that remains in the "median of the spectrum." Only men, who live outside the feminine cave, can achieve heights of genius (1992, 107–9).

Another telling case of misogynist gender difference is John Gray's 1992 *Men Are from Mars, Women Are from Venus,* which has sold more than four million copies in eighty-six languages. Gray starts from the premise that men and women are different species—Martian and Venusian respectively. According to Gray, men (Martians) are goal-oriented strivers toward autonomy "as a symbol of efficiency, power and competence" (1992, 17). Women (Venusians), on the other hand, are purveyors of "love, communication, beauty, and relationships" (ibid., 18). Does this distinction enhance women's power or create more mutual understanding between the sexes? Not the way Gray uses it. Rather, he explains, to create harmony, women must change. Women should extend love to their favorite Martians and look patiently for the loving intention underlying men's selfish or churlish behavior. Men need change nothing, since their strident personalities are innate, immutable facts of nature (Bader 1996, 51–53).

Reversing Gray's analysis would not really help, however. Suppose women's identities were defined as natural and men's as adaptable for the good of the species? The world would not improve with the male sex in thrall or service to the female, no matter how appealing such an idea might seem in the short run. Why does feminism need complete capitulation by men, except for revenge? Such utopian constructions will only lead feminists to replicate the errors of utopianism—overlooking similarities in behavior and desires as well as differences, attaching too much importance to gender in inappropriate situations, assuming that one sex has all the virtues when virtue might, in an egalitarian world, have little to do with gender. Such problems haunt feminist utopian analyses just as they haunt the discourse of a Gray or Paglia.

Difference without Utopianism

Gender difference can, of course, be discussed without engaging in utopianism (as we shall explore more fully in chapter 6). Differences can be articulated as useful generalizations, aggregates of observed behaviors and characteristics that have been carefully correlated with sex and have satisfied the *ceteris paribus* clause of the counterfactual condition, which shows the singular importance of sex in the correlation. Even Deborah Tannen, whose 1990s books on gender and language emphasize (and even assume) gender difference in language use and understanding, couches her conclusions within a realistic framework of caveats: conversational differences arose in a cultural context of women's restricted roles; "conversational style differences do not explain all the problems that arise in relationships between women and men"; male dominance is not the whole story; women and men share interests, such as status and success, involvement and connection, but they often (not always) approach them from different perspectives (1990, 18, 25). We can describe differences without prescribing them. In addition, Tannen notes in her 1994 work *Gender and Discourse,* we must devise ways of identifying differences in linguistic strategies that do not reinforce dominance, that instead take into account the different potential meanings of the same linguistic strategies in different situations (Cameron 1998, 949).

Recognizing the utopian tendency to exaggerate and misinterpret gender differences makes us better consumers of difference claims. Indeed, careful research often modifies hyperbolic claims about sex differences. For example, in the federal elections of the 1990s, the media anticipated a so-called gender gap in which women's vote would turn the tide. Even after the results were in, the gender gap was given credit for election outcomes. Careful reading of the election results, however, unraveled that claim. For the 1994 Congressional election, the National Women's Political Caucus did find a gender gap that was bigger than in previous elections. But they also found that women were by no means a monolithic voting bloc. In fact, differences in marital status, income, geographical location, and race among voters of both sexes were at least as significant for the outcome as—and in some cases many times more significant than—differences between men and women, where the "gap" was 11.1 percent (Berke 1995, A10). Studies of the 1996 election reveal that the gender gap in the vote for the House of Representatives actually shrank between the two elections, from 11 percent in 1994 to 9 percent in 1996. Much more significant in the 1996 House elections was marital status, with a 26 percent gap between married and unmarried voters. Also significant to the outcome was the fact that there was a decline of ten percentage points in support for Democratic candidates for the House among black voters (*New York Times* 1996, B5).

Utopianism creeps into analyses of gender difference when sex becomes a metaphor for difference, as in Shaker Elder Frederick Evans's proclamation about gendered Creation at the beginning of this segment of chapter 4. That is when assumptions too easily replace observation. We forget to ask what the differences really signify. Are they mean differences? What is the range and overlap of distributions? What is the setting in which the differences are observed, a factor that clearly determines the size and direction of gender differences in behavior and attitudes? We forget to distinguish between stereotypes and actual or observable differences. We are subject to preconceptions about the complementarity or opposition of the sexes (Hare-Mustin and Marecek 1988, 456).

Utopians would be right in reminding us, at this point, that the discourse of gender difference has also produced some benefits for feminism. It has made men see that they are also affected by gender as a social and cultural construction, which helps to dispel myths of male dominance based on a male standard for humanity. "Speaking of 'gender' got some men to do housework; helped girls play sports and study science; spurred women to become doctors, construction workers, and bosses." Gender awareness has also empowered women "to postulate dichotomous categories and then to valorize the previously devalued female part" (Gordon 1991, 92–93).

But those benefits have been accompanied by the risks and negative consequences that are typical of utopian constructions. Utopian feminist constructions of gender difference may create dichotomies that diminish what many women value, such as the love of/for sons and brothers and fathers. Sonia Johnson's remarks that help introduce this segment of chapter 4 represent that risk. Johnson saw no alternative to abandoning her sons once she had constructed her utopian gender opposition. Sons are men; men are irredeemable; therefore, feminists must forgo their sons. In contrast, Audre Lorde's observation recognizes a post-utopian ambiguity and contradiction between her social analysis of the sexes and the world of her affections. Indeed, her attachment to her son enhances her ability to theorize because it makes her cautious.

A focus only on difference renders gender both dichotomous and omnipotent. Absolute categorizations produce unintended ironies: to love difference, as Linda Gordon observes, "can mean a retreat from anger at the limitation of possibility, while hatred of difference can mean self-hatred for women." In addition, a "focus on difference makes . . . varying capacities seem more fixed than they need be and contributes to the pursuit of the mythic 'separate but equal.'" Frequently, the privileging of gender difference results in idealization. Feminists "who speak of (female) difference are usually praising it." Feminist theorists often capitalize on the rhetorical appeal of a particular sexual difference, such as female nurturance, and take it to its limits without considering possible unintended consequences of that journey (Gordon 1991, 94, 98–99, 94).

Test Cases: Separatism and the Feminine Golden Age

To illustrate utopianism in the feminist discourse of sexual difference, I will focus on two theoretical strains that build upon gender difference in order to extol female value or virtue: arguments for female separatism and idyllic constructions of motherhood and the mother-daughter relationship. Together these two strains demonstrate utopian levels of idealization, demonization, foundational thinking, and even coherentism, as they predicate female happiness on the company of women, on shared reproductive physiology, or on shared sexuality. Although philosophically distant from one another, these two utopian strains evoke related foundational stories about the power and inherent goodness of a female principle or influence in the world that remains "deeply embedded in the memory of our species" (Johnson 1989, 269–70).[4]

SEPARATISM

The discourse of female separatism is predicated on the notion that women's inherently positive qualities have been obscured and deval-

---

4. One such story is contained in Riane Eisler's *The Chalice and the Blade* (1987), in which an ideal society is defined as one predicated upon the nurturant qualities of the

ued by the influence of men and the abuses of patriarchy. For some feminist theorists in the 1970s, separatism even became the equivalent of feminism. Rita Mae Brown, for example, claimed that "'women-identified collectives are nothing less than the next step toward a Women's Revolution'" (quoted in Shugar 1995, 57). In turn, lesbian identification became the acid test of a revolutionary mentality. Separatism often implied living and interacting only with women, even sexually.

Such views of separatism often play on the utopian quest for purity. According the Lavender Woman Collective, for example, lesbians are the quintessential women, because they are most likely to survive entirely without men. According to the Radicalesbians, they are also "purest," because they are furthest from "'the three material conditions that determine the class position of women—reproduction, production (domestic labor) and sexuality,'" a utopian measure of purity or perfection through distance from reality. From the quest for feminist purity followed a desire for all-female separatist spaces. The premise of such spaces was absolute gender dualism necessitated, according to the Gutter Dyke Collective, by the fact that "'men are the enemy, and we make no distinctions among them. Men are not reformable'" (quoted in Shugar 1995, 67, 27, 43).

Although the separatist communities of the 1970s gave way primarily to separatist fiction in the 1980s, the utopian thinking underlying the concept of separatism remains an enduring and, to some, rhetorically attractive legacy (ibid., 182). Evidence of the resilience of the separatist stance can be found in feminist theoretical literature of the 1990s in which female virtue is defined in opposition to male vice, which is the only source of its defilement. Often a lesbian identity is proffered as the most evolved form of that female virtue. Such a connection is evident in Marilyn Frye's 1990 "Willful Virgin, or Do You Have to Be a Lesbian to Be a Feminist?" While it is not a separatist manifesto, Frye's article represents the genre; it also illustrates the genre's utopian characteristics.

Frye eventually answers her own question with a "no," but her path

---

Goddess. In it, women assumed a kind of power that was (and could again be) equated with responsibility and love and created (and could again create) partnership rather than dominator societies (28). In addition, many women who have read the works of Carol Gilligan and Nancy Chodorow (cited in note 3 above) have responded to its rhetorical persuasion about women's characteristics and behaviors surrounding motherhood and felt redeemed by its confirmation of qualities and behaviors they recognize in themselves.

to that answer enters utopian territory. Her foundational premise is the equation of patriarchy with heterosexuality: "the global phenomenon of male domination, oppression and exploitation of females" results from its imposition of "a near-universal female heterosexuality" ([1990] 1992, 129). Thus, Frye makes a general causal claim for heterosexuality as the major constitutive factor of patriarchy. On the basis of that claim, she concludes that male domination could be overthrown if women refused to participate in heterosexuality, with its abuse, harassment, and "(hetero)sexualization of every aspect of females' bodies and behaviors." In order to be "thoroughly antipatriarchal," feminism must also be antiheterosexual. Frye stops short of prescribing universal lesbianism for feminists because becoming a lesbian in patriarchy is so difficult. Thus she recommends universal virginity, interpreting the term *Virgin* according to its original meaning of a woman unpossessed by and unattached to a man (ibid., 130, 132, 133).

Frye's argument explains women's suffering and redeems a version of female innate virtue with rhetorical appeal. But her analysis depends on numerous utopian constructions. Like celibate utopians, Frye reduces her politics to one characteristic—sexuality (albeit defined differently). She dichotomizes the sexes absolutely and universalizes her claims. She idealizes some women—Virgins and lesbians (who qualify as Virgins by definition)—by claiming, for example, that "[lesbian/]Virgins have strong, reliable, creative, enduring, sustaining, ardent friendships with women," and they desire only to "empower women and create friendship and solidarity among women." Her idealization also extends to the society Virgins would construct. Without patriarchy/men (an untestable *ceteris paribus* condition), women's conflicts and competition among themselves would disappear, they would become unconcerned with appearance or attractiveness, and femininity would become either unproblematic or nonexistent. Frye overlooks the irony of that last claim, which undermines her premise that uniquely feminine qualities underlie the lure of separatism in the first place ([1990] 1992, 135–36, 134).

To support her idealization of women, Frye demonizes men by attributing to them only acts of domination and exploitation of women and girls. Frye also demonizes heterosexuality by associating it exclusively with women's sexual accessibility to men, servitude (her synonym for marriage), and the negative aspects of childrearing. At the same time, she dismisses the role of women's own desires in heterosexual behavior and in motherhood by suggesting that heterosexuality as an institution delimits and confounds women's real desires ([1990] 1992, 129).

Her argument flirts with coherentism on that point, since she bases her conclusion on her own definition of heterosexuality as the global subjugation of all females to all males in order to fulfill male desires and to justify the abuse of women and girls. That claim is never challenged, however, because Frye ignores other meanings or possible meanings for heterosexuality, including those that might be offered by heterosexual women. She thereby overlooks the complexity of the sexual universe, in which heterosexuality, like lots of other behaviors and social structures, correlates with both desire and satisfaction, on one hand, and abuse, exploitation, and coercion, on the other, depending on whom you ask and when. She also overlooks how difficult it is, even for lesbians, to separate the sexes from one another completely. We all have complex attachments and interdependencies via parenthood, sexual desire, business arrangements, and other alliances. By the same token, Frye ignores evidence that lesbianism as a sexual practice can create female solidarity and sexual satisfaction for some women and promote competition and abuse for others.

Also utopian is Frye's compulsion to defame heterosexuality in order to valorize lesbianism (Soper 1995, 120). Such a utopian "good/ us" versus "bad/them" generally backfires, as "we" inevitably see ourselves in "them." That boomerang is evident in Frye's treatment of women's agency. Her argument requires her to assert lesbian agency, since lesbians can determine their own sexuality in defiance of social norms. That lesbians exist signifies that women have sexual agency. Logically, then, Frye should (but does not) acknowledge the agency of heterosexual women, whose history illustrates both resistance and conformity to, as well as the total rejection of, exploitative heterosexual practices and expectations without necessarily rejecting heterosexuality altogether. By the same token, she should (but does not) acknowledge varying levels of agency and approaches to sexuality among lesbians. Rather, she projects her own rebellious personality on all lesbians as if they were a homogeneous group. Perhaps most important, as Frye herself observes, if any women have sexual agency, wherein lies the social power of heterosexuality as an institution ([1990] 1992, 133)? Where do lesbians come from if the system is so coercive?

Having isolated sexuality as the primary salient feature of human life and, on that basis, privileged the lesbian viewpoint, Frye also engages in the utopian myth of the truth teller. She constructs lesbians as sexual authorities for all women because of their greater commitment to self-determination and their greater purity, as measured by their distance from social institutions. But she cannot test the validity of that claim because her utopian approach precludes counterarguments from other sources, such as heterosexual women.

Indeed, so utopian is Frye's analysis that it ignores counterarguments even from within lesbian separatist literature, which, in contrast to her depiction of Virgin society, openly acknowledge how illusory is the expectation of easy harmony and mutuality among women just because they share a lesbian sexual orientation. For example, as early as the 1970s, members of the Gutter Dyke Collective discovered that lesbianism was not a sufficient condition for creating a community. Joan Nixon observed that reality at the 1973 West Coast Lesbian Conference, where an "'army of shouting lovers fell into combat with each other.'" She concluded that "'the oppression we share as lesbian women in a burning patriarchal world was not enough to bind us together.'" Indeed, in practice, separatism has often worked to excuse women's oppressive behaviors toward one another (quoted in Shugar 1995, 74, 52).

The same literature reveals further chinks in Frye's causal claims for patriarchy. As tempting as it is to blame patriarchy for all the difficulties separatist communities have experienced, many separatists have had to admit that divisiveness often comes from within. For example, was it the racist legacy of patriarchy or a utopian intractability about foundational principles that led to the dissolution of Sassafras, a mixed-race separatist community? Its members blame the latter. Was it patriarchy or unexplored class differences, differences of physical ability, and disagreements over children among women of color that made one woman's sojourn in La Luz "one of the cruelest experiences" of her life? Again, that woman blames the group's internal differences (Shugar 1995, 97–99).

Many all-female, separatist collectives have found that issues of land ownership, money, investment, and commitment, as well as individual women's varying values and priorities, are the most challenging obstacles to group harmony. Ironically, the most successful collectives, such as Adobeland or Green Hope Farm, have been controlled by one or two women, thereby challenging separatist dreams about women's inherent ability to work and share property collectively (ibid., 94–96). Outside of utopia we must recognize that sometimes the enemy we meet is us.

THE FEMININE GOLDEN AGE

Another utopian strain in the feminist discourse of gender difference evokes a kind of psychological Golden Age, a repressed but powerful "feminine" psychic force reflecting each woman's experience of a harmonious, symbiotic relationship with her mother (or female caretaker). Certain French theorists, for example, claim that maternal-child symbiosis leaves a kind of psychic residue of "feminine" values and joy that endures (albeit in repressed form) in women (and sometimes in men) as they grow and reproduce themselves. In her 1975 essay "The Laugh of the Medusa," Hélène Cixous explains that residue as a song in women's speech "which never stops resonating" and comes from the "first music from the first voice of love [mother] which is alive in every woman." "A woman is never far from 'mother'. . . . There is always within her at least a little of that good mother's milk. She writes in white ink" ([1975] 1992, 199–200).

Cixous's "song" reflects what French theorists define as the *imaginary*, the repressed "feminine" memory and effects of maternal nurture and care, which endures despite the imposition of the *symbolic*, the culturally acceptable sexual identity and personality formed under phallic influence, via the Laws and Language of the Fathers. It is the symbolic that requires the sequential thinking of language, imposes the incest taboo, and asserts male cultural power and the heterosexual norm. In contrast, the imaginary embodies maternal influences, which are prelinguistic, phantasmagoric, undifferentiated, and unhierarchical. Cixous and some others believe that women are better able to retrieve those maternal forces, whose "phantasms" are likely to appear in their music, painting, and writing, because of their closer attachment and bodily resemblance to the mother. Tapping into that imaginary, women can produce "a resonant vision, a composition, something beautiful" ([1975] 1992, 197). Some theorists, like Julia Kristeva, believe that men can also tap into their own repressed feminine force.

Although predicated on an appealing reversal of conventional Freudian scripts for female gender identity, this discourse flirts with utopianism in the very qualities that make it attractive: the valorization of the mother-daughter bond, maternal influence, and female sexual physiology and diffuse sexual pleasure. But its utopianism can lead theorists to idealized, even romantic conclusions. For example, Kristeva once related female menstrual and gestational cycles to "the eternal recurrence of a biological rhythm which conforms to that of nature" itself, as well as to a cyclical, monumental (synchronic) conception of time. On these grounds, she claimed that the "feminine" imaginary has mystical links with ancient civilizations that have been lost to phallic imperialism (Kristeva [1979] 1992, 216). Although such visions may inspire, they can also risk (with utopian irony) reoppressing women in their association of "female" with "natural" or "archaic."

Like the discourse of separatism, Golden Age psychological discourse is utopian in its assertion of absolute sexual difference on the one hand and inherent female virtue and value on the other. Indeed, it even occasionally promotes separatism, with all its attendant risks. For example, Luce Irigaray recommended in 1977 that women "avoid men long enough to learn to defend their desire notably by their speech, let them discover the love of other women protected from that imperious choice of men . . ., let them forge a social status which demands recognition, let them earn their living in order to leave behind their condition of prostitute" ([1977] 1992, 205–6). While reinforcing women's independence, Irigaray's advice loses touch with reality by suggesting that avoiding men and earning a living are consistent goals. It also defines gender pride and sexual expressiveness as utopian guarantees of self-worth, whereas "social status" requires more than the defense of desire, even for men.

American texts in this category, primarily those in the object-relations school of thought, flirt with utopianism by idealizing mothers and the mother-daughter relationship. For example, Nancy Chodorow offers a rhetorically appealing alternative to Freudian explanations of gender-identity formation. Instead of glorifying the male psychic norm as Freud did, Chodorow's 1978 *The Reproduction of Mothering* defines women's "relational, affective-nurturing" capacities as the foundation of a relationship-focused, flexible sense of female gender identity that is clearly preferable to the rigid and exclusive ego boundaries men presumably develop (Washburn 1994, 2–3). But her appealing analysis does not entirely avoid utopian pitfalls. The assertion of female interest in relationships can be just as restrictive in its way as any misogynist script. Through a utopian reversal, women are still relegated to a specific personality and preference.

Carol Gilligan extrapolated her theory of women's relational morality from Chodorow's work, claiming that women make moral choices that preserve relationships rather than enforce rules and abstract notions of justice. What the utopian reversal endemic to this approach overlooks is the possibility that women have made such moral choices because of the primarily private or domestic contexts in which they have historically had to make them. Indeed, Gilligan's research concerns a "private issue"—decisions about childbearing versus abortion. In another context, say service on juries, women might well enforce rules and abstract notions of justice just as men presumably do.

Golden Age maternal discourse in the late 1970s initiated a celebratory decade for motherhood in feminist theory in the 1980s that displaced earlier probing work, such as Adrienne Rich's discussion of maternal violence in *Of Woman Born*.[5] As affirming as it may be, maternal celebration also obscures the reality that motherhood entails both satisfying nurture and care and "an open invitation . . . to unending hard work [and] also to trouble and sorrow" (Ross 1992, 397–98). As motherhood developed immunity from negative feminist scrutiny, many theoretical texts omitted such issues as the value of motherhood for the mother herself, the discrepancy between a woman's physical and emotional capacities for reproduction, and even the connection between motherhood ideals and women's economic dependence on men. The reproductive romance also prevented discussions of the different motherhood experiences of women depending on their location, age, race, or class.

Utopian perspectives on motherhood, resulting from utopian views of gender difference, confine us, limit our understanding, and silence dissent. If "'women' are collapsed into the 'suppressed feminine' and men into the 'dominant ideology,'" as Chandra Mohanty observes, then how do we account for women's agency in their own drama (1992, 81)? If we idealize women's maternal power, we risk perpetuating the misogynist myth of menacing female power that boys must reject as they mature (Amoros 1993, 417–18). Thus, the exaggeration of maternal power can, ironically, reinforce male dominance. If we use maternity as a premise for feminism, what happens to the women who resist motherhood or do not identify with the nurturing role? What happens to the woman who has been poorly mothered? Like Linda Gordon, we must ask, "What do we miss if we theorize the variations as exceptions?" (1991, 99).

Critics of the generalized and idealized configurations of motherhood have addressed what can be seen as their utopian characteristics. For example, Lynne Segal and Ann Snitow have challenged the

---

5. Chapter X of that book, for example, describes a mother who murders her children and analyzes the causes of the crime.

assertion of a pure feminine culture.[6] Rayna Rapp, Shellee Colen, and Barbara Omolade have resisted overly globalized and generalized theoretical accounts of motherhood by producing highly particularized ones. Rapp has focused on decisions about amniocentesis, Colen on New York City child-care workers from the Caribbean, and Omolade on young women in the Sisterhood of Black Single Mothers (Ross 1992, 403–4).

Yet even those responses do not satisfy Ellen Ross's hopes for feminist theorizing about motherhood. Ross's 1992 "New Thoughts on 'the Oldest Vocation'" offers a phenomenology of mothering that theorizes varied feminist positions based on differing circumstances and rehabilitates the mother-blaming psychosis of the past (to which Golden Age rhetoric can, unfortunately, contribute). Instead of a collection of stories, Ross argues for complex answers to complicated questions: How do mothers feel about their children? How does mothering change women's relationships with jobs, husbands, friends, and lovers? Ross wants to explore how motherhood has inspired political activism, how single mothers and mothers of large families survive, how the meaning of motherhood and fatherhood changes in different communities. She suggests theorizing around the issues of infertility and the loss of children—or the dream of perfect children—because of illnesses, disability, and death (1992, 399).

Utopian Discourses of Gender Difference

Salient differences between men and women probably do exist. And in them may lie important insights into gender issues that concern feminist theory. But utopianism does not produce the deepest possible understanding of those differences. Instead, it distorts them by ignoring the malleability of gender and the variability of its significance over time and in differing social contexts. Gender may matter more, for example, in labor and social relations than in other aspects of human life (Gordon 1991, 96). By assuming gender difference a priori, we assert its eternal importance and create the dualisms we resist. We tend to overlook other influences on behavior and attitude, such as race, religion, income level, political-party affiliation, and individual psychology. We exaggerate reproduction. Utopian visions tempt us to concentrate only on the factor that interests us the most, a tendency that can badly distort the view. Divisions of the world into dualistic differ-

---

6. See Segal in Maureen McNeil, 1992, 24. See also Snitow 1992, 32–51.

ences, attributions of narrow, either idealized or demonized sets of qualities to particular persons or groups, quests for purity, reliance on unitary theoretical explanations for complex phenomena, as well as their obverse, fanatically pursued, are all utopian tendencies that obscure reality and diminish the usefulness and accuracy of theoretical constructs.

The utopian feminist discourse of gender difference reflects these qualities as well as others. But recognizing gender difference, seeking certain all-female spaces, validating motherhood, and celebrating lesbian sexuality are not in and of themselves utopian. They can all be accomplished without pitting social constructionists against "essentialist" proponents of women's values and virtues, without mistaking problem reversal for problem solution, and without asserting female superiority as the answer to male dominance. Recognizing gender difference need not fool us into believing that a good idea gets better when taken to extremes or that our desires must be validated by deprecating the desires of others.

THE DISCOURSE OF DIFFERENCES AMONG WOMEN: "WHAT CHOU MEAN WE, WHITE GIRL?"

Given the differences in experiences among Black and white women, between working-class and middle-class women, between all of us, what then are the prospects for sisterhood? . . . I would argue for the abandonment of the concept of sisterhood as a global construct based on unexamined assumptions about our similarities, and I would substitute a more pluralistic approach that recognizes and accepts the objective differences between women.
—Bonnie Thornton Dill, "Race, Class, and Gender: Prospects for an All-Inclusive Sisterhood"

One "becomes a woman" in ways that are much more complex than in a simple opposition to men. . . . One may also 'become a woman' in opposition to other women.
—Norma Alarcón, "The Theoretical Subject(s) of This Bridge Called My Back and Anglo-American Feminism"

That women are different from one another has generated a significant feminist discourse dedicated to articulating and theorizing those differences. Indeed, for some writers and thinkers contributing to that discourse, women's differences have overwhelmed their similarities. For Norma Alarcón, for example, the very fact of women's differences defines what it means to be a woman.[7] As a discourse devoted to complicating a category, to preventing oversimplification and generalization, this body of work should be post-utopian at its core. And in many ways it is. But as we shall see, the discourse of differences among women can also reside on utopian territory.

Although long a feature of feminist thought and theory, the discourse of differences among women really gained momentum in the United States in the early 1980s, after the publication of *This Bridge Called My Back* (1981), an anthology of writings by women of color. *This Bridge* revealed—for the first time for many white feminists—the extent of the problems and resentments that had emerged from the emphasis on gender-difference analyses in feminist theory. Essays in the anthology expressed the anger many women of color felt at the suggestion that all women should or would unite to promote the issues and interests that had been identified only by some. Writers such as doris davenport, Gloria Anzaldúa, Cherríe Moraga, Chrystos, and many others of African American, Native American, Latina, or mixed descents and identities both disowned these falsely universal constructions and proclaimed in various ways that they would define feminism for themselves through their own writings, based in their own cultures, nations, or movements.

One target in writings within the discourse of differences among women is the concept of sisterhood, which many women of color regard as impossible across racial or ethnic lines. Bonnie Thornton Dill, for example, rejects what she implies is a utopian idea of universal sisterhood. Maria Lugones and Pat Alake Rosezelle emphasize variations in the meaning of feminism for women in different cultural contexts and explain the connotations of *sisterhood* for women of color: "When Black feminists use the term in the expression 'Third World sisters' they are extending to all women of color a different metaphor than the one used by white feminists, a metaphor that is charged with the history of political use of the terms 'brother' and 'sister' in the Black community." *Sisterhood* alludes to the struggle under slavery to maintain families. In that context, *brother* and *sister* are symbols of "redeeming, of respect, of resistance" within minority cultures (1992, 408, 409).

Abandoning sisterhood has not prevented theorists in this discourse from considering the possibility of cross-racial feminist coalitions, however. Patricia Hill Collins (1990), for example, explores

---

7. The subtitle for this section comes from Lorraine Bethel's 1979 article by the same name.

the structure of social relations among women and recommends that feminist constructs always focus on gender in the context of race, ethnicity, and class. Several theorists, such as Native American writer Barbara Cameron, have approached the prospects of coalition from a decidedly unromantic point of view. Cameron observes how structures of race stratification function among minority groups themselves. "I've grown up with misconceptions about Blacks, Chicanos, and Asians," she admits. "I'm still in the process of trying to eliminate my racist pictures of people of color" (1981, 49). Cameron's confession elevates discussions about coalition beyond utopianized categories of "them" and "us."

Many theorists of color also emphasize the contributions of women's differences to the richness of feminist thought. Audre Lorde, for example, redefines difference "as a fund of necessary polarities between which our creativity can spark like a dialectic" ([1980] 1981, 99). Some have developed approaches to the issue of representing and analyzing "the other." For example, Chandra Mohanty warns that the recognition of "other" women must not result in new universals, even if they are sympathetic, that project powerlessness and victimhood onto women viewed from half a world away (1991, 57–58). The discourse of differences among women also asks who can speak for whom, establishes historical contexts for social practices, and defines women's power in culturally relevant ways. Many of these observations and inquiries successfully counter and prevent utopianism as they interrogate themselves and resist the formulation of static or stereotyped views.

Despite such counter-utopian characteristics, however, the discourse of differences among women has also suffered from utopian thinking. In some instances, it has idealized certain identity groups and demonized others. Forgetting the generative quality of language, it has considered its own labels and metaphors as literal and transparent representations of immutable facts. It has indulged in the myth of the truth teller and even advocated foundational thinking and coherentism. And sometimes it has waved the utopian magic wand.

Many feminists believe that white women should be focusing on their own racial identities and leave theorizing about color and marginality to the people who experience them. Marita Golden, for example, warns us that race is "the tar baby in our midst; touch it and you get stuck, hold it and you get dirty" (1995, 3). That reminder must give me pause as I embark on this discussion of texts conceptualized and composed by women from racial and ethnic groups that do not include me. But we must also remember here, as in other cross-identity discussions, the myth of the truth teller and the utopian argument that certain foundational ideas or precepts are sacred because of their subject matter or source. There is danger in segregating texts or arguments on the grounds of their authors' or readers' race or ethnicity, a separation that only compounds the problem of differences among women.

Therefore, all readers can note that utopianism lurks in this discourse when writers claim or imply that feminism alone will overcome racism and eliminate injustice in American society. While it is not utopian to connect feminism with the goal of eliminating racism or to predicate feminist knowledge on a racialized consciousness, it is utopian to assume that feminism makes the fulfillment of that goal self-evident, automatic, or uncomplicated. Otherwise, we begin to believe in the feminist magic wand.

The hope for a feminist magic wand appears in Chrystos's 1981 lament of feminism's failure as "a tool which can eliminate racism" (69). Her desire was grounded only in her wish, rather than in an analysis of the way in which the projects of antisexism and antiracism might fruitfully be connected. The hope for a feminist magic wand also inflected bell hooks's 1991 claim that all feminists need to do is to recognize "the reality of classism" and make "political commitments to eliminating it" in order to end class conflicts in "feminist movement" (39). Hooks's approach makes a utopian connection between problem identification and problem solution, with predictable results. Essential as it is, sincere commitment to the eradication of such intractable problems as racism or classism or homophobia in America is insufficient to the task. Instead of utopian magic wands, the eradication of racism and other forms of discrimination require clear critical thinking, honest communication, a good grasp on reality, and other time-consuming problem-solving processes.

Sisterhood discussions have also demonstrated utopianism by suggesting problem reversal: a term that was once used too much and too carelessly should not be used at all. Although *sisterhood* clearly has different meanings for different groups of feminists, perhaps discarding it altogether is unnecessary. An alternative post-utopian approach could accept the conflicted genealogy of *sisterhood,* which includes both white women's hope for its meaning with respect to cross-racial alliance as well as women of color's concern with its specifically racialized history, without seeing either as absolute. Because terms can also be generative, *sisterhood* might create the meanings people would like for it to have. Although such resignification would not by itself change the racial power dynamics of American society, it could be a tool in the larger project of conceptualizing a more inclusive feminism.

Test Cases: Identity Politics and Epistemic Privilege

The feminist discourse of differences among women contains two related utopian concepts—identity politics and epistemic privilege—both of which equate racial, ethnic, or class identity with political identity. Identity politics predicates political action on identity-group membership. Epistemic privilege predicates the validity of knowledge claims on the knower's identity-group membership, thereby promoting the myth of the truth teller. Many feminist theorists have found these concepts rhetorically appealing without exploring their self-defeating utopian connotations.

IDENTITY POLITICS

The term *identity politics* was popularized in the feminist discourse of differences among women via the African American Combahee River Collective manifesto, written in 1974. Responding to the overly generalized utopian feminist discourse of gender difference, the Collective demanded a feminist politics that took into account multiple and interlocking oppressions in American society. In describing that politics, they expanded the sentiments of Stokely Carmichael and Charles Hamilton, who explained in 1967 that African Americans needed "'to reclaim our history and our identity from . . . cultural terrorism . . . [and] struggle for the right to create our own terms through which to define ourselves and our relationship to the society'" (quoted in Kauffman 1990, 70). The Collective decided that "focusing upon our own oppression is embodied in the concept of identity politics. We believe that the most profound and potentially the most radical politics come directly out of our own identity, as opposed to working to end somebody else's oppression" ([1977] 1981, 210–12).

The concept of identity politics has attracted many women of color who theorize about feminism. In 1980, for example, Michelle Cliff credited identity politics with allowing her to claim an African American identity she had been taught to despise. Even more recently, some women of color have used identity politics to redefine the "subject of Anglo-American feminism" according to the experience and perspective of women of color. Thus, Norma Alarcón rejects the "autonomous, selfmaking–self-determining subject" of white feminism and embraces the subject who exists on multiple registers, whose "subjectivity cannot be arrived at through a single discursive 'theme,'" such as gender (1990, 357, 365–66).

Identity politics allows groups to define and control their own political struggles in order to preserve their integrity and prevent the distortion of their issues by dominant outside influences. The *identity* in identity politics is understood as a function of certain politically charged characteristics, such as race, sex, sexuality, class, and disability. The *politics* are broadly defined as a function of all institutions and relationships in which power differentials exist.

Since identity politics can be regarded as a basic premise of feminism, it might seem inconsistent (or even racist) to object to its utopianism when women of color adopt it as a mechanism for giving new voice to women who have previously been overlooked or silenced in the feminist discourse of gender difference. Indeed, identity politics might even seem like a counter-utopian response to gender-difference discourse.

But such a conclusion overlooks the fact that identity politics has been a dead end for white feminists, too. Despite its apparently fundamental contribution to feminist thought and action, identity politics has promoted utopian generalizations—about women and men of color as well as about other groups—by ignoring differences within those groups. After all, white women's identity politics is what angered feminists of color in the first place. In addition, promoting identity politics has given implicit support to feminist detractors and racists. If *some* political action can be predicated on particular identity characteristics, as opposed to ideas or beliefs, then why can't *all?* Identity politics is therefore as compatible with "white rights" as it is with more liberatory political agendas. Furthermore, identity politics has interfered with building coalitions among women of different races, sexualities, ethnicities, and cultures by emphasizing characteristics that cannot be changed or negotiated away instead of the ideas and projects about which various groups could reach agreement. Thus, identity politics has promoted political antagonisms and paralysis rather than action. Those conflicts lend credence to Linda Kauffman's admonition that "the only basis for a radically pluralist politics, as opposed to a fragmented mosaic of political groups, is the principle of solidarity" (1990, 76–78).

Identity politics fails all feminists because it overlooks overlapping identities, such as Jewish lesbian or disabled African American. Broadly constructed identity categories do not accommodate the mixed-identity person with divided or contradictory loyalties. What are the identity politics of a Rosario Morales, for example, who considers herself "Puerto Rican/ . . . U.S. American/ . . . New York Manhattan and the Bronx . . . Afro-Cuban . . . naturalized Jewish-American/wasp" all at the same time (1981, 14–15)? Expanding nomenclature by stacking up labels will not solve the problem. It will only result in more exclusions. Consider, for example, what happens to the category "Latina" when "lesbian" is added to it. Identity politics therefore inspires the proliferation of increasingly specialized categories with no means for bridging them in political movements. It also assumes too much about the origins of political views. Identity and politics do not always converge. Lesbians are registered as Democrats and Republicans, as are African Americans. The divergent politics of such groups suggests that the best interests of an identity group are not always clear or self-evident.

Identity politics also promotes the utopian quest for purity. It assumes that there can be *the* authentic African American or Latina or lesbian experience. That quest for purity can have the unintended consequence of reinforcing oppressive systems. The authentic quality or characteristic of a racial group, for example, is often the result of its present social location, just as nurturance as a female quality reflects women's historical assignments in the sexual division of labor. To make those qualities the premise for political practice can reinforce the status quo and ensure that the "new" identity politics will be "inevitably entangled with power and domination," just like the "old" politics it purports to replace (Bar On 1993, 91–94). Indeed, as Maria Lugones tells us, the process of drawing the limits of identity—to keep some people in and others out—is itself a product of the ethnocentric racist imagination of the "old" politics. Lugones explains that the "rural mexican/american" valorized by identity politics "is a product of the anglo imagination, sometimes enacted by persons who are the targets of ethnocentric racism in an unwillful parody of themselves" (1994, 470).

By the same token, identity politics utopianizes cultures, especially cultures of origin. But no culture, no matter how precious to us, is entirely good or pure or self-contained. "People and cultures are not so easily put into fixed categories based on race and ethnicity," writes Susan Friedman; "claims for such purity are often based on the binary opposition of pure/impure in which mixing constitutes a form of pollution" (Freedman 1995, 14). Anzaldúa agrees: "'Racial purity, like language purity, is a fallacy'" (quoted in ibid.). In truth, cultures partake of one another, and the culture we claim as our own may owe as much to another as to its own heritage.

Such pitfalls suggest that, among other things, identity politics suffers from utopian present focus. As Judith Butler explains, "Making a conception of identity into the ground of politics, however internally complicated, prematurely forecloses the possible cultural articulations of the subject-position that a new politics might . . . generate" (1990a, 327). Embracing and fixing identities, then, can obscure the generative aspects of all identity labels as well as prevent their evolution. Bell hooks explains that identity is a stage in the production of subjectivity. In order to create black subjectivity, hooks seeks to revise identity politics so as "to explore marginal locations as spaces where we can best become whatever we want to be while remaining committed to liberatory black liberation struggle" (1990, 20).

Identity politics may reverse the problem encountered by oppressed people—by turning the source of oppression into a source of pride and resistance—but it does not necessarily combat oppression. Indeed, identity politics may actually undermine its own power by overlooking the processes and politics of identity formation itself. Identity politics accepts the idea of identity, which may be the source of the problem of oppression in the first place. Until we understand how we really know our "own people," or how we legitimately balance socially constituted identity groupings with individual psychology, family dynamics, and educational levels (Lugones 1994, 469), among other variables, the truly political nature of identity remains underexplored.

In short, identity makes a shaky, utopian foundation for politics. Racial, ethnic, class, gender, and sexuality identity categories are inevitably too narrow or too broad. In addition, identities constitute one another, as Kum-Kum Bhavnani observes: "Categories of identity are not discrete and uninfluenced by each other—for human consciousness and language both create and are created by the relationship of the categories to each other." It is impossible to know when one category—such as race—takes precedence over another—such as sex (1993, 40). Race is sexed just as sex is raced. Gender is formed by sexuality just as sexuality is constituted by gender. A focus on separate or mutually exclusive identities also reduces the likelihood of alliances, which are ultimately necessary for successful political action in a pluralistic society.

Thus, although identity issues have challenged the concept of feminist politics, we must find an alternative to identity politics as we pursue feminist causes. That alternative should entail an understanding of how issues vary depending on social location, but we must not settle for understanding only those variations that have relevance for our own lives and needs. Rather, as Sandra Harding explains, we must all develop the consciousness and analytical tools necessary to address issues of identity and power, regardless of our race, class, or social location. Furthermore, "oppression does not provide all the identities and social locations" oppressed people need for their struggle (Harding 1993a, 150).

EPISTEMIC PRIVILEGE

A close cousin to identity politics is *epistemic privilege,* a concept of knowledge validation also based on specific group identities and experiences. Proponents of epistemic privilege argue that the perspectives of socially marginalized groups are not simply valuable to the development of inclusive and valid knowledge claims but are actually more legitimate, even truer, than the claims of dominant groups (Bar On 1993, 83). The source of epistemic privilege is often oppression. Thus, Charlotte Bunch argued in 1975 that "'since lesbians are materially oppressed by heterosexuality, it is not surprising that we have seen and understood its impact first.'" And bell hooks claimed in 1989 that African Americans inevitably produce "'counterhegemonic discourse'" because of their racial memory either of a time (a Golden Age) before oppression or of resisting voices from the more recent past (Bunch and hooks quoted in Bar On 1993, 88). Advocates of epistemic privilege often claim that "oppression can be quantified and compared and that adding layers of oppression produces a potentially clearer standpoint" (Collins 1990, 207).

Again skeptics will recall that epistemic privilege has been a feature of feminist theorizing for a long time. In response, we must also recall that epistemic privilege based on sex has distorted feminist analyses by producing the effects we observed in the discourse of gender difference: hyperbole, generalization, falsely universalized claims about "women's knowledge" based on sexuality or reproductive functioning, and underexamined experience as the basis of legitimate knowledge. Epistemic privilege is no worse when invoked by women of color, but it's no better, either.

The usual justification for epistemic privilege is its ability to empower women who have been silenced. But, as Catharine Stimpson observes, that benefit comes with a cost: "The admirable desire to

help each woman develop her voice has had an unintended consequence: neglecting to [theorize] how to move effectively in the rhetorical spaces between autobiography and wild overgeneralization, between saying 'I hate my father' and 'All men are hateful.' In this
over-reliance on the personal voice, we have sometimes permitted individual stunts and childish exhibitionism to substitute for [knowl-
edge]" (Stimpson 1996, 71).

Equally dangerous, claims of epistemic privilege can distort and
idealize the groups it celebrates, with unexpected consequences. For
example, Gloria Anzaldúa has introduced the term *mestiza* to describe
and celebrate mixed-race women, especially white and Latina women
like herself. She defines *mestiza* as *tolteca,* or earth women, who "put
bones, pieces of bark, *heirbas,* eagle feather, snakeskin, tape recorder,
the rattle and drum in [their] pack. . . . We are the people who leap in
the dark, we are the people on the knees of the gods. In our very flesh,
(r)evolution works out the clash of cultures" ([1987] 1993, 431). She
therefore implies that *mestiza* produce heroic knowledge (via their tape
recorders) of their exciting identity-based journey through life. Undoubtedly, may of Anzaldúa's readers are inspired by her depiction,
but along with that inspiration they get stereotypes and restrictions on
the *mestiza* identity. To be privileged in epistemic privilege, individuals must often live up to idealized generalizations and concepts of
group purity that distinguish them from other, nonprivileged, groups
(Lugones 1994, 473).

Declaring epistemic privilege on the basis of identity alone means
engaging in the myth of the truth teller, which, in turn, rejects counterarguments or evidence from outsiders. The privileged/marginalized
group thereby becomes an isolated monolith with no external scrutiny
and little internal diversity of opinion or perspective.

The isolation implicit in epistemic privilege promotes yet another
epistemological weakness, the *ad hominem* fallacy. That is, knowledge
produced by those outside the privileged group is judged on the personal or identity qualities of the thinker rather than on the quality of
her thought or argument (Mullen 1995, 141). Typically, that judgment
is negative (as a complement of "insiders'" positive qualities). Epistemic privilege thereby promotes insider thought as absolute truth and
violates its own premise that truth is contingent on a thinker's consciousness and intention (Flax 1992, 452). Thus, it undermines its
own justification by exempting certain knowers from judgments about
their consciousness and intention.

This analysis of epistemic privilege suggests support for objective knowledge, but only as that concept has been redefined in terms of situated knowledges. Thinkers like Sandra Harding, Donna Haraway, and Patricia Hill Collins, among others, have engaged in a decade-long discussion of *situated knowledge* and *standpoint epistemologies* that recognize the role of identities based on social positioning in the production of knowledge as the beginning rather than the end of inquiry. Situated knowledge and standpoint epistemologies have evolved from critiques of scientific objectivity, which has itself been guilty of utopian assertions. That is, scientific objectivity has valorized what Donna Haraway calls the "god-trick of seeing everything from nowhere" (Haraway 1991, 189). It has declared as objective the unrecognized knowledge standpoint of, typically, white male scientists who have achieved distance and emotional and political detachment from what they observe.

Feminist theorists argue that a great deal is lost in that detachment. Haraway and Harding have both challenged traditional empirical methods that lack "rules, procedures, or techniques for even identifying, let alone eliminating, social concerns and interests." At the same time, they have criticized traditional methods for excluding observers (such as women) with varied social backgrounds and beliefs (Harding 1993b, 57). Collins has criticized the absence of emotions in scientific discourse as well as its reliance on adversarial debates and its exclusion of life experience, especially that of African American women (1990, 205).

Despite such criticisms, however, feminist theorists do not necessarily want to abandon notions of objectivity. Harding and Haraway discuss an alternative, feminist definition of objectivity within standpoint epistemologies and situated knowledges. Their definition assumes that all knowledge is partial and embodied. They argue that recognizing an observer's limited social location produces more rather than less objective knowledge than does pretending to see everything from no particular stance. Objectivity in situated or standpoint epistemology consists of combining "partial, locatable, critical knowledges" and recognizing "the possibility of webs of connections called solidarity in politics and shared conversations in epistemology" (Haraway 1991, 188–90). Knowledge must be seen as "saturated with history and social life." Few claims can be made for its universality. Standpoint epistemology "allows us to find out what others think of us and our beliefs and actions, not just what we think of ourselves and them" (Harding 1993b, 57, 72).

In Harding's recent approach, standpoint epistemologies entail starting inquiry from the most challenging position, by taking account of social situations that have been marginalized in the past. Unlike epistemic privilege, however, standpoint epistemology regards the best starting position for knowledge as a place other than the knower's own, wherever that is. It also claims that even self-knowledge can be achieved by taking into account the perspectives of others (Harding 1993b, 54, 66; 1993a, 147).

Also unlike epistemic privilege, standpoint and situated epistemologies do not assume that any particular marginalized position inevitably produces valid claims to knowledge. Collins observes that although it is tempting to assert that black women's oppression gives them the "best standpoint from which to understand the mechanisms, process, and effects of oppression, this simply may not be the case" (1990, 207). These epistemologies, therefore, avoid the utopian myth of the truth teller that plagues the concept of epistemic privilege. A speaker's or writer's association with a specific identity does not assume greater importance than the substance of her words. These epistemologies also avoid the quest for purity in the knowing subject, as in epistemic privilege's practice of "abstracting from the actual lived practices [of a group] and generalizing from normatively approved ones . . . presupposing that there are practices that in one way or another are more authentically expressive of something about the oppressed group" (Bar On 1993, 92).

Also in contrast to epistemic privilege, recent feminist standpoint epistemologies encourage the comparison of viewpoints. While starting from marginalized perspectives, they provide the "reality check" of multiple perspectives, and they require a continual reexamination of the foundations of knowledge. Standpoint epistemologies explore rather than assume the relationship of autobiography to generalization. In Gayatri Spivak's terms, they "make visible the assignment of subject-positions" (1989, 241).

While acknowledging that all knowledge is located and affected by experience, new standpoint epistemologies make no assumptions about the specific knowledge that any specific experience might produce. Perceptions of experience can be limited as well as generated by a particular social location. "Women know much . . . about their own pain, but some of the underlying causes of that pain may be very well hidden from them," writes Sherry Gorelick (1991, 463). "Experience is at once always already an interpretation *and* in need of interpretation. What counts as experience is neither self-evident nor straightforward; it is always contested, always therefore political. . . . Experience is . . . not the origin of our explanation, but that which we want to explain," according to Joan Scott (1992, 37–38). Furthermore, basing knowledge on any predetermined location misses the point: "Splitting, not being, is the privileged image for feminist epistemologies," writes Donna Haraway. "The topography of subjectivity is multidimensional; so, therefore, is vision. The knowing self is partial in all its guises, never finished, whole, simply there and original" (1991, 193). Indeed, by basing knowledge on identity, epistemic privilege has it backward: identities do not completely precede experience and interpretation; identities are also constituted through the interpretation of experience (Mohanty 1991, 88–89).

Standpoint and situated knowledges avoid the utopianism of epistemic privilege by beginning with questions and challenges rather than with predetermined conclusions about the world and its truths. They avoid monolithic utopian constructions of power and utopian dichotomous divisions between good and evil. Whereas epistemic privilege locates all power in an identifiable center and values knowledge according to its distance from that center, standpoint and situated knowledges recognize complexity, what Grewal and Kaplan call "scattered hegemonies," or decentralized and transnational loci of power that interact with the multiple subjectivities of each individual and produce complex effects. No one exists safely or solely either in the center of power or on the margins, they explain, because individuals and communities both resist and collaborate in oppression, and identity categories both serve and disadvantage their members (Grewal and Kaplan 1994, 7, 27–28). Finally, these epistemologies avoid creating competitions among oppressed groups to see who is more epistemically privileged, a project that undercuts both the purpose of creating liberatory knowledge and the significance of epistemic privilege. If many groups can equally claim it, what can it mean? (Bar On 1993, 89).

Utopianism in the Discourse of Differences among Women

That certain utopian aspects of this discourse have inspired and affirmed the experience of women of color, lesbians, and working-class or other marginalized women does not diminish its potential for harm. By overemphasizing identity and promoting the terms of the racist debate, for example, the utopianism of identity politics and epistemic privilege threatens to backfire on those most vulnerable to racist or homophobic arguments. Racial and ethnic pride comes at a price, as world events have taught us. The disenfranchised are also ill-served by the utopian hyperbole and overgeneralization in this discourse which can alienate outsiders, obscure the diversity of such groups, and distort history. Legitimate social power rightly rests upon validated knowledge.

Even more dangerous is the risk of fanaticism. Identity politics and epistemic privilege pit identity groups against one another and impede communication among them. Their tenets indirectly support fanatical predispositions to characterize everyone exclusively by race, ethnicity, nationality, or sex and to attribute good and evil primarily along those categorical lines. In such an extreme economy, identity can be used as a reason to commit violence, and individuals are perceived only in terms of characteristics conferred upon the group. Targeting an African American, a Palestinian, a Jew, or a lesbian seems justified as a way to rid the world of evil.

Feminism should contribute to reducing such dangerous confusion, rather than fueling identity-based hatreds, by providing tools for determining which sex- and race-based injustices and disputes should be pursued on identity terms and which should not. Utopian feminist constructions of sex and race do little to create helpful distinctions between legitimate generalizations about groups and fanatical attributions of identity characteristics.

THE DISCOURSE OF LINGUISTIC CONSTRUCTION: IS "WOMAN" JUST AN EMPTY CATEGORY?

Genders can be neither true nor false but are only produced as the truth effects of a discourse of primary and stable identity.
—Judith Butler, "Gender Trouble, Feminist Theory, and Psychoanalytic Discourse"

A plausible feminist utopia would be a society in which it was not *the case that a woman was beaten by a male intimate every seven seconds [and] . . . four million women a year suffered physical injury at the hands of men who are allegedly their partners in life. . . . We can do this most quickly from within the content of some of our most powerful unifying metaphors. . . . I assure you: language is the only real high technology. . . . Legislation . . . is chicken scratches when it runs counter to the will of the powerful.*
—Suzette Haden Elgin, "Washing Utopian Dishes, Scrubbing Utopian Floors"

Neither power nor discourse are rendered anew at every moment; they are not as weightless as the utopics of radical resignification *might imply.*
—Judith Butler, *Bodies That Matter*

Having complicated the categories of gender, race, and sexuality, we should welcome a discourse that undermines them further as primarily constructions in language.[8] The discourse of linguistic construction is such a discourse. At its most extreme, it recognizes sex and gender as epiphenomena—a "truth effect," as Judith Butler has said—of language that constructs as its represents sex and sexuality, subjectivity, and their intersection with cultural norms. There is no natural or necessary form of gender or sexuality to describe, rationalize, or even contest.

As a product of postmodern thought, this discourse does help to dispel the utopian universalizations of the previous two discourses, by promoting "pragmatic and fabillistic" theory tailored to specific tasks and by using multiple categories. It even interrogates the term *feminism*, "forswearing the metaphysical comfort of a single feminist method or feminist epistemology." It argues instead for conceptualizing feminist theory and practice as "a patchwork of overlapping alliances, not one circumscribable by an essential definition." It envisions the "practice of feminisms" through "multilayered feminist solidarity . . . which is essential for overcoming the oppression of women in its 'endless variety and monotonous similarity'"(Fraser and Nicholson 1990, 34–35). Thus, in its attention to the constructed nature of all it surveys, this discourse seems made in post-utopian Heaven, if there is such an oxymoronic place.

Of particular relevance to the utopian discourse of differences among women, the discourse of linguistic construction deconstructs the language that defines all identities, thereby undermining utopian foundationalist assumptions of identity politics and epistemic privilege. As Judith Butler explained in 1990, in the discourse of linguistic construction, identity—even gender identity—is a text, composed in particular times and places against the backdrop of certain conditions of oppression (Butler 1990a, 331). We have all been duped into thinking that *what we are called* is *what we are*, she observed. That deception applies to the mitigating factors of class, race, age, and ethnicity that fragment the category *woman* and are constitutive rather than descriptive of identity (ibid., 324–27).

8. The subtitle for this section paraphrases the title of an article by Laura Lee Downs: "If 'Woman' Is Just an Empty Category, Then Why Am I Afraid to Walk Alone at Night? Identity Politics Meets the Postmodern Subject." Criticizing both the discursive constructionism of Joan Scott and the essentializing nature of identity politics, Downs sees a model for subjectivity in "the possibility of communication, of meaningful encounter across the boundaries of difference, which will allow us to reconfigure subject, knowledge and community" (1988, 435).

Thus, the discourse of linguistic construction intends, as Joan Scott explains, not simply to enumerate and claim various identity categories but also to challenge all categories and understand "the operations of the complex and changing discursive processes by which identities are ascribed, resisted, or embraced, and which processes themselves are unremarked, indeed achieve their effect because they aren't noticed" (1992, 33). Butler concurs: we must "challenge the place of the category as a part of a feminist normative discourse" by "honoring the diversity of the category and insisting upon its definitional nonclosure." No terms are foundational, no unified core of identity exists beneath the labels (Butler 1990a, 327). It is appropriate for feminists to argue over the definition of the term *woman* (Butler 1992, 16). But what we should really be discussing is whether it is possible to know "what [if anything] exists prior to [woman's] discursive articulation" (Butler 1990a, 327).

Also reflecting its relationship to postmodernism, the discourse of linguistic construction resists all the "grand narratives of legitimation" that have characterized three hundred years of modernism, preferring "plural, local, and immanent stories" to broad theoretical schemes, such as Marxism or liberalism or (to some) even feminism. Those schemes produced by white males are especially suspect (despite that judgment's utopian error). While looking for stories, as Fraser and Nicholson explain, postmodernism is ever cognizant of contexts and power relations that constitute subjects and their experience discursively. History itself must be reconceptualized, according to Joan Scott, as the writing of stories that focus on "processes of identity production, insisting on the discursive nature of 'experience' and on the politics of its construction" (1992, 37). Thus, women's history is no longer about the so-called experiences of women or the facts or chronological narratives of their lives (Hoff 1994, 443), but rather about the discursive production of gendered "subjects whose agency is created through situations and statuses conferred on them" (Scott 1992, 34).

In the discourse of linguistic construction, then, experiences, like identity categories, serve to reinforce existing structures of difference—racial, gender—rather than explain them. If a young black man attracts unwarranted attention in a store, for example, it may be because a racist merchant considers such persons likely to shoplift. When the young man perceives that attitude, his resentment creates new tensions that reinforce the merchant's original expectations. Everything that happens in the exchange reinforces existing racial antagonisms, although no act of stealing or even accusation has occurred. More importantly, the players have enacted the script and internalized its messages so that they become the racist, suspicious merchant and the defiant youngster the script demands. On the strength of such a cycle, linguistic constructionists explain that recounting experience should be replaced by exploring "how difference is established, how it operates, how and in what ways it constitutes subjects who see and act in the world" (Scott 1992, 24). Thus, this discourse reveals "the power of discourses to construct . . . and to anchor difference in social practices and institutions" (Canning 1994, 370).

Despite this long list of post-utopian qualities, however, the discourse of linguistic construction is not entirely post-utopian. In fact, this discursive world includes many utopian characteristics.

Consider the cartoon reprinted here.

"Despite my best efforts, you're still the man and I'm still the woman."

Reflecting the "linguistic turn" in contemporary theory, many feminist linguistic constructionists might observe that the cartoon woman has identified her principal problem: human beings are pawns in a linguistic game that is bigger than they are, more powerful than the woman's "best efforts" to change her life circumstances. As up-to-date as the couple depicted try to be—as indicated by their personal style and surroundings—their attempts to disrupt traditional gender categories have failed; the old definitions overwhelm their efforts. Persistent gender categories have scuttled their goals of equal parenting or shared domestic responsibilities, so that *man* in the domestic sphere signifies for yet another generation leisure and comfort (reading papers and sipping wine) and *woman* still signifies work and service (food preparation and child care). Change will not occur, the cartoon suggests, simply from individual resistance. In the terms of the discourse of linguistic construction, change will occur only when we resignify those labels so that *man* and *woman* mean and therefore enact something different from what they've meant and enacted for centuries.

That reading of the cartoon woman's lament certainly captures part of the problem, but its singular focus on signification obscures other truths, other forces at work. Among them are material forces, like law and economics, that cannot be entirely reduced to language, as well as the biological/physical reality of childbearing and the child itself, once of the woman's body and now in her arms. Susan Bordo's work, for example, challenges purely discursive analyses by identifying reproductive physiology as gender's material base that "fixes the knower in time and space and therefore situates and relativizes perception and thought." It is not entirely possible to "escape from human locatedness," Bordo concludes, and adopt "endlessly shifting, seemingly inexhaustible vantage points, none of which are 'owned'" (1990, 143–46). Experience constructs gender just as gender constructs experience.

The difference between that "material base for gender" analysis and the utopian "reproductive romance" discussed in the discourse of gender difference is this: materiality does not necessarily dictate a *particular* identity, personality, role, or consequence. Rather, it simply contributes a complication in the fashioning of social and individual lives and roles and, therefore, in the fashioning of feminist analyses of those lives and roles. By contrast, utopian constructions of motherhood—the reproductive romance—depend on defining maternity as a pure gift or pure burden of womanhood. In complex reality, it is both, simultaneously. Children tax women's energy and spirit and threaten their autonomy, but they are (or can be) also a precious product of women's bodies, a unique attachment that imbues the burdens they impose with transcendent meaning. Thus the cartoon woman's maternal responsibilities, even though problematic, may not be wholly negotiable even from her own perspective.

By the same token, the woman's stubbornly traditional role, no matter how unfair or irritating, may not result solely from the misogyny, phallocratic, or otherwise masculinist self-affirming discursive constructions of her husband and, through him, the society at large. That her role and responsibilities chafe her sense of justice does not reduce them to a case of signification. Rather, they exist within a wide range of "extra-linguistic" social practices and human desires (Cameron 1998, 970). They are an effect of the labor-force expectations and policies of the corporate world, for example, which tend to merge childbearing, childrearing, and domestic responsibilities.

Identifying the distinction between discursive and nondiscursive influences on gender roles, sexuality, gender identity, and a host of other issues related to feminist theory requires a better theoretical analysis of linguistic construction than we have had so far, according to linguist Deborah Cameron. It must include properly theorized and formalized linguistic data and analysis as well as "textual" interpretation (1998, 969). Such linguistic analyses suggest that terms like *woman* and *man* have little ontological power; that their meanings can be contradictory in the same context; and that gender terms do not construct gender identities in simple or straightforward ways. By the same token, linguistic studies debunk the utopian hope that problems created by linguistic construction can be solved solely by changes in language use. At best, resignification is only one element in the complex process of social change, which requires "people using their new awareness that what counts as 'reality' is constructed, contingent, and (crucially) unjust and on that basis taking different actions in future (including discursive ones . . .)" (ibid., 965–66).

Test Case: "Woman" and Performance

Nevertheless, feminist theory must grapple with the power of language to produce social change, the changing of metaphors as a way to protect women better than the changing of laws. Elgin, whose quotation opens this section of chapter 4, represents a group of theorists who have taken the "linguistic turn" in feminist theory.[9] Such feminist thinkers might well believe that a new metaphor would get

---

9. *Linguistic* in this discourse refers in a nontechnical way to *discourse analysis* rather than to the analysis of sounds, words, or sentences as language elements. Linguists would take issue with such a definition, since to them *discourse* is a "highly organized

the cartoon man off his chair and in front of the stove, baby on his hip. After all, in a discursive universe, even bodies can be manipulated by linguistic conventions. Therefore, the maternal woman can be redefined to read the paper and sip wine while the paternal man cooks.

Following that logic, gender itself can be seen as "a kind of impersonation and approximation . . . a kind of imitation for which there is no original," according to Judith Butler's early 1990s work (1991, 21). Indeed, in Butler's account, "the gendered body has no ontological status apart from the various acts which constitute its reality" (1990a, 336). That is, gender, sexuality, and the self have no existence until they are enacted in a social context. *We are what we perform,* and we are under tremendous pressure to perform according to conventional heterosexual gender scripts. Reflecting the cartoon woman's lost hope, Butler has also advised feminists to abandon any belief in an essential identity for *woman* and pursue more fluid human identities and alliances via coalition politics. Affirming Elgin's sentiments, Butler has predicated changes in gender roles on the resignification of subject positions (ibid., 339).

The rhetorical power of these precepts is striking. We can see only too vividly how gender "scripts" produce conventional femininity and masculinity; how desires are created through imposed gender norms. Then why quibble with these prescriptions for fluid foundational principles or doubt their ability to do more than merely disrupt categories, stereotypes, idealizations, and dichotomies? Because lurking within the non-utopian intentions of the discourse of linguistic construction are utopian precepts.

Even if we deny a material base for gender identity or roles, it is utopian to claim that causation for human behavior can be narrowed to a single albeit capacious category—signification and resignification. Indeed, that claim seems inconsistent with this discourse's key premise that everything, including gender identities, is and should be fluid and flexible. How can fluidity result from a discourse that reduces all plausible causal factors into one—language—and discounts all other explanations, such as religious or psychological conceptions of truth (Deseger 1994, 664–65)?

Even if language can be shown to play an enormous role both in constructing gender and in creating confining gender roles, behaviors,

---

linguistic phenomenon whose formal characteristics" are the primary object of study (Cameron 1998, 947–48).

and sexualities, "the world is not after all reducible to a text" (Smyth 1992, 333), and "life is not literary criticism" (Flax 1990, 47). By the same token, changes in language will not necessarily alter gender hierarchies and structures of dominance. Indeed, to think so is to engage in the utopian process of problem reversal as problem solution.

To the extent that the discourse of linguistic construction identifies language as an absolute "first principle," then, it risks utopian foundationalism and even coherentism. The precept that language plays a significant role in the creation of gender identities and roles, as well as in the social structures that enforce them, is better as a strand in the rope of knowledge than as a monolithic footing for all feminist thought. It works as long as it only goes so far. And one realm it does not reach is political action (Smyth 1992, 336). Indeed, no matter how important linguistic construction and gender performance may be in explaining the ontological status of a particular self-understanding, it is not sufficient to explain "the deprivation of political rights, the depreciation of interests, the differences of wages, or the lack of respect that women (along with other groups) have faced and continue to face" (Deseger 1994, 668). Even "at the end of a hard day's deconstruction" there is still "no clue as to what, in the realm of feminist politics, might actually be done about anything" (Cameron 1998, 965). The prescription for fluid sexualities within this discourse may be even less political. Indeed, without "contestation with a hegemonic heterosexual Symbolic," lesbian and gay identities—emblematic of such fluidity—may lose their political impact (Soper 1995, 120).

Also utopian are claims that the new world imagined in the discourse of linguistic construction, in which no gender or sexual categories exist, will be free of pressure on individual identity formation. Indeed, according to the very precepts of this discourse, no world can be free of social structure or devoid of "constitutive conventions" (Butler 1993, 227). Therefore, we must understand that ideas of gender and sexual fluidity would themselves impose certain conventions in the "new" world without gender conventions. Among them might be pressures against language—and practices—associated with conventional femininity, which would be interpreted routinely as a "mask" for the "refusal of female homosexuality" (Butler 1990b, 53). As such new norms emerge, new pressures for conformity would not be far behind.

Other utopian reversals also beset the discourse of linguistic construction. Having identified the hidden powers of heterosexual normative language to create oppressive gender identities, for example, some linguistic constructionists assume that the opposite—homosexual normative language—would create the opposite effect. Yet, by the very tenets of the discourse of linguistic construction, all sexual desire must be constructed in language, since there is no material base for such desire. And without a material base, there is "no reason to suppose that heterosexuality is any less voluntary or pleasure-motivated than lesbianism" (Soper 1995, 120). By the same token, all sexual theorists, including presumably Butler herself, must be seen as promoting a particular politics of gender and sexuality.

The mergence of *performance* and *performativity* within this discourse is also problematic and peculiarly utopian. Although the terms sound alike, they are in some sense polar opposites. *Performance* denotes human action that is aware of itself as acting (that is, as separate from the actor's personal identity). *Performativity,* according to linguistic philosopher J. L. Austin, denotes language that transforms through utterance, such as threats, warnings, promises, bets, oaths, and vows. In Foucault's terms, performatives create the objects of which they speak. The difference between performers and performatives lies in one's reinforcement of irony and the other's reliance on sincerity. Performers can have ironic distance from their roles; they can pretend to be what they know they are not. But performatives are meaningless without sincere reference to an underlying truth value. Thus Austin's performatives make something happen only as *constatives* that can be judged as true or false. A promise is made only if the speaker has represented himself accurately. A bet is legitimate only if the bettor has money to back it up (Deseger 1994, 662–63).

Gender as performance, then, implies both ironic distance—or ironic mastery—and a constative referent to some kind of gender norms. Even if gender is performance, we are still agents who can distinguish to some extent between our "selves" and our roles. In addition, we gauge our performance against perceived or actual norms whose constative foundation gives meaning to that performance. Because there is no way to measure the level of performance in performativity (Cameron 1998, 949), there is no way to free performativity from the actor's agency or awareness of self within a role. Further, pure manipulation of gender without constatives becomes a meaningless parody (Deseger 1994, 666–67). Both cross-dressers and "real" women or men depend equally on gender constatives, and they may have equal ironic distance from their roles. Thus, gender performances—whether conventional or subversive—do not in and of themselves undermine the very existence of constative gender, as

Butler has claimed (Butler 1990a, 338). Nor do they necessarily conflate one's self and one's role.

Moreover, although the discourse of linguistic construction depends on recognizing the generative powers of language, its assumption that existing language creates only one kind of meaning—that is, restrictive meaning—overlooks the full range of those powers. Why would only *re*signification, or new language, have variable meanings—restrictive as well as expansive? Indeed, *existing* gender categories may already have "pluralistic and multifaceted" meanings instead of (or in addition to) their fixed or confining ones (Deseger 1994, 668). By the same token, *women* in some contexts already connotes resistance and resignifiability just as it connotes in other contexts domestic service, sexual accessibility, low cultural status, and other markers of disadvantage.

Finally, linguistic constructionist precepts are utopian to the extent that they include no mechanisms for assessing themselves. Without a means of reassessment, the new identities or political alliances that form on the basis of new, presumably non-essentialized categories, like utopian societies themselves, could become as uncompromising and destructive as the old ones they replace (Deseger 1994, 671). We have already observed how the retreat from gender essentialism in the discourse of linguistic construction has created a kind of utopian boomerang from its own essentialisms. Thus, in reversing conventional notions of fixed gender identity and sexuality, linguistic constructionist precepts of gender or sexual fluidity become new norms themselves.

A Bridge to Realism

Uncovering the utopian qualities of the discourse of linguistic construction helps to prevent the boomerangs, paradoxes, and ironies that have often vexed feminist thought and theory. Interestingly enough, Judith Butler herself has facilitated this process. In her 1993 work, *Bodies That Matter*, she acknowledges that the concept of "radical resignification," of which some would say she has been guilty herself, is "utopic," and she renounces it. Without addressing her own relationship to it, she explicitly rejects the utopian Nietzschean idea that everything is a "continuous sign-chain of ever new interpretations and adaptations whose causes do not even have to be related to one another" (224).

Butler's use of the term "utopic" strengthens the arguments of *Higher Ground*, for it both identifies (as "misreadings" of her intentions) and revises the utopian aspects of linguistic construction that we have been critiquing. Butler denies having claimed that all human attributes are discursively constructed or that language in any deterministic way produces subjects as its effect. She acknowledges the existence of agency by affirming that people both enact and contest social scripts. She also acknowledges that "the compulsory character of [social] norms does not always make them efficacious" (1993, 8, 12–13, 237). She even affirms that the category *women* has its uses: "This speaking will occur, and for feminist reasons, it must; the category of women does not become useless through deconstruction, but becomes one whose uses are no longer reified as 'referents,' and which stands a chance of being opened up. . . . Surely, it must be possible both to use the term, to use it tactically even as one is, as it were, used and positioned by it, and also to subject the term to a critique which interrogates the exclusionary operations and differential power-relations that construct and delimit feminist invocations of 'women'" (ibid., 29).

Other feminist theorists agree with Butler's newer, more complex, post-utopian view that it is possible both to use or valorize a term and to critique it. For example, Nancy Fraser explains that "generalizing claims about 'women' are inescapable but always subject to revision; they should be advanced nonfoundationally and fabillisticly. Further, the assumptions underlying such claims should be genealogized, framed by contextualizing narrative and rendered culturally and historically specific" (1995, 70).

Such views "de-utopianize" for feminist theorizing the discourse of linguistic construction and its associate, postmodern theory, by emphasizing the importance of simultaneous acceptance and skepticism, of asking continuously "But what about . . .?" Instead of reducing the mother's attachment to the baby to pure cultural or discursive manipulation, post-utopian feminist theory also considers the mother's physical attachment and often ambivalent feelings about her child. Instead of assuming that older feminist constructions must necessarily be replaced, post-utopian feminist theory considers what would be lost in that process. Indeed, even *modernity,* that pariah of contemporary theory, deserves another look, as Catharine Stimpson explains. Stimpson revisits the "narrative of modernity" and asks how we can "cast aside" a discourse that "encourages us to believe in pluralism over monism, secularism over fundamentalism, democracy over totalitarianism, inclusiveness and equality over hierarchy, acceptance of individual differences over conformity to group norms, and reasonable inquiries over dogma and militant revelations" (Stimpson 1996,

74). How indeed, we must ask, and at what cost? As we question the new, however, we must also resist the utopian urge to jump backward with both feet to a Golden Age gone by. There is no innocent haven, no single answer, time, configuration, construction, or cause . . . except in utopia.

III TOWARD HIGHER GROUND

Approaching Realism in Feminist Thought and Theory

INTRODUCTION

I have sought to say that in protecting and advancing the institutions of freedom we need to be guided by a realistic, non-utopian, anything but complacent, but nevertheless optimistic view of human nature.
—Robert F. Goheen, *The Human Nature of a University*

One key attraction of utopian dreams and desires is the sense of optimism they convey. How else, we may ask, can we rally our hopes for the future, especially when the realities of today are so discouraging? But there are other sources of optimism. Indeed, realism and optimism are compatible partners, as Robert Goheen, the former president of Princeton University and director of the National Woodrow Wilson Fellowship Foundation, suggests. Recognizing how much in this world needs improvement could make us cynical, Goheen continues, "but most of us, if we have courage, would prefer to have such clear sight as we can. We would prefer to know as accurately as possible where we are and in what kind of world. Whatever it be, we wish to see it clearly." To acquire that courage we need a "searching mind and probing conscience" (Goheen 1969, 115–16). Scott Russell Sanders, another educator, gets more specific: "Knowledge . . . offers us frameworks for making sense of the fragments. . . . Knowledge helps us imagine how we might act." And knowing how to make sense of the world and how to act upon it gives us hope (1999, B5).

In seeking the higher ground of realistic feminist thought and theory, the chapters in part III strive to establish a connection between realism and optimism. Chapter 5, "Searching for Realism," begins by exploring the meaning of *realism* in various intellectual traditions, including political science, literature, law, and philosophy, in order to establish the parameters of realistic thought. It then suggests some of the qualities that constitute post-utopian/realistic feminist theory, including both traditional and new approaches to knowledge acquisition.

Chapter 6, "Toward Realistic Feminist Discourse," revisits the three discourses of feminist thought and theory whose utopian aspects we explored in chapter 4—gender difference, differences among women, and linguistic construction—in order to explore post-utopian, realistic approaches to those topics. Instead of gender dichotomy, realistic feminist theorizing disaggregates the elements of gender identity and sexuality and offers numerous variations on the concepts of male and female. Instead of identity politics, realistic feminist theorizing explores the politics of coalition among persons who are internally as well as externally diverse. Instead of epistemic privilege, realistic feminist theorizing focuses on located knowledge and examined subjectivity. Instead of gender as pure performance, realistic feminist theorizing connects discursive and material aspects of sexualities as well as gender roles and identities.

THANK YOU FOR BACKING UP YOUR OPINIONS WITH HARD DATA

THE CHRONICLE OF HIGHER EDUCATION   MISCHA RICHTER AND HARALD BAK

FIVE *Searching for Realism*

I do not want to leave my analysis of utopianism in feminist thought and theory at the point of complaint—to be like the bartender's opinionated customers who have prompted him to post his wry little sign. Unlike feminist detractors, I prefer to back up my criticism of feminist theorizing with an equally detailed discussion of positive alternatives. Thus, the following chapters explore post-utopian, realistic theoretical approaches to gender difference, differences among women, and linguistic construction.

In conceptualizing that alternative project, I have been inspired by a familiar gospel hymn, "Higher Ground," which informs the title of this book. "Lord, plant my feet on higher ground/New heights I'm gaining every day. Let me stand . . . on heaven's table land." [1] "Higher ground" works as a mixed metaphor that keeps its eye on the earth even as it seeks transcendence. The image of "higher ground" maintains a tension between firm footing on the one hand and exploration on the other. It suggests a solid platform of inquiry underlying dreams and visions. It recognizes the importance of incremental change on the way to the loftiest goals.

The realistic feminist thought and theory advocated in *Higher Ground* seek that kind of theoretical and epistemological traction. They value ideas that are simultaneously solid and transcendent,

---

1. Composed by Johnson Oatman, Jr., and Charles H. Gabriel, copyright 1907. Published in *Songs of Zion*, Supplemental Worship Resources 12 (Nashville: Abingdon Press, 1981): 39–40.

rooted and exploratory. They require effort, rigor, and vigilance. They advocate no fixed notion of reality but identify realism as a commitment to accountability. They insist that we back up our opinions in the best possible way. Realistic feminist thinking opens itself to questions, goes beyond hopes and wishes, seeks internal consistency (even as it recognizes inconsistent and contradictory realities) and external verification, combs both the past and present for guidance, makes selective use of solid thinking from other (even opposing) idea systems, includes mechanisms for reconsidering its own principles, regards its conclusions as provisional pending new discoveries, and freely admits that even at its best it can never encompass all of life's complexities and mysteries.

Following the hymn's suggestion of perpetual striving, my idea of realistic feminist theorizing achieves no final destination. Success is always just beyond the horizon. As Polly Young-Eisendrath says, "Feminism is not a salvation theology nor a complete explanation of women's or others' suffering" (1988, 155). Rather, it is best conceptualized as a process, a journey—worthwhile in and of itself—toward better but not ultimate understanding. It approaches but never reaches a full explanation of the puzzles, challenges, and complexities of sexual difference, of gendered beings, and of the variety of significances associated therewith. Here realism intersects the "eutopia" of utopianism, the *no place* that can and should never be achieved.

THE LEGACY OF REALISM

What Vladimir Nabokov said of "reality" is equally true of its close cousin,
"realism": it is one of those words "which mean nothing without quotes."
—Michael Davitt Bell, *The Problem of American Realism:*
Studies in the Cultural History of a Literary Idea

Realism, the term I have chosen to represent an alternative to utopianism in formulating feminist thought and theory, has a complicated history. Indeed, it has probably been even more contested and fraught than *utopianism.* Even in ordinary conversation, *realism* has no fixed or definite meaning. Like its cousin *reality,* it often functions less as a descriptor than as an invitation to debate. To explore the term's usage in various intellectual contexts, including philosophy, law, political science, and literary and cultural criticism, is to further complicate its meaning. Within each of those knowledge domains realism has particular applications, which sometimes bear little resemblance to usages in other fields. Even oppositional meanings or connotations can be found for the term across disciplines. For example, philosophers invoke *realism* to refute the proposition that human perception constructs reality, while legal scholars invoke *realism* to explain how human perception and behavior (specifically the perceptions of judges) actually construct reality—that is, the law itself.

By the same token, *realism* serves rather different social ends in different contexts. For example, political theorists use realism to justify a politics based on existing circumstances rather than on ideals. Thus, a political realist recommends formulating foreign policy on the basis of conflicting national interests, attending to what is possible rather than to political ideals—such as human rights—which are desirable in abstract terms (Brown 1993, 515). *Realpolitik* goes even further to suggest that social ideals and values are simply stand-ins or even pretenses for what a nation or leader really wants and is prepared to fight for (Scruton 1982, 395). Many literary realists, on the other hand, regard realism in the fictional depiction of characters, events, social trends, or circumstances as a way to inspire social change rather than to reinforce the status quo. Charles Dickens and Rebecca Harding Davis can be considered realists in that sense of the term. Thus, George Eliot's endings, in which the heroine is punished or dies for her independent acts, are not meant to prescribe such a fate for independent women but rather to "bring into fiction the collision of the unsatisfied, perhaps even illimitable, desire of her heroines with the restricted possibilities of the world as it could be imagined by realism" (Boumelha 1988, 90). Eliot's readers thereby confront stark reality and long not for it but for its modification. Realist feminist fiction, then, depicts women's struggles against stifling cultural conventions and "facilitates readers' own processes of consciousness-raising" (Hogeland 1994, 298).

It is partly because of the term's complex and contradictory meanings, however, that *realism* has appeal for my project. As Nabokov reminds us, everyone recognizes *realism* as a contested term and understands that it must be explained and explored in order to be useful. That recognition in and of itself makes *realism* a better paradigm for feminist theorizing than *utopianism*, which, as we have seen, is more likely to inspire automatic allegiance than to invite debate. Thus, *realism* puts us on the alert. We instantly wonder what it could mean and how it is being used. Such a questioning stance enhances the utility of the term for feminist thought and theory as the word itself connotes inquiry, uncertainty, and complexity.

In addition, the issues historically embedded in the term *realism* include many that are key for feminist thought and theory. As self-identified realists have confronted and debated antirealists or counter-realists (or idealists or formalists) in fields from philosophy to political science, from law to literary studies, they have asked: What works? What courses of action toward social change best utilize *what is* while also promoting genuine improvement? How do we decide what improvement would look like? Can realism promote change or does it confine us to the familiar and conventional? Is reality as we have described it, or do the limits of our language deceive us? How are our representations—in language, symbol, or picture—related to reality? How do we know what *really* happened in the past, or even today? Do realities exist independent of our cognition?

Translated into the terms of feminist analysis, those questions address representation, material conditions, experience, and identity: Do women exist as a category apart from social definitions? In what ways do the racial, ethnic, and class identities that divide women really exist, and in what ways are they artifacts of our perception? To what extent is language the creator of sexism and racism? To what extent are the forces that affect women's lives knowable to them? How do we explore or account for realities that we do not easily perceive? To what extent can a change of language or label change the realities of the oppressed? Given these uncertainties, how can we determine what changes in women's realities would represent real progress?

A few examples from law and philosophy can illustrate the contribution of *realism* to these analytical processes that are so important to feminist thought and theory. In both fields, *realism* raises questions about the relationship of human cognition, behavior, or perception to reality or truth. Do we locate the real in our own depictions or manipulations of the world or in a world beyond our perceptions? Those questions, in turn, open up possibilities for conceptualizing both the natural world and human institutions. Recognizing that there are things we cannot know invites theorists to leave certain questions open and to focus on the process of knowledge acquisition rather than on the defense of certainty. At the same time, recognizing that human beings also shape their own realities helps to situate theory in the context of human behavior and interaction and highlights the importance (and obligations) of language use and representation.

Philosophy

Realism among philosophers concerns the relationship between human cognition and the world. Realists assert that facts or states of affairs involving them—that is, truth or reality—can exist independently of how anyone thinks or feels about them. Antirealists, noncognitivists, and idealists, on the other hand, define truth or reality in epistemic terms—what human beings believe after the best possible application of their cognitive faculties (Craig 1998, 116–17). *Moral realists* are concerned about the source of moral standards and behavior. Can a moral precept be a fact like other natural facts that exist independently of human belief and are discoverable as other facts are discoverable? American moral realists say yes. Or is "moral judgment . . . a matter of recognizing the reasons for action as they present themselves in the present case, and responding to them as such"? British moral realists say yes (Dancy 1998, 536), thereby heading toward a kind of compromise with idealists.

Although these questions may seem a bit arcane for the kind of feminist thought and theory we are considering, they actually have great significance for the cultural analyses in which feminist theorists engage. The interpretation of any issue—sexism in the workplace, for example—depends at the very least upon our idea of agency and structure. We need to know whether people create their own realities (Are women oppressed because they act as if/believe they are inferior?) or whether realities—facts—can and do exist apart from our perception (Are women's disadvantages built into workplace structure?). Or both. We need to know whether social and institutional structures determine human behavior or whether human behavior creates social and institutional structures, or both. We need to consider whether there are aspects of our situation that we cannot perceive because we are too embedded in them.

Realism has been significant to the exploration of such questions. For example, Roy Bhaskar developed *critical realism* in the late 1970s as a strategy for blending philosophy and the human sciences. His purpose was to develop a methodology for discovering social laws and structures without reducing the complexity of human societies and motivations to the workings of the natural universe. Starting with the realist notion that material objects exist independently of our perceiving them, Bhaskar concluded that social "facts" also exist apart from our perception and are not exhausted by the conceptual and the empirical. "Critical realism holds that there is more to 'what is' than 'what is known,' more to powers than their use, and more to society than the individuals composing it." At the same time, however, Bhaskar conceded that human perception typically affects what we can know of "what is": "[Critical realism] rejects the widespread view that explanation is always neutral—to explain can be to criticize" (Collier 1998, 720).

Although critical of positivism, Bhaskar appreciated the positivist desire to discover constant conjunctions in the human world. At the same time, however, he agreed with hermeneutic assertions that human sciences must differ from natural science. He understood that the "experimental condition" of sociology can distort reality and that experimenters seeking reality can shape it as they do so. "Transcendental [critical] realism insists that the empirical is only a subset of the actual, which is itself a subset of the real" (Bhaskar 1989, 190). Thus, he recognized that while stated reasons for actions can indeed be their causes, they can also be rationalizations of actions whose causes lie elsewhere. Indeed, some beliefs may be incompatible with their own true explanations, including moral beliefs (Collier 1998, 721).

The tenets of critical realism exemplify the possibilities contained within the contradictory and contentious history of *realism* as a philosophical concept. Feminism is not reducible to critical realism, but critical realism exhibits the kind of flexibility that contributes to realism in feminist thought and theory. *Realism* for Bhaskar encompasses both a conceptual and a material dimension. He rejects both a "hyperstructuralist view of people as the mere effects or dupes of structures over which we have neither knowledge nor control" and an empiricism that "empties the social world of an enduring structural dimension, making, as Raymond Williams put it, 'long-term adjustments to short-term changes.'" Critical realism focuses on the interaction between social structures and human agency. Each is affected by the other: human agency creates social structures, but people may also be oblivious to those structures because networked interrelationships not of the agents' creation make the social world opaque (Bhaskar 1989, 3–4).

Environmental philosopher, Kate Soper, posits another version of realism that demonstrates its potential for "both/and" rather than "either/or" thinking. As a realist Soper recognizes that the natural world, including the sexed human body, has material qualities that exist beyond human culture, influence, or perception. But she also recognizes that human culture influences nature: "There is an extra-discursive and biologically differentiated body upon which culture goes to work and inscribes its specific and mutable gender text" (Soper 1995, 133). The "natural body" shapes the possible forms of human activity and is, in turn, subject to processes of growth, reproduction, illness, and mortality about which human beings can do little. In fact, we have "no choice but to experience [our bodies] in some form prior to whatever form we impose upon them. . . . They are not artefacts of culture" (ibid., 137). Indeed, as in the case of gender as performance discussed in chapter 4, the body's material reality is what makes gender inscription possible: there is "no possible understanding we can bring to the idea of the body as a site of gender inscription if we do not presuppose the body as a natural organism subject to causal processes of a continuous and constant kind. . . . It is precisely this conception of the body as a natural organism that must inform the idea of its being 'produced' (confined, disciplined, distorted . . .) by discursive formations and social and sexual norms and powers (ibid., 132–34).

At the same time, however, Soper's realist perspective on the body does not imply a normative position or a particular attitude toward nature. Nature sets certain limits and we must observe them, she explains, but their existence supplies only limited guidance. In fact, reference to natural limits does little to settle difficult questions because presumably people on many sides of such questions can agree on at least many of those limits (Soper 1995, 159).

Law

Like philosophical realism, *legal realism* seems to present simply one side of a dichotomous view, in this case concerning the definition of law. Legal realism developed in response to the legal *formalism* (or idealism) of the nineteenth century which emphasized the importance of legal rules, doctrines, and scientifically deduced legal principles. Formalism was the brainchild of Christopher Columbus Langdell, dean of Harvard's Law School, who introduced the case method of legal instruction in 1870 to promote the discovery of "common law as a set of logically interconnected core doctrines and principles." Legal realists objected to the scientific pretensions of Langdellianism. If law is a science, the realists countered, it is a social science with jurisprudential importance (Duxbury 1998, 522–23). "It is judges not rules who decide cases and . . . rules can be no more than general guides to the making of what are essentially political decisions about who is to get what, where, when, and how." The political role of the Supreme Court supports the realist view (Campbell 1993, 188–89).

Although the realist-formalist debate has created a mountain of defenses for one side or the other, especially since the 1930s, it has also engendered a "both/and" position. Today legal realism focuses on social as well as legal factors—such as particular rules and previous legal decisions—that most influence judges in making law. "Law is not a certain set of rules; . . . legal doctrine is nowadays conceived in the context of the wider legal process; and . . . the legal process . . . [is] part of the wider social system" (Duxbury 1992, 137). Thus the formalist position and the realist position are no longer as oppositional as they once seemed, and realism is not as disdainful of democratic processes as critics (such as Roscoe Pound) once charged (ibid., 142–45).

In the end, realism has made it impossible to ignore the importance of society's interaction with the legal system. Most importantly, perhaps, realism has disabused us of the notion that clear, stably imposed rules necessarily create the most just societies by pointing out instances, such as Nazi Germany, in which the clearest, stablest rules have served the most awful purposes (Campbell 1993, 189).

REALISM IN FEMINIST THOUGHT AND THEORY

Seen in its historical context, *realism* becomes a useful framework for feminist inquiry which contrasts with the framework of *utopianism*. To attach ourselves to realism is to embrace the discussions that have characterized the term in various contexts and conceptual systems. Realism invites us to consider the relationship of the way things are to the way things ought to be and to recognize that the issues that engage us can camouflage more important, hidden forces. Realism guides us in challenging notions of fixed identities and leads us to recognize that however deep our knowledge of people may be, it is never complete. Realism suggests that the desire for normative feminist standards in realistic feminist theory must be tempered with attention to new developments, ideas, experiences—and realities—which predetermined norms cannot predict and should not preclude. From realism's role in philosophy, political science, literary criticism, and law we learn to question the role of our own perceptions in our understanding of ourselves and the world.

Although few feminist theorists have employed the term, my survey of feminist theoretical works reveals that realism as a process of thought has not escaped feminist notice. Indeed, there is a long but as yet undefined tradition of realism in feminist thought and theory of which we have already seen evidence. That tradition does not reside exclusively in complaints about "utopic" or "utopian" feminist ideas and strategies, although those complaints exist. Rather, it resides primarily in persistent and probing thought processes that lead to more effective and more lasting forms of social change than those that are possible through utopian means. There is no finite set of "realistic" feminist beliefs or values, or even a line of feminist theory called "realistic feminism." Nor should there be. Such codification would contradict realism's utility as a process for the formulation of feminist thought. Therefore, the evidence for realism in feminist theorizing exists as a core sample of arguments, questions, and concerns from a broad spectrum of feminist views. It includes parameters for thinking and inquiring about feminism in a way I hope readers will find important and relevant to ideas and theories they both generate and consume.

The Dangers of Definitions

Some critics of my approach (primarily those of the linguistic-construction persuasion) might suggest that we simply redefine *utopianism* so that it encompasses what I am calling realism. Lucy Sargisson, whose *Contemporary Feminist Utopianism* (1996) was discussed in chapter 2, might be among them. Sargisson nearly does redefine *utopian* so that it connotes both itself and its presumed opposite, which we might call realism. She claims that people who have seen in utopianism a desire for perfection or a blueprint for the future have been blinded by the content or form of utopian fiction and have missed entirely the importance of its function, which is to provide a space for oppositional, subversive, and transformative thought (47). What could be more feminist than that? she asks.

Sargisson insists that contemporary feminist utopian fiction has abandoned all ideas of designing the future and has concentrated instead on creating open-ended, flexible, realistic worlds. Such feminist utopias combine *eutopia* with *dystopia* and *anti-utopia,* she claims. Indeed, the connection of such works with present reality—what I have called their limiting and misleading present focus—may be their strongest suit, according to Sargisson. Utopias are valuable, she asserts, because of their engagement with contemporary social arrangements (1996, 41). What they do best is provide good social criticism. Utopianism "is critical of the present, destroys certainties, challenges dominant perceptions and, in the process, creates something new. . . . Transgressive thinking of this kind is transformative thinking" (77). And that is what feminism needs. Indeed, how will feminism move into the future unless it imagines such transformation?

Before concluding that I have misunderstood utopianism altogether and simply called what I am advocating by the wrong name, we should remember the pitfalls of the utopian present focus and recall how vehemently feminist utopian novels and novelists have disavowed utopia as they have moved toward open-ended and ambiguous worlds and denouements.[2] We should also note the ways in which Sargisson "utopianizes" feminism by mandating that it aspire to produce "something new" and by failing to acknowledge its diversity. In addition, she characterizes feminism in absolute terms: feminism is ultimately about opposition, providing dislocations of and challenges to the present (225); its goal is to undermine all dualities and provide "new conceptual spaces from which to reapproach the world in a non-dualistic way that is not driven by the desire to possess" (168). Such mandates contradict Sargisson's claim that she disdains unitary, coherent definitions of feminism.

Like most utopian constructions, her definitions are not meant to be interrogated. Thus, Sargisson does not explain how or why the desire to possess is bad. What about possessing joy or freedom? Nor does she explain why feminist thought requires an oppositional stance. What about selective conservation and creative borrowing? As Sartre once noted, we may make history, but so does everyone else. There are lots of good ideas and methods out there. Why deny feminism the benefits of considering them?

Sargisson also fails to interrogate her claim that something called female desire forms the basis for feminist reconstructions of the world. She does not explain what that desire is, how we know it, or what it is worth. We are left to assume that any and every speculative novel written by a feminist embodies a collective feminist desire. Yet, such a dangerously utopian vision of uniformity contradicts her expressed concern with women's diversity. She does not explain how the world's diverse women can share a single desire.

In the end, Sargisson delivers a version of feminism that conforms to the now familiar parameters of utopianism: unscrutinized foundational principles, idealized solutions, reversals of problems to create solutions, and no methodology for interrogating itself. Sargisson uses utopias to advance so-called feminist interests, but what is the good of advancing our own interests unless we first determine what constitutes those interests (Wilson 1993, 250)?

2. See chapter 2.

Despite Sargisson's claims for its open-endedness and experimental play, her utopian model for feminism is not as open, self-reflexive, realistic, thorough, or intellectually honest as I hope feminist thought and theory can be.

Simply redefining utopianism to encompass realism does not allow us to establish the parameters of the divergent—though not oppositional—paths of utopian and realistic feminist thought and theory. It is important to clarify both the connections (or continua) and the distinctions between them. Realism is legitimately associated with greater complexity and higher levels of self-reflection than is utopianism. Realism invites debate, while utopianism discourages dissension. Because such distinctions are significant, they should be emphasized as we explore post-utopian realistic feminist thought and theory.

REINFORCING REALISM

Realistic feminist ideas, analyses, and constructions do something very different from what Sargisson discusses. Although realism does not preclude speculation about new ideas and frameworks for human arrangements, neither does it assume that such speculation is the best foundation or the pinnacle of feminist theorizing. Rather than providing a place to generate perpetually speculative, unscrutinized, and untestable ideas, as Sargisson's utopias appear to do, realism leads us toward a more grounded theoretical laboratory, where many minds inquire, scrutinize, wrestle with, and test feminist ideas.

Nancy Hirschmann describes a version of this concept in the Italian feminist practice of *autocoscienza,* or women's discussion groups, which resemble American consciousness-raising groups from the 1970s but with a twist. Instead of simply accumulating data about sexism, members of *autocoscienza* groups consider collectively both existing and alternative social practices. They do not imagine that life as we know it must vanish before feminist goals—variously defined—can be enacted. Rather, members see the groups as a source of their own empowerment for approaching existing social contexts from a new perspective. They adapt the group's insights to their own situations and interests. There is no feminist "company line," but rather a process of sounding out grievances and possible actions, and of engaging continuously—sometimes to resist, sometimes to adapt, sometimes to recreate—with existing lifeworlds. The groups themselves do not constitute social change, as utopias often mean to do. Rather, the *autocoscienza* groups provide a new context—which is itself recognized as political, partial, limited, and provisional—within which to contemplate social structures and individual desires and to consider alternatives and combinations of alternatives in specific historical locations (Hirschmann 1996, 56–62).

Realistic feminist theorizing also differs from utopian scenarios like Sargisson's by refusing to assume an automatic or necessary connection between existing identities, desires, and ideas and preferred directions for social change. Realism allows for the possibility, as Rey Chow observes, that the best strategy for feminist theorizing might be to embrace identities, desires, notions, or values that are different from or even alien to what we think of as our own. Indeed, Chow warns against developing ideas that are simply self-serving by making our own social location—ethnicity, sexuality, or sex—the "ultimate signified." Chow explains that we must also keep our eye on larger goals, such as support for democracy and human rights, which are more important than individual identity (1993, 25).

Realism also recognizes that we sometimes do the best theorizing about our own situations by "wielding the tools of [our] enemies" (Chow 1993, 22). Acknowledging that realistic "mastered irony," Chela Sandoval recommends a kind of identity flexibility which both embraces tactical subjectivities and creates a "differential consciousness." Together those strategies allow us to navigate among choices and redistribute power (Sandoval 1991, 12–15).

Also in contrast to utopian views, which often assume an innocent "we" in opposition to a guilty "they," realistic feminist theorizing must recognize "our" complicity in the systems we protest. Chow explains, for example, that just as Western capitalists were implicated in the socialism of the Soviet Union (and vice versa), so too are feminists implicated in patriarchal systems. That conflicting systems and values are linked implies numerous other linkages as well: the same social relations that limit our options also produce them; the social conditions that oppress us also generate opportunities and nurture our ability to resist. "Things simultaneously create and destroy, prevent and promote, prohibit and require," in the words of Nancy Hirschmann (1996, 63). Even as we recognize inequities in the distribution of power among various groups, including women, Hirschmann observes, "'less free' does not mean 'unfree,' and 'more difficult' does not mean 'impossible'" (ibid., 57). Furthermore, there is no such thing as innocent knowledge, as Jane Flax (1992) explains. Thus, feminists must "learn ways of making claims about and acting upon injustice without transcendental guarantees or illusions of innocence" (459).[3]

Realistic feminist theorizing must recognize its own—albeit inadvertent—capacity for evil. Instead of a utopian externalization of evil—the "devil made us do it"—realism recognizes that the enemy we encounter will sometimes be ourselves. Susan Gubar, for example, notes that feminist and misogynist ideas sometimes utilize identical rhetoric, such as denouncing the concept of womanhood. Gubar also demonstrates how some feminists even respond to their own ideas with misogyny. She cites, for example, Kate Millett's novel *The Basement* (1979), which depicts a woman sexually oppressing a young girl, thereby contradicting her own critique of such practices in *Sexual Politics* (1970) (Gubar 1995, 145).

Freed of its presumption of innocence, feminist thought can begin the process of exploring assumptions of innocence in related idea systems. Some third-world feminist theorists, for example, have begun to investigate and denounce sexism in precolonial cultures. African feminist Anima Mama, for example, resists the idea that women's subjugation in postcolonial societies is the result only of the forces of imperialism and colonialism. In truth, Mama notes, "colonial gender ideologies were the product of both internal and external factors, and were fed by cultural and material conditions which interacted in complex ways." Therefore, "as we enter the postcolonial epoch . . . we must recognize that there have been pernicious continuities between colonial, nationalist, and postcolonial systems" (1997, 61). Mama cites as an example the deterioration of conditions for women in Zimbabwe since liberation. Today, domestic violence is more common and tacitly accepted than it was under colonial rule, and women's access to education has diminished (ibid., 54). To absolve native governments and peoples of all error and malfeasance creates a utopian shield against social change.

Freed of the utopian tendency to externalize all enemies and injustices, feminist thought can also free itself of the utopian assumption that all enemies and sources of injustice are eternal. Realism requires

---

3. As in part II, I will be using theorists in this part to illustrate realistic feminist thought whose entire opus might not qualify as realistic. Because utopianism has not been an acknowledged characteristic driving feminist analyses, it is not a consistently applied theoretical position. Thus, my use of a portion of a particular theorist's work is not necessarily an endorsement of all of her ideas or writings as realistic; similarly, my observations of a theorist's utopianism does not constitute a judgment that her entire opus is utopian.

us to admit that, like feminism itself, the forces to which feminism reacts also evolve. Indeed, although many feminist thinkers lament the way patriarchy creeps into and undermines feminist rhetoric, few acknowledge the way that feminist ideas have continuously invaded mainstream thinking. Susan Gubar calls this the "interlocutionary nature of representation" (1995, 145).

If utopianism suggests that we must see feminism as comprehensive, encompassing all of life's ideological, political, philosophical, and theoretical elements, then realism allows us to see that feminism may not (yet) address all of life's complexity. And even when feminist thought correctly promotes significant social change, it may inadvertently produce frustrating paradoxes. Just as the revolution in information technology has produced the "productivity paradox," in which devices designed to promote efficiency have actually generated more work, feminism too may promote change that backfires. Feminism, like information technology, can raise expectations. Indeed, Americans now routinely expect many women to do two full-time jobs rather than the one they used to do. In that way, feminism resembles the effects of communication technology, which has made some things worse while making other things better. More communication now borders on too much communication. Software that produces reports more quickly also creates the demand for elegant layouts. What was once handled by a simple memo now requires numerical modeling. And, of course, the machinery breaks down and requires the services of specialized technicians (Attewell 1996, A56).

We must expect that feminist desires for social change will generate such paradoxes. As we seek autonomy, we might begin to long for community, or family, or other forms of attachment. Conversely, as we experience feminist collectives or communities, we may long for solitude and self-reliance. It comes as no surprise, and as no defeat to feminism, for example, that women in post-Soviet eastern Europe have reacted against Communist promises of gender neutrality by seeking recognition for their femininity, their gender specificity. We must also expect that the things that complicate our lives, like work and family, also imbue our lives with the greatest meaning. We cannot seek happiness in the simple terms of choosing one thing over another, since so many choices that seem oppositional are really interdependent. Feminist theory must acknowledge and even address such interconnected but contradictory and paradoxical realities of life.

Feminist theorists must also heed what Patricia Williams calls the

"broken barometer syndrome," which occurs because the time lag between social action and its salutary results is often so great that new
political, economic, or technological developments can obviate its
benefits by the time it takes effect (1995, 160). Feminist thinkers must
be especially sensitive to this paradox, inherent in the utopian present
focus, to avoid causing harm by recommending changes that are inadvertently place- or time-limited.

The utopian desire to form a wholly new human subject, a new social context, and new institutions is another trap. Realism requires us
to recognize that there will never be a pure perspective or a "pure
woman" who is completely free of contradictory desires and a divided
will (Hirschmann 1996, 56–57). While utopianism depends on uniformly enlightened human beings who do the right things for ideolog-
ically consistent reasons, realism accommodates the gap between human beliefs and practices. People typically deny what they fear the
most or what discomforts them. The desire for status or personal freedom or a false sense of immortality can undermine reasonable, even
sane behavior. Why else would so many smart people smoke or resist
using condoms to prevent life-threatening diseases?[4]

Utopias have few strategies for combating such inherent contradictions. Acknowledging the difficulty of achieving perfect consistency
should make realistic theorists humble about our suggestions and
analyses. It should alert us to the many cases in which social change
should be pursued incrementally, provisionally—in jagged rather than
in straight lines.

Realistic feminism must also deal with human diversity, not only
among recognized social groupings but also among individuals. In
addition to other variables, feminist theory must deal with the probability that "feminist" designates a wide range of self-perceptions, levels of activity, and attitudes. Indeed, the term's definition can vary
widely depending on an individual's age or number of years of self-
identification. For example, Nancy Downing and Kristin Roush have
described stages of feminist self-identification, starting with a prefem-
inist phase of *passive acceptance* of gender hierarchy. As a feminist
identity develops, they claim, passivity changes to a phase of *revelation*
about discrimination, which in turn becomes a phase of *embeddedness-*

4. See, for example, the work of Elliot Aronson on getting college students to use
condoms to prevent STDs. Christopher Shea, 1997, "A U. of California Psychologist
Investigates New Approaches to Changing Human Behavior," *Chronicle of Higher Education* 43.41, 20 June A15.

emanation or the "discovery of sisterhood." What follows is *synthesis* or the development of a "flexible truce" with the world and with individual men. Finally, *active commitment* is achieved, as the feminist selects meaningful action on behalf of specific issues (1985, 698–702).

Whether or not we accept Downing and Roush's phases—in number, in order, or in definition—the idea that individuals bring varying degrees of anger, acceptance, experience, self-confidence, and commitment to the notion of feminism is compelling. Realism demands that feminist thought and theory take account of such variations, despite individuals' denial or ignorance of their own phases of understanding and commitment and without necessarily determining who is the "better" feminist.

Such complexities render nearly moot the concept of a complete feminist victory or of cost-free solutions to the problems addressed by feminist theory. Like the free lunch, there may be no such thing. The pursuit of everything worthwhile—autonomy, community, commitment, freedom, power—necessarily entails challenges and costs. Every act has its consequences, and those consequences exact a toll.

Thus, rather than debating the details of the ideal feminist future, realistic feminist theorists do better to concentrate on considering various solutions and compromises and assessing their consequences. "Wouldn't it be wonderful if . . ." must be tempered by "Here's what will likely result from." Arguments should be made, challenged, and reconsidered. Identifying feminist values must entail recognition that even the most positive of values must be tempered in order to prevent negative excess. Without sympathy and fairness, for example, the anger that motivates social change can become destructive. Even sympathy and fairness require self-control, however, and a sense of duty to keep from becoming mere self-satisfaction and narrow loyalty (Wilson 1993, 246). Specifically feminist values also require correctives to reduce their potential for excess in the pursuit of beneficial social change.

CAVEATS

Such a measured view of realism may seem to rob feminism entirely of its purpose, even to border on lassitude and appeasement. Must we never rebel? If we are busy clarifying our thinking by resisting coherentism, confirmation bias, fanatical closure, *ad hominem* reasoning, *post hoc* errors about causation, and the myth of the truth teller, when will we actually work toward social change? As we face history's revisions and reversals, the mysteries of human interaction and individual psychology, the need to scrutinize ideas outside of feminist boundaries, the interconnection of good and evil, the many paradoxes connected with social and individual change, the diversity and complexity of feminism, the complicity of everyone in existing social realities, and the inadequacy of simple sets of values—among other complications—how can we ever act?

Those are important and appropriate questions, since *Higher Ground* purports to connect feminist thought and actual social change. But the need to act should not blind us to the need to evaluate the nature and direction of change and to develop strategies that produce effective and responsible results. Realism does not necessarily preclude rebellion or dramatic change. It simply insists that such acts evolve from a thorough vetting of reasons, motives, and probable consequences. It challenges rebels to go beyond agitation and to be accountable for the change they propose.

THE JOURNEY TOWARD HIGHER GROUND: GENERAL METHODS AND STRATEGIES OF REALISM

Before turning to specific realistic theories within the three discourses of our analysis—gender difference, differences among women, and linguistic construction—we can establish some general principles for formulating realistic feminist theory. Primary among them, perhaps, is a willingness to redeem—rather than to dismiss out of hand—certain traditional forms and methods of knowledge acquisition. Equally important, of course, is establishing criteria for judging new methods of knowledge production and new practices, such as interdisciplinarity, that promote realistic feminist aims.

Reason, Critical Thinking, and Knowledge Justification

We have already discussed the importance of redeeming reason as a benefit for realistic feminist theory, as well as the importance of seeing the connections between reason and other mental processes, such as intuition, instinct, and compassion. Reason and the demand for critical thinking and argument help prevent feminist thought from degenerating into the very prejudice it was designed to overcome or from simply reversing the effects of oppression. Feminist theorizing needs to reclaim reason and critical thinking skills despite their past misuse against women or feminism.

Elizabeth Anderson (1995) offers yet another justification for embracing reason for feminist theorizing: reason is the key to realistic change, the very "power to change our attitudes, intentions, and practices in response to reflection on the merits of having them or engaging in them." Reason is also "the power to acquire, reject, and revise our cognitive attitudes (beliefs and theoretical commitments) and our practices of inquiry through reflection on our reasons for holding them and engaging in them." If reason is to be prevented from supporting misogynist or other prejudicial thinking, it must be connected not with the isolated knower but with groups. Collective thought corrects and checks the individual biases that lead reason astray, Anderson notes, provided the collective includes a judiciously selected, diverse group of inquirers (1995, 52, 80–81).

Anderson's redemption of reason leads her to reconsider empiricism, which has also been the target of feminist critique as "a doctrine that imposes *a priori* substantive restrictions on the kinds of entities and concepts that can ultimately figure in science." But empiricism is an important tool of feminist reason, so Anderson advocates a revision that she calls modest empiricism, which rejects such a priori commitments and remains open to what it finds. Modest empiricism "is promiscuous in its permissible ontology and opportunistic in its methods and models," she concludes (1995, 52–53).

We have also already advocated critical thinking as a tool of realistic feminist theorizing. Historian Jane Tompkins (1994) supplies yet another justification for that position by reminding feminist theorists how often we are called upon as knowledge seekers to determine the validity of information: what really happened, who is responsible, who deserves compensation, who has been injured? Sometimes "talk about language-based reality and culturally produced knowledge" is an appropriate response to our research concerns, but in many cases,

> reasons must be given, evidence adduced, authorities cited, analogies drawn. . . . I must piece together the story . . . as best I can, believing this version up to a point, that version not at all, another almost entirely, according to what seems reasonable and plausible, given everything else that I know. . . . If the accounts don't fit together neatly, that is not a reason for rejecting them all in favor of a metadiscourse about epistemology . . . one encounters contradictory facts and divergent points of view in practically every phase of life. . . . It is only the nature of the academic situation which makes it appear that one can linger on the threshold of decision in the name of an epistemological principle (200).

Tompkins's reliance on educated judgment provides another stepping stone toward feminist higher epistemological ground.

Critical thinking in feminist theorizing also entails scrutinizing feminism's own sacred methods and approaches. Thus, many theorists are beginning to question feminist conventions of knowledge acquisition, such as the use of personal testimony as a knowledge source. Linda Kauffman describes that convention as a belief in "the personal as inherently paradigmatic . . . coherent, unified, morally inspiring" ([1992] 1993, 263). Kauffman demonstrates how "cheap and easy personal testimony is" by recounting her father's career as a grifter who fabricated personal testimony in order to peddle his wares. She also points to Supreme Court Justice Clarence Thomas's invocation of personal authority in his confirmation hearings, which disguised his opportunism, his debt to the civil rights movement, and his cynicism. "Feminism is far more than the effort to 'express' 'women's personal experience,'" Kauffman admonishes. Instead, we must "continually . . . cast doubt on the status of knowledge—*even as we are in the process of constructing it*—a perpetual project" (ibid., 274). If we overcome our obsession with experience, we can pay more attention to the interconnection of feminist issues with other injustices. We can protest the use of the rhetoric of equal rights against women, as, for example, in arguments that frame reproductive freedom in terms of the rights of "unborn women" (ibid., 272).

Critiquing the same feminist affinity for personal testimony, Susan David Bernstein (1992) recommends adopting a "confessional mode of reflexivity," in which the "I" of personal experience is interrogated along with other categories and terms in a feminist analysis. "Reflexive uses of confession in feminism complicate and defamiliarize the 'self' that these first-person [narratives] represent," Bernstein concludes (140).

Interdisciplinarity and Other New Methodologies

Among the new(er) strategies for knowledge acquisition that have particular significance for, and have been defined in part through, feminist thought is interdisciplinary scholarship that attempts to synthesize knowledge and knowledge claims and to interrogate conclusions reached via one disciplinary analytical approach with other disciplinary or extradisciplinary considerations. Rosi Braidotti calls such processes "hybrid thinking." Examples include the analysis of autobiographical texts not simply for an "authentic voice" but also for the evidence they reveal about social, historical, and emotional influences on gender. Braidotti's own attempts to combine materialist and semiotic analyses of women's lives also illustrate the genre (Braidotti and Butler 1994, 58). Cross-cultural comparisons also provide reality tests for feminist thought, promote caution, and interject precision and specificity into our conclusions.

I would like to suggest adopting a strategy I call the scholarly "line-item veto," in which we evaluate theories by recognizing both successful and unsuccessful, realistic and utopian hypotheses or analyses within a single work. That approach contrasts with the more typical dismissal of a colleague's or predecessor's entire opus because of a quarrel with a particular point or conclusion. Using the same reasoning, realistic feminist theorizing must both critique and value the past, recognize competing forms of feminism, and remain skeptical about finite precepts and definitions. Because realism is temperate, it distrusts missionary zeal (McNeil 1992, 25).

Certain scholarly venues can also be more conducive than others to realistic feminist theorizing. Examples include dialogues among scholars with apparently opposed views, such as the 1994 exchange between Judith Butler and Rosi Braidotti published in *differences*. They also include particular anthologies or clusters of articles responding to an especially provocative piece, such as commentaries by Mary Hawkesworth and Susan Hekman in successive 1997 issues of *Signs*.[5] Although it sometimes promotes the familiar "assert and defend" mode of analysis, such interactive scholarship can also help clarify differences, articulate continuities among seemingly opposed viewpoints, and promote new syntheses of ideas.

NEW METAPHORS: FROM BUSINESS TO FAMILY

Looming in the background of these discussions is the specter of feminism itself. What, if anything, we may wonder, constitutes the feminist bottom line? As we develop realistic approaches to feminist thought and theory, however, we may want to replace the metaphor of the bottom line with something more flexible, even indeterminate. Feminism begins to seem analogous to a term like democracy, which encompasses a variety of social and governmental forms that nevertheless constitute a recognizable group. Granted, such a capacious view may seem to reduce feminism to a cipher. But that result can be

---

5. Details about each of these articles follow later in chapter 6.

prevented if the new metaphor itself encompasses both connection and disconnection, consistency and limits.

My suggestion reclaims an image that has been associated more with right-wing than feminist rhetoric, but that can be rehabilitated for feminist theory: "family resemblance." Following Linda Nicholson, who borrows the concept from Wittgenstein for other purposes, "family resemblance" can be illustrated by a discussion of *games,* which Wittgenstein defines as "'a complicated network of similarities overlapping and criss-crossing: sometimes overall similarities, sometimes similarities of detail'" but not necessarily requiring that any one specific feature be held in common (quoted in Nicholson 1994, 100–101).

Using that model, feminism acquires both substance and indeterminacy in a process that identifies, justifies, questions, and reconsiders both connections and disconnections among "family" members. Linda Gordon proposes one such substantive but indeterminate definition of feminist theory: "any body of thought that perceives women to be subordinated, perceives this subordination to be neither just nor immutable, and connects descriptions and analyses of women's conditions to hopes and plans for improving these conditions." Deborah King offers another: feminism encompasses "'many purposes, goals, and activities which seek to enhance the potential of women, to ensure their liberty, afford them equal opportunity, and to permit and encourage their self-determination'" (Gordon 1991, 105; King quoted in Gordon 1991). Grewal and Kaplan offer yet another: feminism, they say, consists of the "practices that different women use in various locations to counter the scattered hegemonies [of fundamentalism, nationalism, and global capitalism] that affect their lives" (1994, 18). Leila Rupp and Verta Taylor offer one more. In studying early twentieth-century women involved in the international feminist movement, Rupp and Taylor began to define feminism as the process of negotiating between solidary identities (perceived differences from men), organizational identities (particular group affinities), and (feminist) movement identity. Thus, they conclude, "the nature of 'feminism' is constructed as it evolves over time, emerging from contests over who belongs and how best to win equality for women. In every group, in every place, at every time, the meaning of 'feminism' is worked out in the course of being and doing" (1999, 382).

Clearly there are both similarities and differences among these depictions of feminism. In utopian practice, we are accustomed to arguing about who is right or more current in her understanding. In realistic practice, we can articulate both points of connection and disparities among varying views, and look for ways that the different concepts can inform one another as well as ways that they represent either different families or different incarnations of the family definition. We can define feminism as a dynamic process rather than a fixed identity.

The notion of "family resemblance" gives weight to my contention that feminism's variety and adaptability to myriad cultural contexts are strengths. It suggests that the expansibility of a category need not lead to its dissolution; rather, it can help refine its meaning through additions, clarifications, and cross-fertilizations that both relate it to and distinguish it from its relatives. To return to the game example for a moment, the concepts of *competition* and *victory* are elements of games, but they also characterize wars. What becomes interesting is the variation in meaning in these different families of activity. Likewise, *separatism* and *sexual difference* appear in both feminist and misogynist discourse. The challenge is to understand the parameters and variations among the terms in different contexts as we establish the "family" constellations. Establishing a feminist "family" also permits subcategories, such as *materialist* or *liberal,* to both intersect with and diverge from one another.

As a metaphor, "family resemblance" is an improvement over "bottom line" because of its more realistic three-dimensionality.[6] It suggests that theory can both expand and contract over time, like families, through voluntary associations, interbreeding, mutation, adoption, and other processes. As a judgment rather than a fixed image, "resemblance" entails self-scrutiny and open-mindedness. Perhaps most important, "family resemblance" recognizes an existing reality: feminist theory *already is* a compendium of shared but diverse sentiments and patterns of thought, contributing to and resulting in a range of values, worldviews, desires, policies, and actions. No unified view will ever satisfy all who identify themselves as feminists. The utopian search for feminist purity necessarily eliminates some portion of self-identified feminists and valorizes others. But the exploration of a "family resemblance" implies a continuous, collective process that can lead to the discovery of commonalities as well as distinctions

---

6. "Family" works here as a metaphor because it encompasses the complexity of rather than idealizes family qualities. When we discuss "family" as a utopian metaphor for feminist community in chapter 6, we will see the dangers of "family" as a metaphor that raises false expectations of harmony and unity.

among the variety of self-identified feminist positions, choices, and preferences.

"Family resemblance" also valorizes the fact that we *already have* de facto indeterminate feminism. It allows us to appreciate that reality and to resist utopian demands to draw hard and fast membership boundaries. Recognizing feminism's "family resemblance" and indeterminacy points to a higher ground where feminism resides as a series of approaches and questions rather than as a list of definitive answers and where its variety is constructively discussed and debated.

Recent collaborative work by M. Jacqui Alexander and Chandra Mohanty represents such an approach to feminist analysis. Although framed in a third-world perspective, their co-authored introduction to *Feminist Genealogies, Colonial Legacies, Democratic Futures* (1997) resists polemic and theorizes around a series of open-ended questions: Who benefits from specific policies? Who benefits from proposed changes or from the status quo? Christie McDonald (1995) conceptualizes feminism itself as a series of questions that focus on the interconnection of gender and ethnicity as well as of personal and positional factors. McDonald explicitly warns against "falling back into inherited schemata of thought" in the construction of feminist theory (240).

Strategies of indeterminacy and family resemblance seem especially important in today's political climate, in which the very term *feminism* sounds to many ears like a curse from the demon world. For example, according to Elzbieta Matynia, calling oneself a feminist in Eastern Europe represents political suicide for women seeking public office (Menon 1996, 16). (The same could probably be said of the United States.) From one perspective, such revulsion indicates the success of feminism's political programs and cultural representation, as well as its failures, since something ineffective would never be endowed with such power. But it does not make for very good public relations. The image of feminist flexibility and responsibility better serves the goal of widespread acceptance than does the image of a rigid feminist monolith, bent on world takeover.

Critics might wonder how feminists can organize politically without a clear feminist political program. Linda Nicholson provides one approach by recommending that feminists develop action plans based on coalition politics among themselves. That is, a diverse group of feminists articulates their concerns at an abstract level that captures their varied needs without prescribing specific actions or policies. In that way, "self-determinacy for women," for example, can unify feminists without violating local or particular values. Or feminists could select specific demands that various groups can unite around (Nicholson 1994, 102–3). Stopping violence against women is an example of such a demand. To critics who advocate feminist "world takeover" I suggest a knowledge-based rather than a coercion-based metaphor. Feminists can work toward the infusion of feminist ideas into all social systems, let us say, rather than adopt the tactics of war.

SIX   *Toward Realistic Feminist Discourse*

The categories of feminist discourse that we have been exploring take on new meanings in the context of realistic feminist theorizing. Now the linkages among the three types of feminist discourse—gender difference, differences among women, and linguistic construction—become even more important. In realistic feminist thought, each category supplies caveats, questions, and challenges to the others. The discourse of linguistic construction, for example, reveals how language contributes to the creation of categories that separate or distinguish women from one another. Likewise, the discourse of differences among women helps to modify concepts of gender difference, since variations in women's social locations construct their gender identity.

Rather than dissolving these categories in the name of realistic feminist theorizing, however, I have chosen to retain them in this chapter as focal points for organizing realistic feminist theoretical works. In the analysis that follows, gender difference, differences among women, and linguistic construction serve as intersecting constellations of ideas around which numerous feminist thinkers have organized their theoretical works.

THE DISCOURSE OF GENDER DIFFERENCE

How can I say it? That we are women from the start. That we don't have to be turned into women by them, labeled by them, made holy and profane by

them. That has always already happened, without their efforts. . . . Your/my body doesn't acquire its sex through . . . the action of some power, function, or organ. Without any intervention or special manipulation, you are a woman already.
—Luce Irigaray, *This Sex Which Is Not One*

The notion of distinct unitary sexual characters for women and men has been decisively refuted. With it, much of the common-sense understanding of sex and gender, together with most functionalist sex role theorizing, should collapse. . . . Practice issues from the human and social side of the transaction; it deals with the natural qualities of its objects, including the biological characteristics of bodies.
—R. W. Connell, *Gender and Power: Society, the Person, and Sexual Politics*

Framing the Issue

Utopianism encourages dualistic thinking about sex and gender, predicating theories and actions on assumed (rather than observed) differences in behavior or character resulting from physical or reproductive differences between women and men. It encourages us to posit difference a priori and to overlook connections and commonalities between the sexes. Often feminist utopian thinking about gender difference leads to the idealization of femaleness, especially in conjunction with motherhood or sexuality. Utopianism in this discourse often leads to problem reversal as a substitute for problem solution by transforming traditional sources of women's subordination and degradation into sources of their value and superiority.

Another consequence of utopian thinking about gender difference is the formation of dichotomized theoretical perspectives. Thus, *difference feminism* is pitted against *gender feminism*, categories represented respectively by the Irigaray and Connell quotations that open this segment of chapter 6. *Difference feminists* recognize and celebrate an essential female subject; they wish to empower woman in her female specificity, to take the material basis of female reproduction as the foundation of woman herself. Luce Irigaray's identification with this position is rooted in psychoanalytic theory. Like others in that tradition, she considers female physiological and (repressed) psychological characteristics a unique female "essence" (or complex of "essences") that translates into a unique female identity. Irigaray has described women's genitals as "two lips that speak together" and contrasted that multiplicity with the unitary phallus, whose hegemonic cultural power has abrogated everything feminine because of the difference. By creating a new sexual economy, difference feminists like Irigaray intend to prevent that erasure of the feminine (Fuss 1989, 108). Variations on difference feminist theories include such historical categories as *cultural feminism* and *radical feminism,* both of which have celebrated female sexuality and/or reproductive physiology as the basis of a unique female sexual character or even a superior gender identity.

Gender feminists, on the other hand, reject notions of "the feminine" (or, for that matter, "the masculine") as "a morass of metaphysical nonsense" (Braidotti and Butler 1994, 47). Gender feminists stress that sexual identity (of men and women) is a function of mutable social, material, or discursive influences. They are social constructionists. Since they believe that people create the gender systems they inhabit, gender feminists advocate the wholesale revision of existing gender definitions and the rejection of traditional or conventional ideas of masculinity and femininity on the way to achieving gender justice. Among well-known gender feminist theorists is R. W. Connell, who attributes current conventions of gender difference to the use of reproduction as the premise of all gender definitions and roles in most societies.[1] The specifics of the link between reproduction and gender identity varies over time and within and among various cultures, and those variations create changing forms of gender hierarchy. Thus, Connell does not accept even the existence of a universal "sex/gender system," let alone a universal conception of feminine or masculine sexual character (1987, 140). As we have seen, Judith Butler expresses perhaps the most extreme of the gender feminist positions when she wonders whether there is anything at all to be said about gender apart from concrete aspects of gender relations in specific situations (Braidotti and Butler 1994, 88).

As in many such supposed theoretical dichotomies, however, we can expect to find utopianism in both prongs of the gender/difference feminist theoretical binary as well as in the fact of the dichotomy itself. Both strains tend to overlook the interconnection of gender characteristics. By the same token, while social or linguistic constructionists might underestimate the significance of reproductive physiology

---

1. In case it is necessary to justify using a male theorist here, I will point out that Connell is often cited for his contribution to gender theory, starting with his 1987 *Gender and Power: Society, the Person, and Sexual Politics.* His 1995 *Masculinities* (Berkeley: University of California Press) was the subject of a written symposium in *Gender and Society* in August 1998. He was a commentator on Mary Hawkesworth's "Confounding Gender" in *Signs* in spring 1997. Hawkesworth recognized Connell as a key gender feminist theorist in that work.

or reproductive experience, difference feminists might overemphasize that physiology and sexual orientation in their theories of political organizing or relational harmony. Difference feminists might also romanticize motherhood and thereby overlook vast differences among women's motherhood experiences, the social implications of those experiences, and the variations among women's attitudes toward motherhood. Difference feminists might further overlook the fact that self-identification as a woman produces no particular reproductive desires, sexual practice, or affectional preference. As Connell reminds us, "Desire [can] be organized around identification and similarity [as well as] around difference" for both sexes (1987, 182).

APPROACHING REALISM IN GENDER DIFFERENCE THEORY

Realistic approaches to gender difference require us to abandon the need for such utopian oppositions and idealizations. We must ask new questions. For example, are we assuming the distinctions we should be testing? As Deborah Cameron observes in her critique of "women's language," it is easy to presuppose gender specificity or hierarchy before testing for it, or to overlook the ways in which women's behavior both reinforces hierarchy and resists it, both relinquishes control and seizes it (1992, 24). Is sexual difference a metaphor for other social forces, such as inequitable economic or social conditions? Deborah Rhode suggests that feminist thinkers focus less on apparent similarities and differences between the sexes and more on the processes that sometimes amplify and sometimes obscure the significance of gender difference (1990, 6). On what grounds can we connect sexual physiology—including genitalia, hormones, and genes—to human behavior, attitudes, desires, and roles? After all, as Linda Nicholson reminds us, transsexuals identify with a gender that does not match their physical body (1994, 97).

If we want to argue that the body does not matter in the formation of gender identity, as gender feminist theorists often do, then we must also explain why many men and women believe that their bodies or genitalia are crucial to locating them in the world. We must also address Susan Bordo's and Nancy Chodorow's observation that an infant's identity develops partly in response to the physiological sex of its primary caretaker. Further, we must consider to what extent both male dominance and feminist politics depend on a material or physical identity for both sexes. We must account for the powerful sexual symbolism, based on sexual physiology, that underlies so much gender analysis and mediates material and social influences on sexual character (Braidotti and Butler 1994, 47).

On the other hand, if we want to argue that the body does matter, as difference feminist theorists do, then we must account without prejudice for variations in sexual orientation among people with the same physical and reproductive equipment. We must consider the ways in which societies influence the very shape of human bodies, through diet, work, and other practices. As Connell explains, "The social definition of men as holders of power [in Western cultures] is translated . . . into muscle tensions, posture, the feel and texture of the body. This is one of the main ways in which the power of men becomes 'naturalized,' i.e., seen as part of the order of nature" (1987, 85).

Negotiating such arguments and data also involves checking for observer bias. What difference do race, class, sexuality, and geographical location make in our very perception of the phenomenon of gender differences? Is sexism constant across cultures, and is it always accompanied by notions of sex/gender difference? What can we as Westerners make of the identification of third, fourth, or fifth genders— such as *berdache* (a gender identity different from one's anatomical sex)—in some traditional societies? What should we think about the gender blending in many Native American societies, which also often attribute more power to spiritual forces than to biology in determining gender identity (Moore 1994, 90–91; Nicholson 1994, 96)? If Papua New Guineans see masculinity and femininity as substances that can be transmitted in adulthood from one body to another, why must Western peoples consider as absolute the physiological sex differences they display at birth (Moore 1994, 90)?

Realistic Approaches: First Steps

Developing realistic approaches to such questions is a long journey. Some theorists, such as Alison Jaggar, Nel Noddings, and Susan Okin, begin the process by challenging not the fact but the meaning of sexual difference. In that vein, Julie Nelson (1992) advocates retaining contrasting sets of personality traits—such as "passive," "soft," "strong," or "analytical"—without ascribing them to either sex. She wants to substitute gender *difference* for *opposition* between the sexes, and she recommends reconsidering the value of qualities like "forceful" and "compliant" in light of the history of women's oppression (141–49).

Related to such efforts are attempts to develop useful generalizations about men and women based on measures of both gender similarity and gender difference. In that category are studies that report little "block difference" between men and women on most traits (sociability, suggestibility, self-esteem, types of learning, cognitive styles, achievement motivation, and sensory modality), observe measurable differences in others (verbal ability, visual/spatial ability, mathematical ability, and aggressiveness), and reveal inconsistent differences in still others (activity level, competitiveness, dominance, compliance, and nurturance) (Connell 1987, 169). Even these measurements should be approached with caution, however, since they depend heavily on definitions of terms. They may also exaggerate differences between the sexes and obscure the importance of our common capacities—for language, intellect, imagination, upright stance, thumb opposition and manipulation, tool making and tool using, and extended childhood and parenting—that distinguish human beings from other animal species (ibid., 119, 71).

First steps toward realistic theorizing about gender difference also include accepting, as Kate Soper does, the tensions and uncertainties resulting from the interaction of genes, hormones, and reproductive organs with cultural influences.[2] Indeed, nature and nurture are so closely intertwined that we may never fully understand the distinctions and connections between them.

First steps also acknowledge the influence of individual psychology on society's gender messages. Nancy Chodorow has recently concluded, for example, that gender identity is tenacious precisely because it is so personalized, so imbued with emotions, including unconscious desires, and so intertwined with individual fantasy, aspects of the self, and images of particular family forms and cultural contexts (1995, 517, 525, 538–39). Of course, that possibility must also be weighed against the equally compelling possibility, as Connell notes, that even "masturbation involves socially constructed fantasies, techniques of arousal and a kind of minimal society in which you are the object of your own cathexis" (1987, 222).

Finally, first steps involve assessing social changes that are already underway. Katha Pollitt, for example, observes that "gender barriers are [even now] slowly breaking down: that women are naturally more caring than men may suit the self-image of nurses and social workers, but doesn't really do much for, say, bartenders and Marines. Little by little, the genders are converging: they are educated more alike and

2. See chapter 5.

raised more alike than ever before" (1994, 195). Furthermore, our increasing awareness of the rest of the world provides a new context for both seeing and challenging the gender norms in United States society.

Thus, first steps entail juggling many balls in the air simultaneously: emotional and psychological aspects of sexuality and sexual identity, "particular historical response[s] to human reproductive biology" (Connell 1987, 286), historically constituted clashes of interests within economic, power, and cathectic relations (Connell 1997, 703–4), and the changing hegemonies of gender (Connell 1998, 475; Pollitt 1994, 195). Personal characteristics, such as birth order, father or mother absence, and self-esteem, must be balanced against social forces, such as economic status, race, and geographical location. They interconnect and mutually constitute one another. Just as race inflects the meaning of father-absence and birth order, for example, gender inflects race and vice versa.

Realistic Approaches: Higher Ground

Subsequent steps toward higher ground entail shifting the foundations of thought about gender difference entirely. That process involves deconstructing the concept of gender difference itself. Philosopher Mary Hawkesworth (1997) embarks on such a project by producing a gender taxonomy that disentangles various, sometimes hidden, aspects of gender—sex, sexuality, sexual identity, gender identity, gender role, and gender-role identity. Hawkesworth argues that *sex* involves chromosomes, hormones, internal and external sexual and reproductive organs, as well as romantic acts of lovemaking. *Gender identity* refers to an individual's feelings about being a man or woman, feelings that have both psychological and social components. *Sexuality* encompasses sexual practices and erotic behavior, while *sexual identity* refers to designations such as heterosexual, homosexual/gay/lesbian/queer, bisexual, and asexual. *Gender role* refers to prescriptive, culture-specific expectations about behavior. It is here that maleness becomes male dominance and femaleness becomes feminine submissiveness. *Gender-role identity*, however, refers to whether an individual accepts and participates in feelings and behavior deemed appropriate to his or her culturally constructed gender (Hawkesworth 1997, 656). There are, of course, many combinations of these elements of gender and gender difference.

Hawkesworth's definitions establish grounds for theorizing gender difference that combine difference and gender feminist concerns. She explains, for example, how an individual can identify with a particular gender grouping (a *gender identity* based on physiology) and still reject the prevailing conceptions of masculinity or femininity (a socially constructed *gender-role identity*). "This distinction breaks any connection between masculinity/femininity and sexed bodies, interpreting masculinity and femininity as culture-specific abstractions notoriously plagued by gender symbolism that marks a chasm between romanticized ideal and lived experience, attributed and actual, propaganda and practice," Hawkesworth explains (ibid., 656–57). While the physiology of gender does not disappear, it takes on an individual rather than a collective cast. A politics based on Hawkesworth's analysis could isolate the location of male-dominance theory in the category of cultural symbolism, separate that from actual bodies or sexual behavior and feelings, and point the way toward social reform involving both the material supports for such dominance and the linguistic constructions that reinforce it.

Hawkesworth's distinctions among the constituent aspects of gender point both to numerous possible variations and to the ways in which gender norms can be mistaken for a natural state when possible variations are overlooked or taken for granted. In contrast to utopian tendencies toward opposed dualities, Hawkesworth's taxonomy simultaneously recognizes culturally constructed aspects of gender and the influence of sexualized bodies on the construction of gender (albeit in no specific direction). It also sets the stage for understanding wide variations in gender both among and within cultures around the globe and throughout history.

CAVEAT: HIDDEN UTOPIANISM

Despite its realistic trajectory, Hawkesworth's gender theory does not escape utopianism entirely. In constructing her taxonomy and analysis, for example, she repudiates the past by dismissing her social-constructionist predecessors who, she claims, remain in the grip of "the natural attitude in feminist discourses" (1997, 682).[3] Her haste to reject the past obscures the contributions of social constructionists, like Connell, to the connections she makes between social constructionism and difference theory. Indeed, almost a decade before Hawkesworth's essay, Connell integrated gender and difference posi-

3. Much of Hawkesworth's 1997 article is focused on disassociating herself from earlier theorists, such as Connell, who seem to her too entrenched in natural explanations of gender. The editors of *Signs* allow those theorists to answer her critique in the same issue, however, thereby instituting a realistic process of theory production.

tions on gender identity in several ways. First, he argued that socially constructed gender differences could not be understood until they were disentangled from preconceptions about complementary reproductive roles. Second, unlike many social-constructionist theorists of that time, Connell did not assume that acknowledging material differences between the sexes was tantamount to supporting sexual hierarchy in social arrangements. Finally, he observed that masculinity and femininity might well exist on "separate scale[s], [but that] the same person might get high scores on both" (1987, 174).

Hawkesworth's utopian separation of herself from her predecessors leads her to a utopian concept of social change. While celebrating expanded gender possibilities, she overlooks the probable difficulties that such an expansion might entail. Less utopian than she, Connell recognized the new social pressures and risks inherent in such changes. While eliminating the "massive inequalities, bitter oppressions, violence and potential disaster" of existing gender arrangements, and promoting greater diversity and expressiveness in gender behaviors and norms, he reasoned, expanded definitions of gender might also threaten human happiness. We are accustomed to a "gender structured culture," he wrote, which has shaped our imaginations and eroticism. Dismantling those structures might create a world so different from the familiar one "that we can hardly know whether it would be desirable or not." Although he recommended "playing with gender . . . by disconnecting elements of sexual character, gender practice and sexual ideology from enjoyment, erotic tension, subversion or convenience," he recognized that "the game analogy only goes so far" (1987, 288–90).

Had she credited rather than disclaimed the accomplishments of previous theorists, Hawkesworth could have incorporated such useful ambiguity into her own work while still emphasizing its contribution: the further dissociation of gender from specific forms of sexuality and reproductive roles, the articulation of cultural differences in sex roles and the norms of sexual experience, and the account of individual variations in sexed embodiedness, gendered divisions of labor, gendered social relations, and gender symbolism (Hawkesworth 1997, 682). Seen as a continuum rather than as a utopian process of repudiation, theorizing about gender difference opens the conversation to even newer data and analysis and paves the way for bridge building between viewpoints stereotyped as oppositional.

Also utopian is Hawkesworth's present focus, which blinds her to her own cultural biases about gender, according to Oyeronke Oyewumi.

Hawkesworth is so imbued with Western notions of gender as a primary category of social organization that she does not see the way she herself is tied to biologism by presupposing the existence of gender before she analyzes it. "Her thinking is yet another example of the problem with gender discourses: the assumption of gender as present everywhere, both historically and geographically." By failing to locate her analysis in the United States, where it properly belongs, Hawkesworth overlooks cultures, such as the Yoruba, in which gender is not primarily constitutive of social structure (Oyewumi 1998, 1059).

A Political Maternal Body

Connecting difference feminist theories and gender or social-constructionist theories, as Connell and Hawkesworth do, is not the final step toward higher, more realistic theoretical ground in the discourse of gender difference, however. Many more challenges remain. Among them is one that neither Hawkesworth nor Connell addresses, and that is how to theorize the potential *connection* between women's reproductive capacity and their gendered identity. In other words, can we synthesize difference and gender feminist views around motherhood (and shed further light on the cartoon in chapter 4)?

As we have seen, difference feminist theory tends to privilege women's reproductive physiology in the construction (social or biological) of female gender identity or personality. It offers a romanticized, universal interpretation of the significance of women's capacity for pregnancy, birth, and lactation when compared with male reproductive physiology. Social-constructionist or gender feminist theory, on the other hand, recognizes pregnancy, birth, and lactation as the empty vessels of reproductive capacity into which societies pour their meanings. Could there be another theory that informs each approach with the insights of the other, a body-based theory of motherhood developed in the context of socially constructed gender?

One theorist who addresses that question is Barbara Rothman, whose work in *Recreating Motherhood* (1989) and "Beyond Mothers and Fathers: Ideology in Patriarchal Society" (1994) manages both to valorize and to denaturalize female birth giving and nurturing capacities and behaviors. Like difference feminist theory, Rothman's analysis predicates public policy and personal decision making about reproduction on the physical realities of women's bodies, but unlike difference theory, it associates no particular feminine personality or characteristics with reproduction.

Rothman takes two related steps toward theoretical ground on which social-constructionist and difference feminist positions can meet. First, she defines women as the agents rather than the vessels of reproduction: women actively create babies through the gestational as well as the nurturing relationship. Although she acknowledges that forces beyond a woman's conscious control may shape her ideas about motherhood, Rothman focuses on an unusual social force—the mother's own interpretation of her circumstances and the world—as the premise for her roles and identities. Pregnancy and childbirth should acquire their significance only from the woman in whose body they unfold, Rothman explains, and not from external social pressures or conventions. What should define reproductive politics is the pregnant/birthing mother's analysis of who she is and wants to be, what she needs in the particular circumstances of a specific pregnancy, as well as the power she acquires from having performed the physical work of mothering (1994, 151–55).

To Rothman, motherhood is best viewed as a "sometime thing," embraced by some women under some circumstances and rejected by others—or even the same women—under other circumstances. Yet it cannot be reduced, as liberal theory tends to do, to a medical condition analogous to a male prostate operation (1994, 147). Thus, like social constructionists, Rothman resists specified ideals of gender, sexuality, or family forms. She assumes nothing about what a woman will think of motherhood or what it will do for or to her. But unlike many social constructionists, she recognizes the unique significance of maternity.

That recognition of women's unique reproductive physiology and role in pregnancy and labor constitutes Rothman's second step toward higher ground. It accommodates difference feminist ideas of female reproductive distinctiveness, but with a twist. Instead of emphasizing only women's identities or feelings about themselves as birth-givers, Rothman's approach politicizes the relationship women develop with the fetus during pregnancy and parturition, and with children during childrearing. Preserving and honoring that relationship, which can also include appropriate men, takes precedence over all other considerations—such as birthing technology and determinations about the "ownership" of children (1989, 250–51; 1994, 148–49).

From that perspective, Rothman claims that woman's reproductive capacity empowers her and sets the tone for the politics of reproduction. In Rothman's politics, women's bodily rhythms—the uniquely slow, continuous experience of gestation and subsequent care of dependent human infants—replace what now dominates reproductive politics—men's disconnected sense that "in goes a seed, out comes a baby" (1989, 98). Thus Rothman challenges male dominance in reproductive matters and creates a politics of sexual/gender difference without destiny. Her "difference feminism" is about women's choices and actions rather than about their essence. Women "deploy their gender," to use Laurie Berlant's terms, without conceding a particular vision of womanhood (Berlant 1988, 239). Indeed, Rothman insists that womanhood must never become a function of the capacity to give birth (1989, 106–13).

Although Rothman does not fully develop the phenomenology of motherhood that Ellen Ross has called for,[4] her approach accommodates the conflicting realities of Ross's analysis. Rothman acknowledges that motherhood represents fulfillment for some women and a burden for others, or for the same woman at different times. She recognizes that motherhood can be "intimate, joyous, terrifying, life-affirming," or any combination thereof (1989, 23). Because motherhood and womanhood are not synonymous, no choice represents automatic betrayal of a presumed gender identity or sexual character. There is no destiny, only a physiological platform for decision making. Rothman's analysis frees theorists to explore wide variations in maternal feeling and practice, differing circumstances that promote such feelings in differing cultural contexts, historical locations, and individual lifeworlds, and varying effects of the child itself on maternal conditions and response.

A Realistic Construction of Gender Difference

Like Hawkesworth's taxonomy, Rothman's approach to motherhood begins the process of defining a "family resemblance" between apparently opposed feminist theoretical positions—the difference feminists who valorize maternity and the gender feminists/social constructionists who seek the meaning of gender beyond sexual or reproductive biology. Rothman's work does not fully satisfy either "camp," of course. Difference feminist theorists will want more elaboration of the psychology and discipline of female sexuality, mothering, and maternal capacity, as well as more cultural/social/political influence for women in general and/or mothers and maternal practices in particu-

---

4. See chapter 4.
5. See, for example, the following works by Sara Ruddick: 1980, "Maternal Thinking," *Feminist Studies* 6(2) (summer): 342–67; 1983, "Thinking About Mothering and Putting Maternal Thinking to Use," *Women's Studies Quarterly* 11(4) (winter): 47; 1992, "From Maternal Thinking to Peace Politics," in *Explorations in Feminist Ethics,* edited by

lar.[5] Gender feminists will question Rothman's acceptance of chil-drearing as women's province (1994, 153). Still, her reasoning creates a new ground for a body-based reproductive politics and suggests how we might conceptualize gender and womanhood by recognizing the interdependence of biological and cultural factors. Also, like Hawkes-worth's taxonomy, Rothman's approach to motherhood recognizes the power of an individual's interpretive acts and decisions as social forces shaping not only individual behavior and lifeworlds but also cultural scripts about gender, sex, sexuality, and reproduction.

Gender difference on such a theoretical ground can be neither assumed nor denied. Its significance will forever depend upon the questions asked, the reasons for asking the questions, and their con-text. Gender difference has significance in some ways and not in oth-ers. People are never wholly constructed by either their physiology or their societies, and the degree of construction by each depends on the particular situation or aspect of gendered reality being explored. Re-productive physiology is integral to that process, but neither the phys-iology nor the process is absolute. That women gestate fetuses and give birth to babies is significant both to them and to culture, but like all significances, those are subject to interpretation and revision.

A utopian critic might wonder if gender doesn't matter in any par-ticular or definable way, then who needs feminism? A realistic answer to that question is, simply, that feminist theory is necessitated as much by complexity and ambiguity as it is by specificity and certainty. Fem-inist theorizing is important for both understanding and shaping the way that gender differences both result from and constitute social hi-erarchies and political institutions. Feminism helps us to negotiate and monitor the gender differences that are meaningful, both to us as in-dividuals and to our various social contexts, and to identify common-alities that link the sexes in a shared humanity.

THE DISCOURSE OF DIFFERENCES AMONG WOMEN

There is no assurance, after all, that methodological centrality retrieves the black woman from her historical erasure. . . . To achieve this may require in-vestigative travel in an initially contradictory direction, into that domain of

---

Eve Browning Cole and Susan Coultrap-McQuin (Bloomington: Indiana University Press), 141–55; and 1994, "Thinking Mothers/Conceiving Birth," in *Representations of Motherhood*, edited by Donna Bassin, Margaret Honey, and Meryle Mahrer Kaplan (New Haven: Yale University Press), 29–45.

cultural relations most underwritten by the African-American woman's his-
torical absence: those among black and white men.
—Robyn Wiegman, *American Anatomies*

Conceptualizing these systems of oppression as difference obfuscates the power
relations and material inequalities that constitute oppression. Doing away
with thinking about differences will clarify the real problem.
—Patricia Hill Collins, "Symposium: On West and Fenstermaker's
'Doing Difference'"

The category "lesbian" is not essentially radical or subversive. Indeed, the
category 'lesbian' is not essentially anything. It does not have a fixed va-
lence, a signification that is proper to itself. . . . "The deconstruction of iden-
tity is not the deconstruction of politics; rather, it establishes as political the
very terms through which identity is articulated."
—Annamarie Jagose in *Lesbian Utopics*

Approaches to difference must be distinguished from visions of difference.
—Dana Takagi, "Symposium: On West and Fenstermaker's 'Doing
Difference'"

A postethnic perspective resists the grounding of knowledge and moral values
in blood and history.
—David Hollinger, *Postethnic America: Beyond Multiculturalism*

Reality, in other words, is understood as not out there, self-contained, but as
all-encompassing; knowers and known are part and parcel of it. Both reality
and individuals are believed to be historically constructed. To the extent that
humans in society have structured reality hierarchically and dichotomously,
furthermore, whether consciously and intentionally or not, the resulting mate-
rial conditions place humans in oppositional social locations.
—Diane Fowlkes "Moving From Feminist Identity Politics to Coalition
Politics through a Feminist Materialist Standpoint of Intersubjectivity
in Gloria Anzaldúa's *Borderlands/La Frontera: The New Mestiza*"

Framing the Issue

In its utopian versions, the discourse of differences among women, including the concepts of identity politics and epistemic privilege, tends
to idealize identity groups, encourage rather than heal divisions, and
mistake problem reversal for problem solution. As Robyn Wiegman
and Patricia Hill Collins suggest, those utopian approaches to differences among women can obscure the real problems and questions to
which feminist theory should attend. If we focus exclusively on differences among women, feminist theory may overlook entirely more crucial forces that determine women's well-being, such as power relations
among men.

First steps in formulating realistic theory about women's diversity entail recognition that women's gender roles and identities co-exist with and are constitutive of numerous other socially mandated and personally chosen attributes, affiliations, roles, activities, opportunities, and commitments. Therefore, they involve understanding the complexity of the category *women* on which feminist theory is based. At the very least, we must always ask what women, what gendered realities, what power relationships we mean when we use that term. We must consider all the social and personal variations that may exist, including race and ethnicity as well as class, sexuality, physical ability, age, and numerous other factors that shape a woman's public and private relationship with her gender category and with social structures.

It is utopianism, however, that tempts us to abandon the idea of a category *women* altogether. It is also utopianism that requires us to reject all feminist theorizing that has not taken full account of women's diversity or to reject out of hand all existing theory on the assumption that it is necessarily inadequate. Instead, we must inquire. Robyn Wiegman observes that "at the same time that we disavow the utopic rhetoric of female bonding implicit in notions of a commonality based on gender . . . feminists often gesture toward a truer version of such myths, toward transcending their fault lines in order to grasp . . . our own post-racist historicity" (1995, 188). Thus, as we approach higher ground in realistic feminist theorizing about differences among women we must recapture as well as re-landscape the terrain on which the matter of women's diversity now rests.

A CAUTIONARY TALE

Many issues at stake on higher ground in feminist theorizing about differences among women are addressed in Wahneema Lubiano's essay (1992) about Anita Hill. In that essay, which documents the complex interconnection between race, class, and gender in the media's representation of Hill during Clarence Thomas's 1991 Senate confirmation hearings for the Supreme Court, difference emerges as a multifanged, complicated, and contradictory beast.

Lubiano focuses on the way that media coverage of Hill's testimony constructed her as the villain of Clarence Thomas's success story. She demonstrates how the media undermined Hill's credibility in relationship to Thomas, in the minds of many blacks as well as whites, even in the face of sworn testimony about his incompetence as an Equal Employment Opportunity Commission administrator, his bigotry, and his mediocrity as a jurist (1992, 343). She explains that the media associated Hill with the two images of black women that everyone—black and white—is supposed to fear: the welfare mother and the powerful black lady. On the one hand, despite her level of education and professional success and despite her conservative political views, Hill became identified with Thomas's sister, who had lived on welfare. On the other hand, she was simultaneously identified as an uppity middle-class black woman whose very success somehow signified the failures of African American males (ibid., 335).

Perhaps most startling, Lubiano convincingly demonstrates that, despite Hill's racial identity, the media constructed her as essentially a white feminist (and therefore a liberal), "the embodiment of black female betrayal or 'white' (by fiat) feminist cat's-paw. . . . With no check on Thomas's evocation of his blackness, with no real check by Democrats or the mainstream press, Hill got whiter . . . with her class privilege so consistently recognized, evoked, and articulated" (1992, 348–49). She therefore assumed the menacing qualities often attributed to white feminists.

In the end, such media transformations elevated Hill's identity as a woman over her identity as an African American. Her outspokenness constructed her as a female threat, both within and outside her race, to the achievements of the much-lamented emasculated black man and, by extension, all men. She could not be allowed to triumph. The health of the nation was at stake.

It does little good simply to lament such devious manipulation and refusals by the media to analyze the intersection of Hill's race with either her feminism or her educational level and class position. Rather, Lubiano's analysis challenges feminist theory to account for the messy and convoluted realities of our society's construction of race and gender, of which media constructions are a crucial element. It suggests a framework for understanding race and gender that is already at work in the culture, a framework in which the markers of difference—such as race, ethnicity, sexuality—rarely signify in discrete, predictable ways. Rather, the boundaries between such categories are blurred. They become entangled with specific, historical circumstances, which increasingly include media representation.

Thus, realistic feminist theorizing about difference must often address issues that have little apparent connection with differences among women. In the Thomas case, Lubiano explains, one such issue was the collusion of masculinity and state power. Thomas's (erroneous) association with the ethos of the self-made man hovered over all discussions of his past and ultimately overrode in the hearings all allegations about his harassing language and behavior. (Lost in the discussion was the fact that Thomas's bootstrap career owed as much to the support of white politicians, who relished his conservatism, as to his own talents and efforts.) America's need for self-reliant men, especially black ones, was ultimately more important than Thomas's qualifications for his position. Therefore, those who interfered with Thomas's tenant-farm-to-judicial-bench success story, for whatever reason, appeared subversive of American progress. "By confirming Thomas," Lubiano writes, "by affirming the black father, the stand-in for state power . . . the black-female threat [Hill] to what 'America' means was wrestled to the ground. . . . America is back and standing tall" (1992, 354). What was preserved by the Senate was male solidarity around issues of masculinity and the state.

Lubiano's approach to the Thomas-Hill story suggests the importance of achieving the largest possible perspective in the formation of feminist theory around issues of diversity. To reach that higher ground, we must be careful not to draw boundaries around issues that create theoretical ghettoes with little connection to complex social realities. While feminists are busy delineating differences among women, the culture at large may be lumping all women together for some purposes and dividing us for others, few of which advance feminist agendas. While it occasionally behooves us to contest such imposed divisions and connections, we should not ignore those with political significance. The media was partly right, after all, in associating Hill with what they called liberal white feminist views, even if they were wrong in assuming that such views necessarily made her either white or a liberal. That link is significant to feminist theorizing and should not be eclipsed by assumptions that the races (or political parties) share no political positions (or metaphors), especially since, as Rey Chow explains, many such categories partake of one another (1993, 10–13).

By the same token, realistic feminist theory should investigate how imposed divisions among women betray us, how language imperfectly creates all categories, and how the interests and conditions of our lives both contrast and collude. Anne McClintock reminds us that even oppressors' roles exist in historical, "dynamic, shifting, and intimate interdependence" with the roles of the oppressed and that oppressors themselves can be ambivalent mimics of their own concepts of power (1995, 61–62). Octavia Butler's fantasy novel *Kindred* (1979) demonstrates such interdependence when her 1970s African American female character is transported back to the pre–Civil War South only to discover that, in order to ensure her own birth, she must save the life of the white man who raped her enslaved great-great-grandmother!

Lubiano's essay further points to the interconnection between the political and the discursive. As feminist theorists contemplate social change, we might do well to keep in mind Howard Winant's admonition that "every [racial] project is . . . both a discursive and a cultural initiative, an attempt at racial signification and identity formation on the one hand, and a social structural initiative, an attempt at political mobilization and resource redistribution, on the other" (1994, 24).

FROM DIFFERENCE DISCOURSE TO "RACIALLY
INFLECTED GENDER ANALYSIS"

In short, higher theoretical ground requires a deeper understanding of the context within which differences among women (like difference between the sexes) acquire significance, always keeping an eye on the pernicious racially (or sexually, or ethnically) inflected effects of "the unequal distribution of economic wealth and political power in this country" (Christensen 1997, 621). It requires moving from an excessive focus on our feelings about race toward a politics of taking responsibility for changing those inequities. White feminists must figure out how "to take seriously the experiences and analyses of women of color and use [their white] race privilege to help change the material conditions, institutions, and cultural traditions that oppress" others (ibid.). Higher ground also requires understanding the connection of racism and sexism to such practices as the funding of schools through property taxes, congressional redistricting, campaign financing, health care, welfare, and hiring and seniority systems that codify past discrimination (ibid., 638–43). Moving toward higher ground inevitably involves building coalitions with other communities and organizations dedicated to the same goals (ibid., 633).

This conceptualization of higher ground in the discourse of differences among women challenges the utopian notions of epistemic privilege and identity politics we considered in chapter 4. Neither idealizing those who have suffered nor relying for our politics on identity alone seems appropriate to the generation of comprehensive knowledge and the production of lasting systemic change.

Identity Politics Meets Coalition Politics

Identity politics involves utopic *visions* of difference, but it offers little insight into the *approaches* to difference that Dana Takagi supports in her quotation at the beginning of this section of chapter 6 and that realistic feminist theorizing and politics require. Identity politics may romanticize and idealize traditional cultural practices and formations and thereby reinforce qualities that have resulted from oppression and from existing and historical hierarchies and injustices. Identity politics may also idealize nonvoluntary communities of origin or place that "'do not necessarily constitute us as selves who agree or comply with the norms which unify those communities'" (Susan Friedman, quoted in Tirrell 1993, 8). In the extreme, identity politics even suggests that oppression itself constitutes the sum of oppressed people's identities and social locations.

Further, identity politics ignores overlapping identities, which "may be stressed or muted, depending on the situation." It posits identity as a pre-existing natural condition rather than as a product of social situations (West and Fenstermaker 1995, 30–31). Identity politics creates its own hegemony by conceptualizing power in conventional terms, often simply replacing the cast of characters—nonmajority versus majority groups—without questioning the principle by which meaning and circumstances are determined by one group for others.

Realistic feminist theory requires another approach both to identity and to politics. Utopian identity divisions omit too much and obscure overlappings among categories. An identity-based politics not only creates difference and separation, it also misses the larger arena in which genuine social change must occur. To reach higher ground, we must articulate *approaches to* rather than *visions of* identity. We must seek new metaphors of connection and coalition.

Higher Ground: Realistic Constructions of Identity

Annamarie Jagose's work on lesbians takes important steps toward realistic identity definition. Jagose outlines an alternative to utopian visions of resistant or nonhegemonic identities by first rejecting the utopic notion that lesbian identity escapes all cultural norms, in this case of "heterosexual exchange and patriarchal nomination." She argues that the lesbian body is not "some natural body that always already exists beyond discourse, culture and representation and which functions as a guarantee of escape from phallocentrism." Nor does she accept that the powers creating the lesbian body are all on some "other side." The lesbian does not represent *simply* resistance and subversion. Rather, like everyone else, lesbians neither create their own reality (a belief Jagose calls "idealist voluntarism") nor act solely as pawns in a "patriarchal/capitalist/colonial world." "The cultural meanings of the lesbian body, like those of any body, are neither fully self-determining nor fully determined" (1994, 160–61).

Second, Jagose considers dangerous any belief that lesbian sexual behavior is inherently safe or that lesbian relationships can avoid the jealousies and conflicts that plague other sexual unions. If, to use Gloria Anzaldúa's term, lesbians live "on the border," then (in contrast to Anzaldúa's depiction) Jagose considers them in a position that both reinforces and transcends the two "sides." "Borders preside equally over hospitable and hostile interaction of familiar and alien," she explains, "and divides while rendering indistinguishable the categories of inside and outside" (1994, 152). In short, no identity allows us to escape involvement with and at least partial responsibility for the world as it is. Indeed, there is always the possibility that whatever we do to distinguish ourselves from others simply enacts a larger social script that masks our epistemic, social, and political involvements. Her warning reinforces Amy Mullin's observation that, in divided societies, "individuals often live out these divisions and contradictions in the form of existential unease" (1995, 27).

Jagose's approach provides a foundation for yet another step toward higher ground in the discussion of identity. Her view of imperfect and culturally complicit identities leads us to the probability that no identity category can ever fully match our complicated selves. It is not simply that each of us has "multiple category memberships and subjectivities," as if we were composed of many personlike, full-identity parts (the lesbian, the African American, and the disabled, for example) (Frye 1996, 1004–5). Rather, none of us quite belongs to any named group. Again according to Amy Mullin, we are all somehow different from or misfit in whatever category we are given or embrace (1995, 21–23). None of us is fully captured by designations such as white, middle-class heterosexual or black, working-class lesbian.

Thus, difference also involves inner diversity. June Jordan illustrates that point by describing her complicated relationship, as an African American, to the black maids at a West Indian resort hotel where she once stayed. Likewise, Minnie Bruce Pratt documents her uncomfortable fit both in her own white southern heritage and in the all-black Washington, D.C., neighborhood where she once lived.[6] For

---

6. June Jordan, 1983, "Report from the Bahamas: Conflicts of a Black American Tourist," *Ms.* 12 (November): 78+; Minnie Bruce Pratt, 1984, "Identity: Skin, Blood, Heart," *Yours in Struggle: Three Feminist Perspectives on Anti-Semitism and Racism*, edited by Elly Bulkin, Minnie Bruce Pratt, and Barbara Smith (New York: Long Haul Press), 9–63.

both writers, acknowledging inner or intrapersonal diversity is essential both to recognizing interpersonal difference and to crossing its boundaries.

Maria Lugones's notion of "curdling" (1994) provides an interesting metaphor for the messy way that inner selves and identities are divided in the real world of identity formation. Lugones envisions impure, curdled subjects whose various parts and identities are "tainted" by other parts and identities, as in the oily yolk and the yolky oil of a mayonnaise emulsion. She postulates a "subject who in its multiplicity perceives, understands, grasps its worlds as multiple sensuously, passionately as well as rationally without the splitting separation between sense/emotion/reason." In contrast to the utopian love of purity, which creates oppressive structures, the power of impurity can resist and threaten those structures (465, 468).

SISTERHOOD REVISITED

The diverse inner self is the opening many theorists use to reach yet another plateau on the way to higher ground beyond difference, ground on which, as Susan Friedman argues, feminists will be saved from "repetitive rounds of denial, accusation, and confession in our discourses about race and ethnicity that stunt . . . our growth as a movement academically and organizationally" (1995, 33–34, 39). "If we cease to view the self as unitary and stable," writes Sonia Kruks, "realizing that it is instead 'split and contradictory' we will see that such a split self can join easily with other such selves: 'The knowing self is partial in all its guises . . .; it is always constructed and stitched together imperfectly, and *therefore* able to join with another, to see together without claiming to be another: our rough edges, our seams, our openings perhaps, are the places where we can join with other and different selves'" (Kruks 1995, 9; Haraway quoted in Kruks 1995, 9). Amy Mullin concurs: the fact of being somewhat out of place in whatever group we enter allows us to attach to those outside of that group (1995, 21–23). Gloria Anzaldúa (1987) claims that survival itself depends on our understanding the divisions among us as "a system of gates that we can open and use as connectors, as 'feminist architecture'" (quoted in Fowlkes 1997, 119).

The joining that theorists like Kruks, Anzaldúa, and Mullin imagine, however, bears no resemblance to the melting pot of 1970s sisterhood. The probability of real and material differences remains as individuals and groups cross boundaries between them. Borrowing an idea from Sartre, Kruks explains that such joining can, indeed must, occur as individuals act in a "practical material field that brings [those acts] into mediation with other individual praxes" (1995, 18). Even if the relations between praxes or lifeworlds is antagonistic, which is the case to which identity politics is the response, "a reciprocal comprehension of praxis exists. Indeed, if it did not exist, conflict or struggle would not be possible. . . . Struggle is possible *only* because we can reciprocally comprehend praxis as intentional action" (ibid.). Despite the fact that we may never know or identify with another person's innermost feelings, according to Kruks, "the fact that all of us engage in a diversity of praxes, mediated through the same or overlapping practical material fields, means that however different our worlds appear, and however antagonistic our interests really may be, reciprocity and the possibility of a mutual comprehension of each other's actions always remain possible" (ibid.).

"Translatability" might be another term for Kruks's approach to comprehension and alliance building across real and apparent differences. Rey Chow suggests that term as she rejects the absurdity of thinking that groups, cultures, and languages are so distinct that they are virtually unknowable to one another. Such thinking not only utopianizes groups and cultures, by suggesting that they contain something pure and inaccessible, it also masks the way that different groups and cultures are "accomplices" to one another (Chow 1993, 3–5). Ignoring that interdependence builds a world of incommensurability, according to Jean Bethke Elshtain, when reality is quite otherwise. Human beings inevitably formulate identities and political programs not in isolation but in "dialogical relations with others," often others who are very different from themselves (1995, 66).

As Linda Nicholson has reminded us, feminists routinely benefit from dialogical relationships with one another around diverse lifeworlds and perspectives. It has been eye-opening to many middle-class white feminists, for example, to learn that women from different classes and ethnicities disagree about the liberatory potential of paid work for women, as well as about the oppressive nature of domestic labor and motherhood. All of feminist theory has been enriched by an exploration of the role of state violence in some women's lives, as well as by revelations about varying levels of trust among women of different racial, ethnic, class, and sexual groups (Watt and Cook 1991, 133, 137).[7]

---

7. Watt and Cook cite the following sources as evidence of feminist theorists' assumptions about these matters: Michèle Barrett and Mary McIntosh, 1985, "Ethno-

At the same time that feminist theory has benefited from such differences in perspectives, however, realism demands that we not lose sight of resemblances among those same perspectives. For example, the term "womanism" expresses a racially specific celebration of African American women's "outrageous, audacious, courageous, or *willful* behavior." Yet its parallel commitment "to survival and to the wholeness of entire people, male *and* female" (Walker 1983, xi) connects it to feminist statements and positions expressed in other racial and ethnic contexts. Third-world feminists often discuss the importance of communal relations that include men as well as women. Some suggest strategies that entail involving men in women's worlds—"these living connections, this dailiness, this burden, this immanence"—and posit "new relations between the sexes" (Mies 1989, 51–52, 55). Realistic feminist theorizing recognizes the extent to which important bridges can be built between apparently divergent views, as well as ways that boundaries around identity have already been redrawn.

COMMUNITY REVISITED

New visions of identity and alliance formation across boundaries of difference also require new visions of community, as both the places we come from and the collectives we seek to join. As the places we come from, nonvoluntary communities of origin or place may or may not be the best source of our identity, self-understanding, or effective social agency. Lynne Tirrell (1993) argues that we must ultimately decide for ourselves whether the rules for membership or the limitations imposed by our communities of origin or place, since such communities can never be perfect, are appropriate for us or not. That decision involves "articulating and rearticulating ourselves in relation to others. . . building new and different sorts of alliances, and . . . reshaping our social practices." Whether our community is one of privilege or disadvantage, we may decide to disaffiliate from it, to separate ourselves only from some of its aspects or activities, or to fight for change within it. Even privilege might be a tolerable concept, for example, if

centrism and Socialist-Feminism—Gender, Ethnic, and Class Divisions" (*Feminist Review* 20: 23–47); Hazel Carby, 1982, "White Woman Listen! Black Feminism and the Boundaries of Sisterhood," in *The Empire Strikes Back: Race and Racism in 70s Britain* (London: Hutchinson), 212–35; Prahtiba Parmar, 1982, "Gender, Race, and Class: Asian Women in Resistance," in *The Empire Strikes Back: Race and Racism in 70s Britain* (London: Hutchinson), 236–75, and 1989, "Other Kinds of Dreams" (*Feminist Review* 31: 55–65); Caroline Ramazanoglu, 1989, *Feminism and the Contradictions of Oppression* (London: Routledge); Fiona Williams, 1989, *Social Policy: A Critical Introduction* (Oxford: Polity).

its benefits can be extended to the many rather than the few (8, 37, 23). By the same token, as Kimberly Christensen observes, remaining involved with hostile communities or families can effect social change, as when a homophobic family learns to live with one of its homosexual members or a racist family learns from an antiracist member (1997, 635–36).

One implication of Tirrell's advice for feminist communities or collectives is the importance of flexibility, of withholding judgment about individuals' and groups' decisions concerning affiliations with various other communities. Such decisions cannot be judged merely on their appearance. Creating that kind of room in the feminist community is another element in constructing an indeterminate "family" of feminism, and it has particular meaning in a transnational context. According to Lauren Berlant (1988), "We must not be horrified by women who refunction their relations to masculine modes of authority in ways that seem senseless to us. . . . Women should not expect all women to have the same 'imaginary relations to the real'" (254).

At the same time, however, realistic feminist theorizing demands that such decisions not be romanticized or exempted from scrutiny. How to question those decisions across lines of cultural, racial, or ethnic diversity has long been a sticking point in feminist theory, around which much ink and metaphorical feminist blood has been spilled: How can we truly know the lifeworld of another or judge another's actions? Are there any absolute feminist truths? Realistic answers to those questions must incorporate such concepts as translatability, reciprocity, and mutual comprehension. They should also recognize the ways in which outsiders teach us about ourselves. In addition, Helena Michie suggests the concept of "correctability," which "allows one to speak, to speculate, to try to formulate ideas about experiences and communities that are somehow 'other' in the full knowledge that one can and will be corrected and challenged" (1992, 11–12).[8] David Hollinger (1995) further suggests adopting "postethnic cosmopolitanism," which entails the mutual scrutiny of all cultures, including our own, as well as the search for points of convergence among *ethnoi* that are presumed to be contradictory (107).

Realistic feminist theorizing on this point must also avoid the utopian myth that perfect communities exist. Separating ourselves from inappropriate or incompatible affiliations does not guarantee that we

---

8. Michie's correctability is reminiscent of the "but what about . . .?" mode of theorizing advocated elsewhere in this book.

will find an ideal alternative. A successful community, as Martin and Mohanty (1986) suggest, requires work and struggle; "it is inherently unstable, contextual; it has to be constantly reevaluated in relation to critical political priorities; and it is the product of interpretation . . . attention to history, to the concrete, to . . . subjugated knowledges. . . . If identity and community are not the product of essential connections, neither are they merely the product of political urgency or necessity. . . . They are a constant recontextualizing of the relationship between personal/group history and political priorities" (210).

Like communities of origins, feminist or other communities of destination will inevitably entail envy, competition, and other unpleasant aspects of relationships, even in the absence of oppressive patriarchy or racism or homophobia.[9] If they are families, then such communities are real rather than ideal families. That is, they are contentious and diverse. Even physical resemblance or shared history is no guarantee of harmony. As in real families, members of such affinity groups both desire and recoil from identification with one another (Michie 1992, 7, 9–10).

By the same token, such communities must resist romantic metaphors about home, which, as Bernice Reagon Johnson warns, can become a barred room in which only folks like you are admitted. That situation is "'inadequate for surviving in the world with many peoples.'" For understanding community, Johnson prefers the metaphor of the beast: "'It's not to feed you; you have to feed it. And it's a monster. It never gets enough. It always wants more'" (quoted in Caraway 1991, 124–25).

FROM COMMUNITY TO COALITION

The realities of feminist communities suggest the next step toward higher ground—coalition. They prepare us to view coalitions as June Jordan does, based on "the need that we find between us. It is not only who you are, in other words, but what we can do for each other that will determine the connection" (quoted in Friedman 1995, 40).[10] Along with Helena Michie, we can begin to conceptualize coalitions as temporary, revisable as our interests and comfort levels dictate (1992, 14). We are ready to learn, as Marilyn Frye suggests, from the

9. See, for example, Evelyn Fox Keller and Helene Moglen, 1987, "Competition: A Problem for Academic Women," in *Competition: A Feminist Taboo?* (New York: The Feminist Press), 21–37.

10. Friedman actually calls the dream of coalition and connection utopian (1995, 40), but her depictions of coalition do not really suggest the elements of utopia.

coalitions women have historically created to enact their gender in collective projects (1996, 1099).

At the same time, however, a realistic view allows us to see coalitions as opportunities to enlarge rather than reinforce our existing views and lifeworlds. As Trudy Govier explains, coalitions can enable us to trust others even where distrust has been the rule (1992, 18). They can promote what Maria Lugones calls "world-travelling," a process of learning to see others within their worlds and of seeing ourselves as we would be in their worlds (1990, 160–64, 170). They allow us to learn about ourselves from others. They create the possibility of emotional catharsis through experiencing vicariously the worldview, struggles, and needs of another person or group, as human beings have done for millennia through literature. None of these concepts of coalition requires us to abandon our notion of ourselves. Rather, they invite us to expand that notion and to connect with others around differences as well as similarities.

Such approaches to coalition converge with realistic views of identity to suggest several key points: none of us is as distinct from others as utopian notions of identity have led us to believe; our very differences both within and between ourselves provide openings for connection and coalition; yet, the collectives we honor or desire will never provide perfect harmony and bliss.

From Coalition to Series: Unity from Diversity

Such realistic approaches to identity and coalition unsettle comfortable, utopian notions of any universalist feminist "we" working to effect self-evident goals and aims. Indeed, they support notions of an indeterminate feminism and challenge the very possibility of feminist action. Therefore, in order to conceptualize realistic feminist action, feminist theory must take a new tack.

Iris Marion Young's concept of *seriality* provides one strategic model for realistic feminist coalition. Through an impressive act of creative borrowing, Young (1994) redefines Sartre's notion of seriality to conceptualize fluid and flexible feminist coalitions that neither assume a particular identity or set of shared feminist goals or issues nor prescribe affiliation with any identifiable collective. Young starts with the premise that feminist politics per se cannot constitute women as a group. In fact, thinking that it can reduces feminist politics to the foundationalism of predetermined feminist issues (1994, 721), a utopian trap. As an alternative, Young envisions coalitions and collective action organized and reorganized around particular but changing and continuously scrutinized goals and ideas.

For Sartre, a *series* connotes a social collective that is formed on the basis of its members' passive unification around specific actions or around the effects of others' actions upon them. Thus, people waiting for a bus that never arrives can become a series that might mobilize itself, for example, to seek alternative transportation. They are united because circumstances require them to respond in some way to the "continuous material environment" around them or to various social structures that "have been created by the unintended collective result of past actions" (Young 1994, 724). Yet, there may be nothing similar in their backgrounds or worldviews.

Young's *seriality* builds on Sartre's notion by describing spontaneous, voluntary, temporary, and issue-focused coalitions among feminists that avoid the pitfalls of identity politics yet allow for unresolved differences among their members. Young regards "each person's identity [as] unique—the history and meaning she makes and develops from her dealings with other people, her communicative interactions through the media, and her manner of taking up the particular serialized structures whose prior history positions her." At the same time, she postulates an undercurrent of nascent commonality: "No individual woman's identity, . . . will escape the markings of gender, but how gender marks her life is her own" (1994, 734). Circumstances will bring that commonality to the forefront, suggesting that the fact of difference is not inconsistent with the motivation for unity.

What Young does not outline, but what may well occur in serial coalitions, is the profound change in individuals that might endure even after the collective has dissolved. That is, seriality may not leave people exactly as it found them, and patterns of "difference" that precede such coalitions may not remain intact. Where utopianism institutionalizes the contending forces its finds, realism keeps open the possibility of merger, interaction, and mutual instruction. Seriality provides one model for such a realistic outcome.

From Epistemic Privilege to Examined Subjectivity

Identity politics has a utopian cousin in epistemic privilege. The two concepts share a tendency for idealization, hyperbole, generalization, and the false universalization of both marginalized and hegemonic groups. Like identity politics, epistemic privilege relies too heavily on existing concepts of identity and identity formation. It also risks creating competitions—hierarchies of suffering—among oppressed groups who aspire to automatic status as knowledge producers.

In addition, just as identity politics can create new hegemonies, epistemic privilege can create new elites by turning the previously despised knower into the newly privileged one. Thus, at its worst, epistemic privilege supports fanaticism—the imposition of one group's unchallengeable ideas on all others. At the same time, epistemic privilege risks losing the benefits of helpful sources of knowledge and techniques of knowledge production, such as reason and empiricism, just because they are traditional, in the utopian belief that anything traditional is inevitably suspect.

To give epistemic privilege its due, however, we must remember its important realistic premise—that truth is contingent at least in part on the consciousness and intention of the knower. That premise underlies the concept of situated knowledges in feminist theory, as we discussed in chapter 4. But that same premise also creates a dilemma for realistic feminist theorizing in the face of different, competing, and conflicting knowledge claims. How can we move away from unmitigated relativism and toward justified, valid feminist analyses and conclusions? If justification cannot be pursued on the basis of trust, what are the grounds for accountability in knowledge production?

Feminist epistemologists insist that social location influences particular knowers' approaches to knowledge, but they increasingly recognize the need for knowledge justification as a corrective to that concept of knowledge standpoint. In addition, many want to develop strategies for going beyond located knowledge to reaching actual conclusions about the world. As Donna Haraway has famously noted, "'Our' problem is how to have *simultaneously* an account of radical historical contingency for all knowledge claims and knowing subjects, a critical practice for recognizing our own 'semiotic technologies' for making meanings, *and* a no-nonsense commitment to faithful accounts of a 'real' world. . . . We . . . need . . . the ability partially to translate knowledges among very different—and power-differentiated—communities" (1991, 187).

Central to the contemporary epistemological debate is the role of experience in producing knowledge. Epistemic privilege is predicated precisely on the point that certain kinds of experience produce the best kinds of knowledge. But as we have seen, that connection is studded with land mines. As realistic feminist epistemology has wrestled with the question of experience, it has increasingly recognized that it is "experience *in its mediated form* [that] contains a 'cognitive component' through which we can gain access to knowledge of the world" (Mohanty quoted in Moya 1997, 137). Even though the social facts of a person's life may produce certain kinds of experiences, and those experiences may create a kind of cultural identity that influences the way she makes sense of her experience, as Paula Moya argues, the resulting cultural identities and interpretations of experience can vary widely among those who share a social location (1997, 138–39). What is more, people can fabricate or manipulate their experiences for their own ends, as Linda Kauffman has described, or use them to bludgeon others, as Chow has argued. If there is epistemological privilege, Moya contends, it is only because some social locations, like "American," are still granted more privilege than others, such as "Mexican" or "Hispanic." "Epistemic privilege exists only in the way one selects an identity stance" (ibid., 137–39).

From Epistemic Privilege to Epistemic Interest

Standpoint epistemology and situated knowledge are key strands in the rope of realistic feminist theorizing about the relationship of identity and experience to knowledge. Although there is no clear consensus about how these strategies should work, many theorists argue for what we can call "examined subjectivity," which contrasts sharply with epistemic privilege.

The contrast between the two approaches is evident in a recent scholarly debate among Susan Hekman, Patricia Hill Collins, and Sandra Harding. Hekman worries that standpoint epistemologies do not sufficiently guard against the proliferation of infinite points of view. But what she is really protesting is the notion of epistemic privilege: anointing any standpoint as automatically complete or comprehensive. Powerlessness is not necessarily less biased or freer of its location and situation than powerfulness, she argues (1997, 347–49).

Collins argues that what we must eliminate in order to eradicate "unexamined subjectivity" is not standpoint theory but epistemic privilege. Because standpoints are a matter of social definition, not personal affiliations, they will not dissolve into infinite numbers of individual points of view. But standpoints must be judged by specific criteria. We must ask, for example, whether the standpoint explains and condones injustice or challenges it and whether the standpoint recreates hegemonic power or resists that power (1997, 381).

To Sandra Harding, examined subjectivity consists of epistemic *interest* rather than epistemic *privilege*. Since suffering should enjoy no particular moral status, she argues, the standpoints of marginalized people must derive from something other than their pain. The epistemic significance of marginalization, then, consists of the perspectives and questions it suggests that challenge hegemonic conceptual frameworks via the complexities (and difficulties) of marginalized lives. People in various cultural locations contribute to knowledge by bringing different interests and discursive resources to the table (1997, 385–86).

Donna Haraway has long agreed with such analyses. "Subjugation is not grounds for an ontology," she argues, although "it might be a visual clue. . . . There is no immediate vision from the standpoints of the subjugated. . . . Positioning implies responsibility for our enabling practices" (1991, 191, 193). Thus, we must resist investing others' powerlessness with automatic moral or epistemic authority (what Rey Chow calls the Jane Eyre phenomenon [1993, 13, 11–12]), as so many senators did for Clarence Thomas when he claimed moral and epistemic authority on the basis of his grandfather's life as a sharecropper (Lubiano 1992, 329). Encouraging such investment often involves base motives—the creation of guilt and the exercise of control—and risks reinscribing in the name of righteousness what we seek to overthrow (Chow 1993, 16–17).

Nor can we trust any particular kind of discourse to convey truth or knowledge. Any form can be tainted with deliberate dishonesty, exhibitionism, sensationalism, exaggeration, or sentimentality. Clarence Thomas claimed in an inflated metaphor, for example, that all opposition to his candidacy for the Supreme Court was "lynching." Confessions can be manipulative, creating false senses of solidarity. Stories can be hypertheorized in order to rationalize troubled or troubling personal disclosure or to disguise its political motivations (Bernstein 1992, 124–25).

Realistic feminist epistemological theory needs speakers and writers who demonstrate how they interrogate their own knowledge and apply theory to or extract it from their own lives and viewpoints, and who "explore the politics of subject construction" through discursive, historical, and ideological means (Bernstein 1992, 142). Marianne Janack suggests some "epistemic virtues" that feminist epistemology should support: "people who care passionately and who recognize the impact of the effects of knowledge production on human lives[,] . . . people who listen sensitively and sincerely to other and divergent perspectives and who can . . . work creatively with the disruption that differences can create" (1997, 137). We need not fight metaphorical fire with fire, turning all professional conflicts into lynching or rape, or all family disagreements into abuse. We can de-escalate the rhetoric and demand accountability for images and metaphors, both from ourselves and from our detractors.

Advocating such guidelines for pursuing knowledge need not dull feminist theory's political edge. As Donna Haraway explains, collective and collaborative knowledge generation should be "power-sensitive, not pluralist . . . [in order to produce] better accounts of the world" (1991, 196). Moya argues that "relinquishing the notion that there is a 'privileged position of oppression that incorporates all other dominations' does not free us of the need to causally relate the intersecting relations of domination that condition our experiences of oppression" (1997, 149). An accurate construction of the world requires oppositional struggles that "call to account the distorted representations of people, ideas, and practices," especially those resulting from "the colonial, neo-colonial, imperialist, or capitalist project" (ibid., 140).

Thus, the realistic generation of knowledge is not a calm quilting bee, with everyone affixing her own equally examined subjective patch. If quilting is the right metaphor, then this is a contested affair, with people offering, retracting, restitching, or reselecting their patches, some patches blending into others or covering them with finer cloth. And the whole, should it ever be completed, will enter a juried show, where others will scrutinize, judge, and possibly reconstruct it indefinitely.

Realistic Constructions of Differences among Women

Utopian constructions of difference lead us to utopian conceptions of identity and tempt us to make utopian claims about knowledge construction and knowledge validity. Realistic feminist theory interrogates both the composition and utility of difference claims, finding surprising similarities in some quarters and constructing effective coalitions, despite differences, in others. On the higher ground of such theory, the most obvious distinctions among women no longer camouflage more important connections. We require accountability for all arguments and knowledge claims.

At the same time, however, as Diane Fowlkes suggests, realistic feminist theorizing acknowledges the role of social location in the construction of the individual and her knowledge, even as it comprehends the "self's" inner multiplicity. It recognizes that experiences contribute to each individual's or group's knowledge of the world, but in no unmediated or predictable way. On the higher ground of feminist theorizing, no social location is exempt from scrutiny and no account of experience is regarded as transparent truth.

THE DISCOURSE OF LINGUISTIC CONSTRUCTION

The world is more than a text. Theoretical interpretations of the world must operate within different parameters than those of literary criticism. Although both theories of life and theories of literature are necessarily dependent on conceptual schemes that are themselves structured by language and, hence, contestable and contingent, theories of life must deal with more than the free play of signifiers.
—Mary Hawkesworth, "Knowers, Knowing, Known: Feminist Theory and Claims of Truth"

Woman cannot just be reduced to the lack of the phallus because the metaphors through which she is represented produce an always-shifting reality. . . . What shifts in language . . . cannot be definitively stabilized.
—Jacques Derrida quoted in Drucilla Cornell, "Gender, Sex, and Equivalent Rights"

Framing the Issue

Utopian critics might, at this point, feel that I have set myself a trap. They have undoubtedly noticed my evocation of linguistic construction in the pursuit of realism, despite my having associated that concept with utopianism. To an extent, they would be justified in gloating. I have indeed identified linguistic reform as a realistic force. I have also observed that language creates misperceptions of gender, race, sexuality, and other identity categories and have defined language as a means of reformulating such identities in realistic feminist theory. In addition, I have focused on modes of representation as constitutive elements of race, class, and gender—as well as their complex intersections—in American society. I have also supported new rhetorical practices, such as metaphorical restraint and the interrogation of experience as a discursive construction. Finally, I have used an essentially linguistic metaphor—translatability—to establish continuities among cultures and groups of women.

Such critics would be wrong, however, to conclude that my recognition of language as a key player in the construction of realistic feminist theory is necessarily utopian. Utopianism enters the picture when all agents of both social construction and social change are reduced to language or when change is envisioned as only or primarily a function of resignification or when the newly signified world is assumed to be free of oppressive structures, constitutive conventions, or conceptual errors, such as foundationalism and coherentism. My observation in chapter 4 that eliminating biological explanations for gender would not necessarily end prescriptive discourse about gender norms demonstrates that I have bestowed no such exemption.

Realism in feminist theorizing does not preclude recognizing the key role of language in the construction of oppressive gender norms or racial or sexual categories. Realistic feminist theory can recognize a reason without "reduc[ing] the multiplicity of reasons to a monolithic 'reason,'" according to Mary Hawkesworth. Realism may recognize that cognition depends on language and that facts are "theoretically constituted propositions"; yet, it need not conclude from those observations that life equals language (1989, 549–50).

Likewise, realistic feminist theory need not engage in "the postmodernist tendency to reject all reasons *tout court*" (Hawkesworth 1989, 556). That language is constitutive of reality does not necessarily threaten the very existence of meaning or reduce meaning to predetermined, arbitrary, or idiosyncratic assignments of terms. That language is constitutive of reality does not mean that language does all the speaking without human agency, or that all depictions or representations of reality are equivalent, or that no standards for determining truth can exist. Rather, as Hawkesworth explains, critical feminist epistemology, "keenly aware of the complexity of all knowledge claims, must defend the adoption of a minimalist standard of rationality that requires that belief be apportioned to evidence and that no assertion be immune from critical assessment. . . . The need to debunk scientistic assumptions about the unproblematic nature of the objective world does not require the total repudiation of either external reality or the capacity for critical reflection and rational judgment" (ibid.).

Indeed, even postmodern theorists recognize that language's role in constructing reality is not unique. For example, legal scholar Mary Joe Frug explains: "For me, the promise of postmodern legal feminism lies in the juncture of feminist politics and the genealogy of the female body in law. It is in this juncture that we can simultaneously deploy the commonalities among real women, in their historically situated, material circumstances, and at the same time challenge the conventional meanings of 'woman' that sustain the subordinating conditions of women's lives" (quoted in Johnson 1992, 1080).

For Frug, language's power is neither absolute nor complete. It intertwines with other constitutive factors—"material circumstances"—that may well contradict its power to sustain women's subordination.

Implicit in Frug's statement is the importance of realities that exist despite and apart from conventional linguistic designations, in this case conventional meanings for and associations with the word *woman*. Language alone does not have the power to enforce boundaries around women's lives. Even Derrida admits that the metaphorical nature of language renders any linguistic construction unstable and therefore constructive of an "always-shifting reality." There will always be more to woman than meets the word.

First Steps: "Words Are Mere Words"

Sometimes reality is a question of language or semantics, but often it is not. "*Words are mere words,*" Kenneth Burke reminds us. "Nothing could be farther from 'food,' for instance, than a mere word for it" (quoted in Heath 1986, 93). There are things in the universe that would exist even if "'all ability to use words (or symbols generally) were eliminated'" (quoted in Schiappa 1993, 406). "'The Universe displays various orders of recalcitrance' to our interpretations, and we are forced to amend our interpretations accordingly'" (quoted in ibid., 409).

Thus, many feminist theorists have taken the first steps toward higher ground by acknowledging that language and nondiscursive reality co-exist in constant tension. Maaike Meijer identifies that tension as a dialectical relationship between representation and reality (1993, 368). Elizabeth Gross discusses an interproductive connection between language and reality. Although language helps create oppressive systems, Gross points out, oppressive systems also construct language (1987, 202). Sonya Rose describes a "'double vision of text and context'" (quoted in Canning 1994, 380). Judith Walkowitz suggests "that material reality is a force that pressures and destabilizes the discursive domain, requiring representations 'to be reworked, shored up, reconstructed'" (ibid.).

Conflicting theories of rape can illustrate feminist concern with the tension between material and discursive reality. On one side is Mary Hawkesworth's (1989) resistance to the conflation of language and the material realities of battery and assault: "Rape, domestic violence, and sexual harassment . . . are not fictions," she declares (555). On the other side is Sharon Marcus's (1992) criticism of Hawkesworth, which suggests that we "understand rape as a language and use this insight to imagine women as neither already raped nor inherently rapable." Otherwise, Marcus argues, rape becomes an "inevitable material fact of life." To prevent that kind of self-fulfilling prophecy, we can recognize rape as a process that is constructed through "rape scripts" and work to counteract those scripts by exploring the "narratives, complexes and institutions which . . . structure our lives" (387–89).

Lurking within the contrast between the two theorists' views, however, are hidden connections. Close inspection reveals that Marcus is actually arguing for a "continuum" theory of sexual violence, in which language is not seen as the equivalent of violent acts. She identifies terrain between the verbal threat and the act of rape where a woman can intervene or "overpower and deflect [through acts and words] the threatened action" (1992, 389). Thus, like Hawkesworth, Marcus ends up distinguishing between language about rape, the act of rape, and the new realities that new linguistic constructions can effect.

That hidden connection points to an even more important paradox to which feminist theorizing about linguistic construction should attend: overcoming the negative effects of discourse that constructs gender or other identities and relationships depends heavily on reengaging with nondiscursive reality—the material causes of oppression and hierarchy. That is, in order to challenge the power of conventional linguistic constructions—from gender terms to rape scripts—we must rely on material evidence from the domains of economics, psychology, or politics. To resignify *women*, for example, we point to the material realities of women's lives—the fact that many women are the sole support of children, for example—that are obscured by existing language, which merely sexualizes them or reduces them to objects.

Separating discursive from material reality, in a utopian approach to linguistic construction, sacrifices the concepts of *agency* and *justification*. Giving language the ultimate power to form identities, relationships, and social structures, as discussed in chapter 4, turns speakers into puppets controlled by the language that precedes them and forms the very consciousness with which they know themselves and the world. They are isolated in a universe constructed by their own experience (which is, in turn, a linguistic construction), unable to communicate beyond its boundaries or to know others trapped in their similarly constructed cages. As Laura Downs explains, ours becomes "a world where no one can apprehend the whole because no one can know (or approach) that which exceeds the bounds of her own experience" (1993, 417).

By the same token, if language speaks us, rather than the other way around, and reality is a matter of linguistic manipulation, then there is no way to judge truth or value. A purely linguistic world includes no

Archimedean points outside of its own terms and definitions by which to provide justification.

AGENCY

Realistic feminist theorists have lamented the death of the subject in linguistic constructionist theory and called for exploring anew the idea that speakers can be agents in constructing their lives, the world, and reality itself. Among them is Nancy Hartsock, who believes that "our various efforts to constitute ourselves as subjects . . . were fundamental to creating the preconditions for the current [feminist] questioning of universalistic claims." Hartsock's observation is not tantamount to "calling for the construction of another totalizing and falsely universal discourse," however. Such a conclusion would condemn feminism to "the alternatives posed by Enlightenment thought and postmodernism: either one must adopt the perspective of the transcendental and disembodied voice of Reason, or one must abandon the goal of accurate and systematic knowledge of the world. Other possibilities exist and must be . . . developed" (Hartsock 1987, 204–5).

Kathleen Canning also sees the need to redeem agency: "Now that the linguistic turn has stripped agency of the 'baggage' of the autonomous enlightened individual," she writes (1994), "it should undergo the same kind of rethinking and rewriting as the terms *experience, identity,* and *class.*" Like Sherry Ortner, Canning wants to understand how the subjects of history have "pushed back" against their historical and political locations (377–78).

Sandra Harding's concept of the traitorous identity, in which we deliberately challenge our own socially/linguistically constructed identities, illustrates subjects' "pushing back" against their own historical locations and preconceptions. "Whites as *whites* can provide 'traitorous' readings of the racial assumptions in texts—literature, history, science—written by whites," she explains ([1991] 1993, 156). Agency depends on intellectual work and political activity that feed one another. Action and interaction can create new knowledge and explode existing discursive conventions (ibid., 157).

Further, subjects are not simply constructed by powerful forces "from the top down," as Foucault seems to suggest. Laura Downs resists definitions of subjects as "either the radically separate selves of a frozen master-slave dialectic or [as] useful fictions, produced by the will to discover the truth/power immanent in the metaphysics of truth" (1993, 435). Instead, Downs explores the way subjects are constructed "through means other than a one-way exercise of power." She investigates gaps between the discourses of power and the way power actually works (ibid., 425). For example, in analyzing Carolyn Steedman's *Landscape of a Good Woman,* Downs notes how fractures in the welfare-family system create "spaces in which working-class children learn something different, something other than that which the system seeks to impress upon them." Thus, the lives of those children can follow very different trajectories than those prescribed for them in a deprived childhood (ibid., 431, 424).

In Jessica Benjamin's *Bonds of Love,* Downs sees a similar gap between agency and discursive forces. Benjamin rejects Freud's narrative of a death dance between an insatiable infant and a servile mother and postulates instead a "chain of dialectics: the child demands, the mother is independent; the mother is seductive, the child is free; the mother supports the child in hands which both hold and restrain the wriggling energy of the infant" (1993, 428–29). Neither capitulates fully to the force of the other; both learn from the other's exercise of cooperation and will.

The consequence is a fissure between the discourse of male power and its reality "on the ground." Steedman recognized that gap as a child when she saw the difference between her father's personal weakness and vulnerability, because of his class position, and the cultural scripts about fathers and masculinity. For Benjamin, the gap occurred between Freud's discourse about a mother's role in the Oedipal phase and her own clinical observation of mothers exhibiting their own desires—"the stuff of which agency is made" (1993, 428–33).

Canning's analysis of female factory labor in late Imperial Germany further illustrates the intersection of constructed and independent, complicit and resistant subjectivities. In many public discursive ways, women factory workers were constructed by social reformers to suit the state's attempts to respond to the rapid expansion of German industry. But that language did not fully constitute the reality of the female labor force. Rather, the workers made their own meanings about their work and work identities in "everyday struggles over pride and honor, gossip and respectability, bodies and sexuality, charity and tutelage—through which workers adapted to subverted ordained locations within the factory regime." They displayed both complicity and resistance (including discursive resistance). Each worker occupied multiple subject positions at any given moment (Canning 1994, 383–84).

Put another way, a realistic view of the gaps and tensions between language and nondiscursive reality recognizes *us*, the women who received all the same messages as our more presumably compliant sisters did but who resisted, reconstructed, reacted, rebelled. (Claims that rebels got different messages only reinforce the existence of gaps in hegemonic linguistic control.) A utopian either-or view of the speaking or historical subject overlooks or undertheorizes the forces that create rebels, as Marilyn Frye has done in attributing only to lesbians the ability to discern "the truth" about sexuality while implying that others have been manipulated, even duped, by messages of compulsory heterosexuality.

Accounting for the complex ways in which individuals and groups receive and adapt cultural messages becomes increasingly difficult as the reach of technology extends ever more widely across the United States and around the globe. It becomes less and less possible to describe what message set(s) any person or group absorbs in the midst of the ever-expanding visual, verbal, and practical clues we receive about possible identities, behaviors, and lifeworlds through TV, print media, movies, the Internet, and the World Wide Web. Utopian notions of enforceable linguistic orthodoxy become less and less realistic in our media-saturated world.

JUSTIFICATION

Also compromised in a strictly linguistic constructionist approach to feminist thought is *justification,* or the validation of propositions and the connection of conclusions to evidence. On realistic theoretical ground, as we have seen, justification and reasoned argument are compatible with other forms of knowledge construction, such as intuition and practical knowledge. Moreover, on realistic theoretical ground, justification and reasoned argument are necessary to prevent feminist theorizing from becoming feminist fanaticism. Mary Hawkesworth suggests an additional benefit. Now that "the preponderance of rational and moral argument sustains prescriptions for women's equality," she argues, it would be too cruel and reactionary "to accept that reason is impotent, that equality is impossible. . . . In confrontations with power, knowledge and rational argumentation alone will not secure victory, but feminists can use them strategically to subvert male dominance and to transform oppressive institutions and practices" (1989, 557).

Nevertheless, realistic theorizing must accommodate the challenges to concepts of rationality and justification represented by the reasonable claims of linguistic constructionists and feminist standpoint epistemologists that no neutral language or standpoint exists. If a detached objectivity is impossible, we must define the grounds on which rational standards can be constructed.

Language Communities Revisited

To undertake that project, we once again turn to the concept of epistemological community. If all knowledge is partial and limited, then truth, especially social truth, is unlikely to be discovered by an isolated individual knower. In order to determine standards of evidence, criteria of relevance, and strategies of argumentation, then, knowers can benefit from consultation with others in different social locations.

That process requires more than identifying "situated knowledges," to use Donna Haraway's term; it depends on pooling multiple and diverse situated knowledges and seeking surprising and unusual points of view. Such a collective approach is most likely to produce "sustained, rational, objective enquiry," a "passionate detachment" that rejects easy relativism and holism (Haraway 1991, 191–92). Also crucial is the notion of examined subjectivity, which replaces epistemic privilege. As we pool knowledge, we must recognize that neither the subjects nor the objects of knowledge are fixed or stable. Both are complex and occupy multiple, even contradictory, standpoints simultaneously. The process is further improved if knowers deliberately adopt knowledge standpoints that are different from their own so they can evaluate their own perspectives. According to Sandra Harding, "Understanding ourselves and the world around us requires understanding what others think of us and our beliefs and actions, not just what we think of ourselves and them." To that end, she prescribes "strong objectivity," consisting of "systematic methods of locating knowledge in history" (1993b, 50, 66–67).

Knowledge communities, like other realistic approaches, must, however, be pursued with caution. Helen Longino and Lynn Hankinson Nelson, for example, warn about the danger of developing utopian coherentism within such communities. To avoid that danger they recommend subjecting whatever standards of evidence are used within a community to continual scrutiny. They also recommend that individuals participate in numerous different communities in order to experience varying points of view and that multiple communities interact in order to prevent coherentism (Nelson 1993, 150). Such multiple and interactive knowledge communities can help to undermine specious arguments and claims, such as creationism, because such ideas cannot bear widespread scrutiny and criticism. At the same time, a broad public base also helps to ensure that politically marginal positions are not dismissed as crackpot (Longino 1993, 118).

Surprise! Language Communicates!

Underlying a belief in collective knowledge production is a notion that challenges those linguistic constructionists who regard language as merely the bars on conceptual prisons. In the communal approach to knowledge, the same language that constructs reality is also a vehicle of communication through which "boundaries of difference" can be reconstructed and "subject, knowledge and community" can be reconfigured (Downs 1993, 435). Such a view identifies language as the key to the "gates" as Anzaldúa calls them, in the fences that language also helps to construct between us. Through such gates, Anzaldúa continues, we can create "feminist architecture" (quoted in Fowlkes 1997, 119). Thus, accompanying its scripts that limit human interaction is the "public nature" of discourse that facilitates connection through the exchange of ideas, insights, and perspectives.

That simple (even obvious) point does not render communication a simple matter, however. It modifies claims of resignification by fiat with a focus on persuasion and dialogue. Edward Schiappa explains, for example, that "the whole process of producing scientific knowledge involves generating discourse and persuading fellow scientists to accept one's claims" (1993, 418). Nancy Love borrows Habermas's theory of "communicative rationality" to discuss the complexity of communicative processes. For Habermas, communicability depends upon exchange in "extra-foundational space" where, despite their heterogeneity, subjects are constructed as symmetrical in their power to assert, dispute, reveal, conceal, prescribe, and conform.[11] What results in such exchange would be "con-sensus" based on "'problematic and unclarified presuppositions.'" Far from easy truths or bland agreements, such con-sensus is necessarily "'diffuse, fragile, continuously revised'" (quoted in Love 1991, 98–99).

Thus, the communicability of language does not eliminate its ambiguity. Nor does it eliminate contradiction. On the contrary, realistic theories of linguistic construction violate the traditional epistemologi-

---

11. It is possible to see utopian connotations in Habermas's conception of "extra-foundational space." In reality, all subjects do *not* have symmetrical power; nor are all voices heard in symmetrical ways. I prefer, however, to focus here on Habermas's definition of "consensus" and to address his utopian point in chapter 7.

cal *principle of noncontradiction* which states that "no being can both have and not have a given characteristic at one and the same time." They recognize instead what Thomas Quine calls "ontological relativity," in which "the same stimuli can [indeed] possess different, even contradictory, meanings. . . . 'Things' can both be and not-be at the same time." Once language abandons absolute meaning, and once meaning varies depending on differing frames of reference, then opposed realities will inevitably co-exist (Schiappa 1993, 413–15).

Unlike utopian thinking, however, which confines meaning to discrete boxes and recognizes few shared borders, realism welcomes contradictions as sites of opportunity, as in the reconsideration of *sisterhood* in feminist theory discussed in chapter 2 and again in this chapter. That meanings are never absolute inspires us all to withhold judgment, to request explanation, to exchange lifeworld observations, and to adjust usage to accommodate varied historical or practical sensibilities.

Realistic Approaches to Linguistic Construction

Linguistic constructionist views have roots in Saussurean theories of language that recognize both its arbitrary nature—based on the arbitrary relationship between the signifier and the signified—and the power of *langue* (the symbolic system that preexists speaking subjects) over *parole* (or the local, historical utterances of any individual or language community).[12] From those premises has evolved a sense that meaning is produced less by what's "really out there" than by the relationship of signifiers to one another. According to theorists in this poststructuralist school, speakers may think they are inventing meaning as they speak the language, but the language is really expressing itself through them.

While the arbitrary and essentially symbolic nature of language can lead to utopian conclusions—what Hawkesworth and others have called the path to escapism and nihilism—they need not do so. The problem—linguistic construction—is not necessarily the source of the solution. Precedent exists for other approaches. Kenneth Burke is among those who have pursued an alternative path. Although he shares with poststructuralists and postmodernists the belief that

---

12. Again it is important to distinguish between linguistic theories and theories of discourse analysis. Linguists are no longer interested in Swiss linguist Ferdinand Sassure's poststructuralist approaches, but discourse analysis has clearly developed from many of his premises (Cameron 1998, 966).

"language develops by metaphorical extension," and that images for the new build upon existing images of the old, he does not conclude that human beings therefore have no agency or that reality can be reduced to language (Schiappa 1993, 406). Rather, he recognizes what linguist Deborah Cameron describes as "extra-linguistic" forces and social practices that construct both reality and discursive situations (Cameron 1998, 970).

Even Foucault, whose work is strongly identified with "battles among discourses and through discourses," recognizes certain extradiscursive domains, such as sexual desire, repressed knowledges, and unthinkable or unformulated experiences that can serve as sources of truth and motivations for new knowledge. Because of such counterforces, Foucault admits that socialization can never be complete; "there is always scope for a kind of 'agency' that might form new interests/desires" (Assiter 1996, 140).

Perhaps what separates a Burke or even a Foucault from utopian linguistic constructionists is a kind of hubris. Realistic linguistic constructionists recognize that their knowledge of the mechanisms of language can never be sufficient to explain the world and people's relationships to it and to one another. Even knowing what we know, some mystery and much misinformation remains. Indeed, linguists themselves recognize how their own preconceptions—such as the importance of gender to speech—skew their research into language structure, acquisition, and use (Cameron 1998, 960). Thus, all observation of language is loaded from the start.

Realistic feminist theorists can afford to assert the importance of linguistic construction without also asserting its foundationalism. We can afford to admit that much lies beyond our representations or perceptions of the world, and that we welcome other, even contrary perspectives to enrich our own. We must be accountable for the conclusions we reach although we recognize them as provisional. We can afford to admit that even given our best collective efforts, we may never identify let alone comprehend all the relevant factors that construct gender identity or sexuality or the many other issues at the heart of feminist theory. No matter how striking our metaphors may be, they might be misguided. No matter how elegant our theories, we must entertain counterexamples, challenges, and contrary evidence. Indeed, we must invite them. Not to do so exposes us always to dangerous utopian traps.

THE HIGHER GROUND OF REALISM

Although realism is not a destination in feminist theorizing, it does constitute a recognizable journey. As this chapter has demonstrated, realistic feminist theorizing works to balance material forces (including individual psychology, economics, politics, and nature) with the forces of representation (including linguistic and visual images) in the construction of theories about women and gender. Realistic feminist theorizing recognizes that, even as gender is its main concern, gender, as well as race, class, sexuality, and age, has variable meanings and levels of significance depending on particular social and personal contexts. It makes no presuppositions of difference, either between the sexes or among women. It understands the multiple components of gender identity. It regards the category *women* as complex, as constituted by variables of race, ethnicity, and social and geographical location, but it does not therefore deny the possibility of commonality or coalition. Nor does it assume a transparent meaning for the variations among women.

As a process of thought, realistic feminist theorizing continuously questions both the existing world and its own attempts to enact social and cultural change. It regards feminism's flexibility and adaptability to myriad lifeworlds and locations as strengths. Among its greatest contributions is its insistence on denaturalizing inherited truths and truisms, including feminist truisms. It is strongest when it criticizes its own foundations along with those of its antagonists and detractors.

The intellectual history of realism as a concept is useful for feminist theorizing because it raises so many of the issues that lie at the heart of feminist thought. Debates about realism emphasize the relationship of language to reality and the interaction of abstract systems, such as law, with human interpretations and behaviors. Debates about realism remind us that we cannot discount the power of the knower in the formation of the known, even as we must accept the existence of the unknown and (possibly) unknowable that lies beyond human comprehension. Yet, those debates also remind us that we have a responsibility to formulate usable, workable knowledge even in the face of uncertainty. We can neither fully accept nor wholly discount the words with which the world is depicted. Rather, we must recognize the gap between representation and the represented and evaluate knowledge according to the clearest and most critical thought at our command.

IV BEYOND FEMINISM

INTRODUCTION

A healthy dose of . . . suspicion towards one's political beliefs is no form of cynicism, or nihilism, but rather a way of returning politics to the fullness, the embodiedness, and consequently the partiality of lived experience. I wish feminism would shed its saddening, dogmatic mode to rediscover the joy of a movement that aims to change the form of life.
—Rosi Braidotti, "Feminism by Any Other Name"

The world of feminist thought and theory is vast, but it is not the whole world. Nor should its focus—even on the issues that most concern feminism—be limited only to its own constructions and conclusions. In every way, feminist thinkers must look beyond feminism if we want to ensure the survival of feminist ideas and increase their influence on the course of social change, either locally or globally. The realistic project of feminism is unlikely to succeed unless it is pursued within a larger realistic political and cultural context.

In chapter 7, which constitutes the main body of part IV of *Higher Ground,* going beyond feminism entails, first, extending the analysis of utopianism and realism to cultural domains and concerns of the wider society. Feminist thinking is not alone in its attraction to utopian thought. Thus, chapter 7, "Confronting the Culture of Utopia," explores many instances of utopian thinking, with a special emphasis on three examples—the culture wars, multiculturalism, and the Promise Keepers. It also suggests alternative, realistic ways to address the issues embedded within these examples. Such explorations beyond feminism offer practice in developing a utopia detector as well as techniques for realistic thinking, which I hope will serve readers well long after they close these covers.

Second, chapter 7 looks beyond feminism in Rosi Braidotti's sense of developing a "healthy dose of suspicion" toward our own political beliefs. Healthy suspicion involves the kind of balancing and critical thinking discussed in part III of *Higher Ground,* as well as methods for the continuous reexamination and reevaluation of cherished goals and foundational principles, including any that might emerge from this book. In addition, healthy suspicion motivates us to go beyond feminism and consider compatible political processes that facilitate feminist desires "to change the form of life." Because feminism(s) will not prevail in the absence of overall support for social justice, chapter 7 confronts the culture of utopia by formulating realistic feminist political strategies in terms of general liberatory strategies for social change. Building on the work of Howard Winant, Nancy Hirschmann, Iris Marion Young, Michael Sandel, Nancy Fraser, Drucilla Cornell, and David Hollinger, chapter 7 proposes processes that accommodate the changing nature of social values and cultivate diversity, ambiguity, and complexity. With any luck, such approaches to realistic feminist social change will not only succeed but also help us to rediscover the joy of the feminist movement that Braidotti believes we have lost.

SEVEN   *Confronting the Culture of Utopia*

*No matter how many levels of consciousness one reaches, the problem always
goes deeper.*
—Shulamith Firestone, *The Dialectic of Sex*

Feminism is by no means the only cultural site that attracts and nurtures utopian thought. Indeed, utopianism is all around us. Shulamith Firestone offers a key reason for identifying that thought wherever we find it: almost any serious problem is bound to be more complex than our analysis of it, no matter how good that analysis may be. Although her insight might seem obvious, it is all too often overlooked. No matter how much we recognize that the most serious problems and injustices we face are also the most complicated and that human insight is time- and place-limited, often reductionist, and clouded with politics and self-interest, we are constantly offered utopian solutions for life's thorniest dilemmas that fail to accommodate those realities. By the time utopian solutions reveal their undersides, however, long after complexity has been reduced to dichotomy, polarization, and idealization, it is often too late.

Among the most familiar utopian voices around us are those of politicians wishing for the good old days (when kids behaved, and men and women knew their roles) or waving magic wands by proposing quick fixes (such as hooking every kid to the Internet or putting more police officers on the streets) to wipe away failure, misery, and risk. But following such leads seldom produces the promised results or accounts for their costs—the repressions and oppressions that propped up the so-called Golden Age or the limitations and unintended consequences of the quick fix.

One recent utopian policy, California's Proposition 209—the anti–affirmative action law enacted in 1996—invited the public to "remember" a time when neither color nor gender mattered and only the meritorious received competitive educational and employment opportunities. But few voters asked for proof of Proposition 209's accuracy or an analysis of its possible unintended consequences, which may well include reducing the emphasis in California (and other states) on quantitative admissions standards, such as S.A.T. scores, for all college applicants (Rosen 1998, 62–63).

Proposition 209 and other similarly utopian political appeals to an alleged Golden Age frequently overlook the significance of changing social values: what passed for justice before affirmative action policies were implemented does not anymore. Too many Americans, including Californians, of all political persuasions now recognize the educational and social benefits of a diverse student body. Slow, individual achievement in a world that is still demonstrably stacked against the success of women and minorities no longer represents acceptable progress (Rosen 1998, 62–63).

In addition, utopian thinkers all around us mistake problem reversal for problem solution. Recent debates about welfare reform offer an example: people receive welfare because they don't work; therefore, to eliminate welfare, everyone should be required to work. Such apparent logic is attractive, and it may even succeed for some recipients. But how can it not be riddled with fallacy? The "solution" depends upon the narrow claim that welfare does more harm than good, primarily by robbing recipients of their initiative. Thus welfare itself becomes the reason that people go on welfare. To accept that tautology means at the very least to overlook other structural reasons that welfare recipients do not work, to ignore the fact that some welfare recipients will never be employable, and to assume that jobs are available for which most recipients could qualify and from which they could earn a living wage.

Utopian voices can also be heard in the pronouncements of tyrants. Pol Pot, for example, proclaimed Year Zero in 1975. He pronounced his black-shirted troops the agents of a new utopia, equal to all that is good in the universe and destructive of all that is evil. To achieve that utopia, two million Cambodians had to lose their lives. In the absence of democratic means for national self-examination or for leadership succession, a lack typical of societies constructed on utopian precepts, such rulers can equate themselves personally with the virtues of the state and render unthinkable any challenges to their power. Under such circumstances, leaders change only at the point of a gun (if then). New leaders promise an even more perfect state, thereby perpetuating the utopian-totalitarian pattern. Without mechanisms for reexamination and accountability, charisma can become dictatorship and even great social ideas can become tools of abusive power. Add the utopian charismatic leader to a utopian monoculture and the result is totalitarian fanaticism.

Political negotiation at home and abroad is often stymied by utopian voices that too quickly judge and label all sides in a dispute, thereby committing the utopian *ad hominem* logical fallacy. How many situations on the world's political stage might be altered if utopian categorical assumptions and proclamations were complicated, if fewer "our sides" were romanticized and "their sides" demonized? How many differing values and interests might better co-exist, or even benefit one another, if national or ethnic identities were redefined as provisional and multifaceted rather than fixed? How often have our own utopian attributions to our "enemies" left us gaping in surprise? Many Americans, for example, including the C.I.A., were astonished to discover at the end of the Cold War that the situation in the Soviet "evil empire" was very different from our construction of it.

Utopian voices are not always as loud and obvious as those of Pol Pot or even welfare-reform enthusiasts. Sometimes they appear primarily as inflections and tones, or as tendencies and proclivities. Utopianism can be a habit or symptom. It can be a longing, as for the perfect society, or an assumption, as in the belief that dissent or debate would undermine social perfection. It can prevent us from examining or reevaluating our favorite foundational principles or make us believe that any system or ideology can fully account for life's nuances and complexities. Utopianism can make us think that history either begins or ends with us or our group, believe that human beings can be molded entirely by social forces, ignore our own present focus when trying to foresee the future, and seek problem solution in problem reversal.

That utopianism is often inspired by the desire for social change, however, does not mean that the desire for social change is in and of itself utopian. As we have repeatedly seen, and shall see again, there are realistic ways to think about social change, and there are realistic approaches to making that change. Realism is less a state of being than a mode of proceeding: respecting the processes by which change should occur, working tirelessly to define the real problems to be addressed, assessing and reevaluating continuously the changes that do occur, insisting on self-knowledge and self-scrutiny, and probing conscientiously all identity labels (right-wingers, capitalists, feminists, etcetera) before we determine who is friend or foe.

Because realistic approaches to social change must be suspicious of all rigid labels, both *utopianism* and *realism* must themselves be constantly monitored. We must explore the fine lines between these categories and recognize their coincidences, interactions, and cross-fertilizations. Realism is not an absolute standard, but rather a useful tool for analyzing thought patterns and tendencies, social plans, and cultural dynamics, and for providing a benchmark for theorizing and future planning.

THE CULTURE WARS

All . . . rules and canons require revision in the light of reason. . . . Those societies which cannot combine reverence to their symbols with freedom of revision, must ultimately decay either from anarchy, or from the slow atrophy of a life stifled by useless shadows.
—Alfred North Whitehead, *Symbolism: Its Meaning and Effect*

Because of the smoke screen of the culture wars, Americans are not prepared for the fact that high-quality education in the coming decades will cost society considerably more, not less.
—Annette Kolodny, "If Harsh Realities Prevail, We All Will Continue to Lose"

The main story about the curriculum is compromise. . . . we are almost all revisionists now.
—Todd Gitlin, "A Truce Prevails; for the Left, Many Victories Are Pyrrhic"

Even if some people in the United States want separate and pure cultures, identities, and histories, they are about 500 years too late.
—Patricia Nelson Limerick, "The Startling Ability of Culture to Bring Critical Inquiry to a Halt"

According to the mass media, Americans have been engaged in a "culture war" for more than a decade. The "sides" have been described and labeled; the lines between positions have been drawn; the military metaphor has been honed to perfection; and Whitehead's prediction of decay and anarchy seems ever nearer to realization. As we prepare for the fray, we have inevitably military responses: Are we generals, victims, or prisoners of this war? Is it a just war? Who will win?

On the face of it, there has been lots of evidence that we are, indeed, a culture at war with itself. Domestic terrorism, as in Oklahoma City, women's-clinic protests and bombings, and assaults on abortion providers and clinic workers, by gunmen like Michael Griffin, Paul Hill, and John Salvi, look very much like a shooting war. Indeed, organized, politically motivated violence is, in fact, war of a certain kind, no matter how sporadic it is or how mentally ill its perpetrators.[1] That is why random terrorism is such an effective political tool, often bringing huge populations to their knees in fear and insecurity. Yet, the "war" metaphor alone may be as damaging to our society as the violent acts themselves, since it inspires a sense of hopeless opposition, generalizes and stereotypes people's feelings and motivations, and typically impedes levelheaded discussion and complex analysis. The war metaphor by itself can create a utopian dualism—a "we" on both sides, which needs nothing so much as an oppositional "they."

The existence of war metaphors in American politics can be attributed in part, according to Deborah Tannen, to the widespread (utopian) belief in the communications industry that truth will emerge from the conflicting rhetoric of two opposing sides of an issue. Tannen disagrees with that belief and laments its effects: "It's a myth that opposition leads to truth when truth does not reside on one side or the other but is rather a crystal of many sides," she writes. "Truth is more likely to be found in the complex middle than in the simplified extremes. . . . The determination to find another side can spread disinformation rather than lead to truth" (1994b, A29).

The media construction of complex social issues into false dichotomies is so powerful, however, that many Americans, including myself, have spent the last decade believing in the war metaphor and accepting the utopian notion that the entire country can be divided into two kinds of people who respond to all issues in predictable and oppositional ways. Both reflecting and constructing that view is the work of

---

1. Three recent books about the abortion controversy in the United States utilize the war metaphor in their titles: James Risen and Judy L. Thomas's *Wrath of Angels: The American Abortion War* (New York: Basic Books, 1998); Cynthia Gorney's *Articles of Faith: A Frontline History of the Abortion Wars* (New York: Simon and Schuster, 1998); and Rickie Solinger's *Abortion Wars: A Half Century of Struggle, 1950–2000* (Berkeley: University of California Press, 1998). As I write this, the first clinic bombing in several years has occurred in Alabama, and the bomber remains at large. So, the war metaphor may remain in use for some time to come.

James Hunter, whose 1991 *Culture Wars: The Struggle to Define America* identifies the two sides of the "war": "the impulse toward progressivism" on one side and "the impulse toward orthodoxy" on the other. Each side, claims Hunter, rests on "different systems of moral understanding . . . [that] always have a character of ultimacy to them." In other words, they are fixed oppositional worldviews reflecting differences in philosophical and theological assumptions about "the meaning of America" (42–43, 50). On the orthodox side is the vocal Religious Right (either Republican or fundamentalist) as well as other less vocal or activist conservative or independent Christians. On the progressive side are the rest of us (religious and political liberals or secular humanists). According to Hunter, the two sides are always and predictably opposed on such issues as homosexuality, gender roles, sex education, school prayer, crime, social justice, affirmative action, poverty, divorce, and abortion. Indeed, these opposed views have even forged alliances across religious denominations in the culture war (1991, 46–47).

As we witness the sporadic political violence of our time, it is easy to accept Hunter's oppositional, religion-based view of American opinion on social issues. But as a utopian construction, such a polarized view should automatically be suspect. It must be scrutinized for its factual accuracy as well as for the implications of its theory of social polarization.

A group of sociologists undertook such scrutiny of Hunter's proposition by probing social attitudes underlying the culture wars. The results of that study by Rhys Williams and others, recounted in *Cultural Wars in American Politics: Critical Reviews of a Popular Myth* (1997), tell a somewhat different tale than Hunter does. That is, on most social issues American public opinion is distributed fairly evenly along a continuum, rather than clustered at the poles. Indeed, even among evangelicals and fundamentalists, there are significant differences of opinion on social issues. Furthermore, Williams and his colleagues found that public opinion varies less according to pre-set, mostly religious ideology than according to the specifics of a particular issue and to the economic and social circumstances of the person holding the opinion (Williams 1997, 284–85).[2]

2. This research appears in Rhys H. Williams (ed.), *Cultural Wars in American Politics: Critical Reviews of a Popular Myth* (New York: Aldine De Gruyter, 1997). Several researchers used pooled data from the National Opinion Research Center's General Social Surveys (G.S.S.) for a spectrum of years from 1974 to 1997. Others developed their own multistate, multiregional, gender-balanced, and multiethnic samples.

Thus, even among orthodox religious people (including whites as well as Latinos, American Indians, and African Americans), opinions vary about the gendered division of labor, race relations, and economic inequality, as well as about family values, and religious affiliation has less to do with the variation than the respondent's race, class, or gender (Davis and Robinson 1997, 57). Since most religiously orthodox people are not wealthy, their economic interest leads them to support such classically liberal actions as governmental programs that "equalize differences between rich and poor and between whites and people of color" (ibid., 40).

Perhaps most surprising is the conclusion that "differences between religious conservatives and religious liberals *declined* during the 1970s and 1980s with significant convergence" on issues such as women's roles, racial integration, sexual conduct, sex education, and legal restrictions on divorce, although (predictably) school prayer remained a divisive issue between the two groups (Dimaggio et al. 1997, 84–85). In fact, "only attitudes toward abortion have become more polarized in the past 20 years, both in the public at large and within most subgroups." But because "abortion attitude measures behave differently than measures of opinion on any other issues," generalizing from the abortion controversy to other issues, or viewing it as "evidence of more deepseated polarization, is profoundly misleading" (ibid., 90).

It may be, then, that a single issue—abortion—is most suited to the "culture war" analysis. Yet, even with that issue, opinions may not be as clearly oppositional as they appear. Indeed, according to a 1998 *New York Times* poll, attitudes toward abortion are complex. For example, even though Americans expressed more reservations about abortion availability and professed anti-abortion sentiments than they had in a survey done nine years earlier, most (58 percent) nevertheless continued to support a woman's right to have an abortion and to respect individual decisions about abortion depending on the circumstances. Even one-third of those who believed that abortion is "murdering a child" also considered it "the best course in a bad situation" (Steinfels 1998, A13).[3]

Adopting the war metaphor for the abortion issue also obscures the magnitude of opinion polarization. According to Williams and his associates, those who prioritize a conservative religious philosophy and oppose abortion in all circumstances comprise only 4 percent of the

3. Detailed poll results appear in the January 16, 1998, edition of the *Times*, pp. A1, A16.

American population and only 9 percent of the Republican Party (Smith et al. 1997, 192). What empowers that 4 percent is what always empowers outnumbered bullies—their willingness to do harm. By threatening revenge at the ballot box or violence in the streets, and occasionally carrying out those threats, a tiny fundamentalist minority has been able virtually to eliminate abortion services and abortion training in mainstream hospitals. Although we must take seriously calls to violence (because of "God's judgment") against Jews, homosexuals, and other groups by such organizations as Pat Robertson's Christian Coalition, and we must respond vigilantly to the theocratic police state such groups advocate, we must not therefore assume that the volume of their voices represents the mass of their support.[4]

Utopianism plays a double role in this issue. First, it infuses the fanatics' ideology, as they idealize the fetus and demonize any pregnant woman who considers abortion at any stage. Second, through the war metaphor's implications of two equal sides, utopianism prevents the rest of us from determining actual numbers. In the assertion of two clear-cut "sides," fed by the media's attraction to a fight, we overlook those numbers, as well as the multiple, conflicting, and intersecting viewpoints that constitute reality. Such widespread complicity with utopian thought strengthens vocal minorities beyond their due.

No one would suggest overlooking religion as a divisive factor in American politics, but sociologists like Rhys Williams suggest that an exaggerated focus on that division obscures other complicating factors. Indeed, Williams argues, if we want to identify the deepest bifurcation in American life, we should look first to political affiliation, not religion. The rhetoric of the culture war is largely a by-product of tactics deemed necessary to build the viable political coalitions that, in turn, support the two major political parties. It is a mistake to take that rhetoric at face value, however, because it is not a reliable guide to public opinion, activist opinion, or even the realities of the coalitions that constitute the parties. Rather, it is "strategically instrumental language" designed primarily to mobilize adherents via the "we-they" dualities that are so familiar in utopianism (Williams 1997, 288).

At one level, then, the most effective utopian force in American democracy may be the two-party system. That is the bad (utopian) news. The good (realistic) news is the counterforce of our political institutions, which tend to have a moderating influence on the dichotomies

---

4. See Bruce Bawer's 1997 *Stealing Jesus: How Fundamentalism Betrays Christianity* (New York: Crown).

of uncompromising conflict. The realities of our democracy require "institutional isomorphism," according to Williams—that is, a centralizing tendency toward compromise and cooperation. In the end, moderation is what we usually get, because "organizational pressures [in our democracy] are centripetal even as ideological tendencies are centrifugal" (1997, 293).[5]

If the researchers in Williams's book have it right, then we can take some comfort from the structures of American political institutions, even as we suffer the agonies of oppositional politics. "Institutional isomorphism" does not mean that our political institutions produce wise compromise on every issue. That such isomorphism exists, however, suggests how important it is to protect political processes that prevent total victory on every issue for any particular worldview, including our own. It also means that the separation of powers is important to just resolutions of intractable issues. It teaches us to cherish and expose the inconsistencies and contradictions as well as the intersections that exist among Americans' opinions on various issues, as well as the ambiguities that characterize each difficult issue.

Given the moderating tendencies of the American political process, feminist activists can consider new alliances, even across the old barriers of utopian polarized thinking. According to Marie Griffith, one such potential alliance might be forged in what would seem to be a very unlikely place: between feminists and Evangelical Christian women. Griffith has studied a group of Evangelical Christian women called the Aglows and discovered that, despite the decidedly nonfeminist implication of their name, Aglows share some interests, attitudes, and projects with their presumed feminist enemies. Needless to say, neither feminists nor Aglows thus far recognize the connection. In fact, Aglows denounce feminists for, among other things, promoting views on sex and reproduction that appear (to them) to absolve men of family responsibility. Nevertheless, Griffith discovered that, despite their determination to bask in the "glow" of their families' and God's love, Aglows, like many feminists, object to the subordination of wives by husbands, refer to each other as sisters, engage in quasi–consciousness raising experiences, celebrate their commonalities as

---

5. Perhaps it is the inevitably moderating effects of American political institutions that led Christian-right spokespersons, such as Ralph Reed and columnist Cal Thomas, to suggest in 1999 that their forces abandon politics as the primary way to influence society toward a conservative agenda. They suggest instead developing parallel social institutions, like home schooling, and influencing elite institutions, like universities and the media.

women, believe feminine activities and affinities should be given greater respect and value, denounce male irresponsibility, express a certain distrust of men, and deplore domestic violence (1997, B7). That some kind of alliance between feminists and Aglows might be possible does not mean that the two worldviews will ever be united, but it does suggest that polarized utopian politics obscure opportunities for convergence that may lurk just beneath the surface.

Multiculturalism

The concept of "culture wars" also exists in the world of higher education, albeit with slightly different meaning. There, too, the war motif reflects divided opinions on a key point—in this case the question of a "multicultural" versus a "traditional" curriculum. As bitter as this fight has sometimes become, however, the multicultural conflict has also been manipulated, according to Annette Kolodny, by conservative forces who wish to cut funding for public education, control the composition of the student body, and shift authority for academic decision making from faculty and administration to regents and legislators. Deliberately obscuring their real motives, such conservatives have succeeded in getting educators to fight among themselves about a presumed conflict, which may not exist, between traditional and multicultural approaches to the curriculum (Kolodny 1998, B5).

Many observers of academia argue that the real academic culture wars are over and that higher education has already lost. Academia and its faculties have been defined unflatteringly by their conservative adversaries, who have set the terms of the debate (Suarez 1998, B8). Faculty have been snookered into performing a familiar utopian dance in which designated role-players attack one another while the real issues are determined beyond the purview of either side.

TRADITIONALIST UTOPIANISM

If it has been a setup, then it has been a brilliant one, because the ostensible issues of the curricular culture wars strike at the heart of what matters to modern educators—diversity, access, and academic integrity. Those issues genuinely engage faculty, students, and administrators who hold out the (possibly utopian) hope that universities can lead society in solving the intractable problems of racism and sexism. Because it has been implicated in producing the problems in the first place, the curriculum has seemed like a good site from which to launch the solution.

To the extent that a truce has been reached concerning the nature of the curriculum, as Todd Gitlin claims, it has been forged on the anvil of utopian polarization.[6] Indeed, the combatants in the real or contrived curriculum culture war have quickly fallen into line with the utopian polarized scheme. On one side are eager proponents of a traditional curriculum, which focuses primarily on Western achievements and literary production as the presumed pinnacles of human civilization. On the other are equally eager proponents of a multicultural curriculum that recognizes and incorporates curricular "newcomers," like women of all races, gays and lesbians, and African American, Latino, Asian American, and Native American males. Multiculturalists question the hegemony of Western history and literature, and traditionalists question the quality of the newcomers' achievements and cultural contributions. Traditionalists question the value of incorporating such contributions at what they see as the expense of a more coherent narrative of human history and time-tested classics.

The two sides of the curriculum culture wars have also frequently characterized one another in utopian terms, portraying their apparently different interests as dichotomous and polarized in the extreme. Traditionalists have characterized multiculturalists as reckless revisionists who would toss out all literature, history, and social science that in any way reflects the traditions of the past. Presented as evidence of their uncivilized behavior is their desire to replace the classics of Melville and Faulkner with the work of such upstarts as Adrienne Rich and Toni Morrison. Such traditionalists are not easily swayed by the fact that Melville and Faulkner themselves were once considered rubes unworthy of serious literary study, or that Toni Morrison has won a Nobel Prize, or that the student body is dramatically more diverse in gender, racial, and ethnic background than in times past.

In the utopian traditionalist view, multiculturalists are Birkenstock-shod advocates of "pigment-privileged programs" and normalizers of sexual deviance, whose decisions about what to study or about how to view United States history can only be motivated by an attitude called "political correctness" (Suarez 1998, B8). Such traditionalists believe that "universities in the United States [have been] transformed by small cabals of political and social radicals who [have] somehow . . . captured venerable . . . institutions of higher learning, converted them to their own agendas, overwhelmed and silenced the vast majority of their colleagues while boards of regents and trustees benignly looked

---

6. See Todd Gitlin, 1998, "A Truce Prevails; for the Left, Many Victories Are Pyrrhic," *Chronicle of Higher Education* 6 (March): B4–5.

on," and that such radicals continue to "mislead generations of gullible and passive college youth who are robbed of their true heritage and thus compelled to stumble forth into the larger world as undereducated and uncultured dupes" (Levine 1996, 29).

Such utopian traditionalists have seen themselves as knights defending the past, the truth, and the quality of education. In his 1987 *Closing of the American Mind*, Allan Bloom, a highly visible traditionalist, accused the student, feminist, and black power movements of the 1960s and 1970s of causing "the collapse of the entire American Educational Structure," thereby evoking images of a utopian Golden Age in mortal struggle with a wholly external evil force.[7] Another self-proclaimed traditionalist, Alan Kors, received a standing ovation at the first meeting of the conservative National Association of Scholars (N.A.S.) in 1988 when he identified as "barbarians" all proponents of multiculturalism, democratization of the university, and feminism. A few years later, Kors warned that the demands of such villains for curricular reform would reinstitute the dark ages. In response to that threat, Kors enjoined his like-minded supporters to preserve "'what is worth preserving amid the barbaric ravages in the countrysides and towns of academe'" (quoted in Levine 1996, 6).

As we have seen, a few self-proclaimed feminists, such as Camille Paglia and Christina Hoff Sommers, have weighed in with the traditionalists by accusing feminists in particular of corrupting higher education. Their attack on an easy target has apparently increased the credibility (and marketability) of the utopian traditionalist cause. In her 1990 book, *Sexual Personae: Art and Decadence from Nefertiti to Emily Dickinson*, Paglia attacks "whining" feminists and charges, "'If civilization had been left in female hands, we would still be living in grass huts'" (quoted in Faludi 1991, 319). So much for studying anything women think or produce. In her 1994 *Who Stole Feminism*, Sommers paints the picture of a feminist cabal in higher education, claiming that "it is now virtually impossible to be appointed to high administrative office in any university system without having passed muster with the gender feminists" (273).

---

7. To demonstrate that the labels applied to the two sides in this battle are inevitably inadequate, I want to note that Bloom's traditionalism about the curriculum included a realistic resistance to the notion that racial differences are in any way absolute. Thus, he resisted curricular innovation partly because he thought it entailed "a dangerous severing of the races in the intellectual world, where there can be no justification for separatism and where the idea of a common humanity must prevail" (1987, 98). Of course, some people would consider such color blindness racist.

Such wild claims and generalizations make good headlines. Thus, the utopian polarization of the curriculum issue has persisted. The pro-oppositional media has been only too happy to validate the rhetoric of people like Kors, Paglia, Sommers, Richard Bernstein, Robert Hughes, Charles Sykes, and Dinesh D'Souza by making such terms as "thought police," "PC claptrap," "feminazis," and "gender feminists" household words. Few in the media call such polemicists to task for substituting sound bites for thoughtful analysis or relying on utopian constructions—such as the evil "them" and the innocent "us"—instead of data. Few note the irony—and utopian boomerang effect—of employing the very slipshod methods they attribute to their foes.

Lawrence Levine's 1996 rejoinder to Bloom's book, entitled appropriately *The Opening of the American Mind*, reveals both the extent of traditionalist utopianism and the weaknesses of its methods. Levine explains that "Allan Bloom presented no evidence whatever to document his assertions that students today appreciate classical music less than they did thirty years ago, or that sexual liberation has robbed them of their ability to relate to the novels of the past, or that students no longer think about or want to visit the countries of Western Europe" (1996, 23). So eager is the American public to buy into utopian proclamations that few of Bloom's readers even asked him to justify his accusations.

Sommers has also been exposed as a data manipulator who checks neither stories nor sources, and who so eviscerates quotations that in her retelling they convey the opposite of their original meaning.[8] For example, to refute feminist claims that wife beating was tolerated in English Common Law, Sommers quotes only the first part of William Blackstone's eighteenth-century explanation of patriarchal familial rule: "The husband was prohibited from using any violence to [*sic*] his wife" (Sommers 1994, 205). Linda Hirschman supplies what Sommers omits, which translated from the Latin means ". . . other than that which lawfully and reasonably belongs to the husband for the due government and correction of his wife," a telling omission indeed (Hirschman 1994, 13). Also hidden by Sommers's pretenses to objectivity (in presumed contrast to her "enemies") is her funding by conservative backers, such as the Olin Foundation; her lack of credentials as an educational researcher; and her disingenuous fabrication of a

---

8. For other critiques of Sommers's work, see *Democratic Culture* 3(2) (fall 1994). Relevant articles include John K. Wilson, "Stolen Feminism?" (pp. 6–8) and "Sommers and Her Conspiracies" (p. 9); Nina Auerbach's "Christina's World" (pp. 10–11); Linda Hirschman's "The Big Lie" (p. 13); Jonathan Entin's "Beyond Polemic" (pp. 14–15); and Celinda Lake's "How Sommers Has Distorted Polls" (p. 17).

feminist self-identity. Evidence of the last includes a statement she made in a 1994 *Esquire* interview, in which she explains the existence of women's studies by saying that the "'homely women in women's studies . . . are just mad at the beautiful girls'" (quoted in Flanders 1994, 3).

MULTICULTURAL UTOPIANISM

Because utopianism rarely resides on only one side of a polarized issue, it comes as no surprise to find self-proclaimed multiculturalists also falling into utopian traps of polarization and self-idealization. Indeed, underlying the label "multiculturalism," as critic Russell Jacoby points out, is a sometimes nonreflective use of the term *culture* and a utopian assumption about *identity* as it is related to culture. Thus, multiculturalists may fail to analyze what it means, exactly, to be a Latina writer, or a woman writer, or what, exactly, constitutes the cultures they represent. Are they distinct structures of work, living, and beliefs, as anthropologists might define them? In what ways do such cultures differ from the hegemonic United States culture in which they are embedded? Are there any significant shared values—such as faith in upward mobility and hard work—among such subcultures of the United States? Do those shared values override differences in any way (Jacoby 1994, B5)? Have multiculturalists taken too literally the provisional distinctions of their own categories and labels and thereby exaggerated divisions and obscured interconnections?

Equally utopian is the multiculturalist emphasis on culture as "a freestanding, self-determining force of its own." In turn, that reification, according to Patricia Nelson Limerick, can represent humans as "automatons [who] march around following culture's inflexible orders." Typical of utopian thought, such a view of culture exaggerates the extent to which human agency results from cultural influences. That exaggeration also "cut[s] the ground out from under intergroup empathy, compassion, fellow feeling, and understanding," as Limerick argues, thereby contributing to the boundary setting common in utopian thought (1997, A76).

Utopian boundary policing, as we have seen in our discussion of identity politics, leads in turn to the utopian idealization and demonization of people based primarily on their membership in particular groups, as well as to the *ad hominem* fallacy. Thus, extremists among multiculturalists have sometimes denounced any and all historical or literary work by "dead white males" and approved too automatically any work by those from the margins of society. Missing in such judgments is a realistic assessment of the exchange of ideas across cultural, racial, and gender boundaries, as when Martin Luther King turned to the essays of Henry David Thoreau in writing his "Letter from a Birmingham Jail."

Exemplifying utopian tendencies for idealization and demonization, certain extremist Afrocentric constructions have idealized African history and isolated it from the white, Western, and presumably imperialist version of that past. Not all discoveries of Afrocentric scholars fall into that category, of course. Indeed, many Afrocentric historians have corrected the historical record and increased the world's awareness of, for example, black Africans' contributions to Egyptian civilization and influence on Greek philosophy. But drifting toward utopianism have been idealized claims about African accomplishments and virtues, on the one hand, and demonized white Western historical obfuscation and invidious intentions, on the other (Pope 1994, B1–3). Often such claims have demonstrated the utopian boomerang effect by adopting the very "sins" of exaggeration and ethnocentricity that infuriate Afrocentric scholars when they appear in scholarship by Western whites.

Some critics identify Martin Bernal's *Black Athena* as an example of Afrocentric excess in its denouncement of whites for deliberately suppressing African contributions to civilization and its claims that Socrates, Cleopatra, and Ramses were black and that Greece stole most of its ideas from African blacks (Egyptians). In making such declarations, Bernal substitutes African rose-colored glasses for Western ones of the same hue. Moreover, he perpetuates the overvaluation of Western historical icons, such as Greece, just as white historians have traditionally done, thereby placing himself and other African descendants directly in the path of the utopian boomerang. After all, such privileging of cultures over one another is what led to the devaluation of Africa in the first place.

In her 1996 refutation of Bernal's scholarship, *Not Out of Africa*, historian Mary Lefkowitz refutes both the particulars of his claims and his cynical view that history is essentially a fiction written differently by each nation or ethnic group solely to aggrandize itself. What is fiction, Lefkowitz argues, is "the ancient Egypt described by Afrocentrists" (1996, xvi). Typical of a utopian *ad hominem* response, one refutation of Lefkowitz's critique is entitled *The Jewish Onslaught: Despatches from the Wellesley Battlefront.*[9]

9. Tony Martin, 1993 (Dover, Mass.: Majority Press).

Multicultural utopian scholars overlook critical distinctions and convergences. For example, Christie Farnham Pope, a white history professor at the University of Iowa, agrees that African contributions have been overlooked in historical accounts, but she disputes the utopian identity politics that has led her black students to reject categorically her right to teach African American history (1994, B1–3). Henry Louis Gates has criticized the self-congratulatory (utopian) thinking of Afrocentric extremists who have turned some black studies programs into "segregated, ghettoized amen corners of quasi-religious feeling, propagating old racial fantasies and even inventing new ones. One of the greater ironies of this situation," Gates continues, "is that the racial ideologies of many Afrocentrists are simply inverted versions of the White racisms of the past few centuries" (1994, 138).

The point of Lefkowitz's, Pope's, and Gates's arguments is not to establish an "innocent" side to contrast with the Afrocentric "guilty" side but rather to establish the grounds on which the multifaceted crystal of historical truth can be based. These critics do not argue that black Africans did nothing to contribute to civilization while white Europeans did it all; nor do they argue that whites have never oppressed Africans or suppressed African history. Such claims, when they occur, are just another utopian version of the debate. Instead, Lefkowitz, Pope, and Gates suggest that the two "sides" work together to ask questions and uncover evidence that reveal the most accurate picture of historical events, recognizing along with Catharine Stimpson that "virtue is the pockmarked, fraught, contested way between two extremes." Stimpson calls for "moderation" in a multicultural curriculum that strives "to teach not one culture, but human similarities, differences, and cross-connections." She also calls for "decorum," which is less "a synonym for remaining imprisoned in conventions" than "the capacity to recognize the nature of all conventions and to assess which matter, to whom, and why" (1994, B2).

ACADEMIC REALISM

Stimpson's comments point the way toward a more realistic version of multiculturalism. The goal is not to declare a cultural "winner," but rather to explore the intricacies of cultural exchange, interchange, and production, and to see how the results of such exchange often transcend their component parts while also recognizing the power differentials that have situated some groups as winners and others as losers in the making of history.

Equally important for realism on this issue is deconstructing the notion of two warring sides in the debate by, for example, revealing overlaps in their concerns. Levine and other so-called multicultural-ists respect many so-called traditionalist views, such as the importance of determining academic excellence, the need to teach mental disci-pline rather than or in addition to particular content, and the desire to identify greatness in human achievement and artistic production. Multiculturalists are simply more likely to ask about the hidden poli-tics of conventional judgments about literary quality and historical significance. They are also less likely to accept the notion of a Golden Age in higher education when American universities were free of cultural influence, even of cultural vulgarities. Levine, for example, points out that universities have always reflected "politically correct" views. Before the 1960s, what was politically correct, and therefore dominant in university curricula, were repressive and prejudiced atti-tudes toward women, minorities, and gays (1996, 28).

A realistic multicultural curriculum would challenge received wis-dom, such as the concepts of "enemies" and "patriotism." Ramsey Clark wonders, for example, how Americans can ever again be moti-vated to fight a war when they can muster sympathy for so many peoples through the literature, art, and history they have studied (Craige 1994, B3). But a realistic curriculum would also embrace the importance of the traditional. Multicultural realism allows us to see, for example, how Ralph Ellison, in writing *The Invisible Man*, "ab-sorbed everything from black folklore to Dostoyevski's 'Notes from the Underground,' creating something entirely new, lasting, and American" (Remnick 1994, 34). It allows us to consider what would have been lost to literature if Ellison, who wrote perhaps the best American novel between 1945 and 1965, had had no opportunity to read Dostoyevski, as well as Eliot, Pound, Faulkner, Hemingway, and Stein (ibid., 36).

At the same time, realistic multicultural lenses allow us to critique apparently progressive or innovative perspectives, as when the Black Arts and Black Power movements of the 1960s and 1970s called Elli-son a race traitor because of his "assimilationist" political views. These movements had a single standard for black genius, one that romanti-cized isolation from the surrounding white culture. Ellison never ac-cepted that standard. Indeed, at the age of eighty, just before his death in 1994, he continued to tout the "constant interplay and exchange" and the unexpectedness of the American experience. "'It just goes to show that you can't be Southern without being black,'" he said, "'and you can't be a black Southerner without being white. . . . There are a lot of subtleties based on race that we *will* ourselves not to perceive, but at our peril'" (quoted in Remnick 1994, 38).

In contemplating realistic multiculturalism, Sheldon Hackney, former director of the National Endowment for the Humanities, decided that jazz is the right metaphor for American society. Like the United States, jazz is both old and new, created from the bottom up, and non-hierarchical. It is *of* one culture—African American—but it speaks to all cultures. Like jazz, America involves individual improvisation in a group setting (1994, A56). If Hackney's metaphor has it right, then it amplifies Patricia Limerick's point earlier in chapter 7: it's too late to rein in the cultural interchange that is at the heart of the American polis. Much too late.

Equally important for achieving a realistic approach to multiculturalism is a commitment to revisit continuously whatever we believe about ourselves as a group or people. Utopian educational tendencies inspire some to whitewash the errors and evils "we" (however defined) might have perpetrated. A shocking example of those tendencies occurred in 1995, when the Smithsonian National Air and Space Museum canceled an exhibition about the atomic bomb because veterans protested the exhibition's criticism of its use in Japan during World War II. John Dower expresses a realistic response to the museum's capitulation to the veterans' concerns by describing the principles he believes must inform all educational activities: "Critical inquiry and responsible revision remain the lifeblood of every serious intellectual enterprise." Serious historians continuously "reconsider and rethink received wisdom." Those maxims are especially important in public institutions, where we cannot allow the fact of tax support to preclude criticism of the American experience. "We must face these terrible ambiguities squarely—and do so at our public, as well as our private, institutions—or else stop pretending to be an honest and open society" (Dower 1995, B2).

The need to reach a multifaceted, self-reflective middle ground between two extremes is certainly one important lesson to be learned from the higher education culture wars. But we should not lose sight of another equally significant lesson from this particular utopian fray. As Annette Kolodny and Ray Suarez remind us, tendencies toward utopianism may have rendered everyone on both sides of the culture war mere pawns in the hands of those who would undermine academia altogether. Utopianism often prevents us from scrutinizing the real problems before us, encourages us to construct eternal verities from our present preoccupations and commitments, and, therefore, makes us suckers for various "let's you and him fight" strategies. Such utopianism has made multiculturalists fear traditionalists and traditionalists fear multiculturalists more than those who disparage them both. As Suarez notes, educators have ignored the real subtext of questions about the "Political Correctness Movement," which has to do with defining the relationship of academic work to the concerns of the middle class, who "were plowing themselves under with loans and on-campus jobs to hang in for the sheepskin." So, while the curriculum fights continued, the academy lost the real war (Suarez 1998, B8). Academics have now joined lawyers as the butt of endless jokes, and public support for higher education has been replaced by ever-growing highway and prison appropriations.

The Promise Keepers

"I'm leaving you and the kids to join the Promise Keepers."

Even today, Americans sometimes get the historical utopian urge to gather in groups and act out a shared social vision. In recent years, that urge has struck thousands of middle-aged men in baseball caps, who have flocked to the outdoor summer rallies of the Promise Keepers. The Promise Keepers' code of seven promises reflect the socioreligious codes of many nineteenth-century utopists who sought individual perfection through new, universally applied familial and social designs. Like many of their utopist forebears, members of the Promise Keepers confess their sins (racial prejudice, domestic violence, marital infidelity, and social isolation) and pledge to change their ways and to live a life of conscience (sexual fidelity, nonviolence, and service). They ask forgiveness from women for having abdicated their God-given masculine roles as family leaders (Abraham 1997, 108). They accept blame for not having fulfilled their promises to God and their communities. Also like most utopian movements, this one has attracted mostly white adherents, although there is some racial diversity in the crowds.

Promise Keepers differs from utopian groups in a number of respects, however. The first difference is its size. From its earliest days, in 1992, when twenty-two thousand men met in the University of Colorado football stadium, to its 1997 membership of 1.2 million, Promise Keepers has hardly been a typical fringe group (Kimmel 1997, 46).[10]

In addition, unlike most utopian groups, Promise Keepers has gained the support of its members' families, including wives and girlfriends (McDonald 1997, 28). Indeed, that support for the men's pledges to practice "spiritual, moral, ethical, and sexual purity" violates the standard of utopian isolation and marginality (Abraham 1997, 55). Perhaps most surprising, even a few feminists have praised the group for allowing men to express their vulnerable, feminine sides. *Ms.* reporter Donna Minkowitz, who attended a Promise Keepers' rally dressed like a boy, saw a suggestion of feminism in that feminine vulnerability. How can society change, she asks, "if men have no support to start acting less like 'men' and more like caring, loving, ethical, and nondominating human beings" (Minkowitz 1995, 67).

Despite such differences from typical utopian organizations, how-

10. As I write this, the Promise Keepers organization is laying off hundreds of employees because of a revenue shortfall. That shortfall has been caused, according to the Promise Keepers, by the elimination of an entry fee to the organization's rallies, a fee that once lined the company coffers. From now on, the group will be primarily a voluntary organization. We will have to see what effect this change will have on the number of attendees at Promise Keeper events.

ever, the Promise Keepers' credo is rife with utopian thinking, which, like most such thinking, can undermine the very reforms to which its members are committed. Primary among those utopian constructions is the Promise Keepers' belief in a Golden Age of family life to which the organization can help all right-thinking Christians return (Abraham 1997, 20). Key to that Golden Age is men's spiritual and material leadership of their families, a role that Promise Keepers claim produced contentment and family harmony in the good old days, in contrast to the family dissolution that has resulted from today's unclear gender roles. As a utopian credo, however, the Promise Keepers' doctrine does not consider the costs and unintended consequences of that Golden Age or question whether it ever really existed. Their doctrine also proposes a single family model and a single model of manhood for everyone, a utopian reversal of the alleged problem of diverse familial and masculine types. Their code also prescribes a single model of gender relations, in which the sexes are fundamentally distinct from one another yet linked through a particular (unequal) relationship, regardless of individual personalities or life circumstances.

Also utopian is the Promise Keepers' assumption that individuals schooled in the group's doctrine can effect dramatic social change. Thus, the Promise Keepers' code urges members to apologize for their own racist actions and attitudes and to perform individual acts of racial reconciliation in order to produce racial justice (Love 1997, 76). That expectation, which exaggerates the potential of the group's members to effect social change, reflects utopian wishful thinking, on the one hand, and apoliticism on the other. Without a program for activism or a structural design for creating a nonracist society, the Promise Keepers are unlikely to produce the results they seek.

Also like other utopianists, the Promise Keepers equate members' dedication to a code of beliefs and behavior with the value of that code. But that equation bypasses members' critical capacities and forecloses scrutiny of the organization's foundational principles, such as the celebration of married men's promise to stop sleeping around (or wanting to) or the assumption that women's sexual fidelity is less remarkable than men's. Nor do they consider what distorted vision of masculinity makes a man's sexual fidelity in marriage such an achievement.

SIN

That utopian pitfall also prevents Promise Keepers from examining perhaps its most utopian, and ironic, foundational principle, its vision of sin. Sin is seen as "out there," a solely external enemy of men. Even though more than a million men have publicly confessed to the sin of sexual infidelity (or temptation to infidelity), the organization sees no reason to believe that sin might exist "in here" or have any connection with behavior and values considered "good." Therefore, the group does not ask its members to probe their own inner lives, motives, intentions, or goals. Nor does it ask them to engage in direct, open communication with the women they have betrayed or otherwise let down. Rather, to eradicate sin, members select three male associates to hear their confessions of sin and direct them toward a better path (Abraham 1997, 48–49). Instead of focusing on improving their intimate relationships with women or on internalizing a genuine desire for sexual fidelity, members of Promise Keepers engage in male bonding. They learn to perform good deeds for male approval.

While such forms of behavior modification can certainly reinforce and produce "good" behavior, they do not necessarily promote good marriages or get to the heart of "bad" behavior. Indeed, they may mask altogether an important reality that is lost in the organization's utopian approach: sexual infidelity might result less from external forces of sin than from certain internalized concepts of masculinity that the group itself perpetuates. Among those concepts is the equation of masculinity with insatiable sexual appetite.

The Promise Keepers' approach to sin promotes utopian problem solving by problem reversal—sinful temptations exist; therefore, sinlessness requires resistance to temptations. But that construction overlooks the fact that sexual fidelity has more to do with committing oneself to a primary relationship in a way that precludes infidelity than with resisting temptation on a daily basis. One *is* faithful rather than *performs* fidelity, just as one *is* physically fit, by *preferring* healthful foods and exercise, rather than *performs* physical fitness by continually *resisting* hot fudge sundaes. A truly committed married man (or woman) asks not "How can I avoid the inevitable temptation to cheat on my spouse?" but, rather, "How can I construct a relationship (and a view of my self and my mate) so that cheating has no appeal?"

WOMEN AND FAMILY

Also utopian is the Promise Keepers' approach to women and the family. As the group defines it, the problem is men's neglect of their families and wives through their abnegation of leadership roles in the household. Their solution is to make men the leaders of their families and of their wives. In other words, men have fallen, so the solution—

a utopian reversal—is to place them on a higher pedestal with women below them. Identifying men's rightful place as head of the family undermines the egalitarian connotation of Promise Keepers' pledges to perform household chores and child care. Their credo of sexual hierarchy takes a utopian leap over several key issues contributing to instability in contemporary family life, including historical changes in family dynamics and social conditions such as women's economic contributions to their families. It ignores the effects of such changes on traditional (even biblical) notions of masculinity and male responsibilities in marriage. It also leaves no room for individuals to decide how their own families might best be managed.

The result is a utopian boomerang. The Promise Keepers' credo of sexual hierarchy backfires because of its historical associations with the very behaviors the organization wants most to eliminate, especially violence. Indeed, studies of domestic violence reveal that families in which decision making is shared by both spouses are less likely to be violent than those in which one spouse makes all the decisions (Berry 1996, 28). Also associated with domestic violence are male expectations that a wife will take full responsibility for housework and child care no matter how much she contributes to the family income (Felder and Victor 1996, 251).

What this utopian credo obscures is the fact that men's family leadership can result in devastating consequences for women that restrict their life options and create debilitating economic dependency. The perception that men and women are necessarily different and must play different social roles also helps to create the sexual stereotypes that interfere with personal growth and genuine, committed relationships (Buss and Malamuth 1996, 182). Such limitations and stereotypes, in turn, set women up to become victims of male violence. Indeed, because the concept of masculine dominance, virility, and superiority requires feminine submissiveness, passivity, and weakness, male dominance has historically depended on force to establish women's subordination (Scully and Marolla [1985] 1996, 289). Furthermore, if male dominance means that the man wishes to control a woman's friends and activities, then it becomes one of the three major causes of spousal homicide (the other two being adultery and jealousy) (Daly and Wilson 1988, 207). Such consequences are not conducive to the family harmony the Promise Keepers seek.

Any prescription for gender hierarchy, therefore, undermines the Promise Keepers' vision of domestic reconciliation. It ignores feminist scholarship that has demonstrated the harm done to women by gender hierarchy. The license to rule another person, no matter how lovingly, tends to objectify her. Her life becomes defined in primarily instrumental terms. To tolerate the uneven bargain implicit in this group's definition of family life, women must ignore contemporary definitions of personhood and train themselves to be obedient when everything else around them, including the divorce rate, conspires to promote self-reliance. I have seen many women who face such a conundrum resort to passive-aggressive behavior in order to exert control in their marriages.

The Promise Keepers' vision also overlooks the fact that few men today can "earn" their headship of the family through providing complete economic support, as they have historically done. The group substitutes a presumed biblical injunction for that traditional role, with men's added commitment to provide service in the home, but neither motivation may ultimately replace the material base of the old economic bargain. Will making the bed, babysitting, cooking a few meals, and taking out the trash earn men familial leadership? Should it? Aren't these "services" (like fidelity) simply part and parcel of a modern marriage?

Given the study of religious believers by Williams and his colleagues, it is hard to imagine religious doctrine alone overcoming the economic and psychological realities of contemporary married life, even if the prospect of turning their lives over to a husband may appeal temporarily to some women. If biblical interpretations do turn out to be more powerful than other realities, however, then the outcome could surprise the Promise Keepers by producing more disharmony and violence than harmony and cohesion in family life, thereby perpetuating the problems the group hoped to solve. That some women accept the Promise Keepers' vision of sexual hierarchy as the price they must pay for men's sexual fidelity and domestic responsibility may say more about those women's desperation than about the solution's effectiveness.

The cartoon that opens this segment of chapter 7 suggests perhaps the ultimate utopian boomerang implicit in the Promise Keepers' design. Any utopian plan risks undermining its mission by making the survival of the organization the paramount goal. An unintended consequence of the male bonding so important to the lure of the Promise Keepers is the possibility that such bonding might become the new life goal for its members, to the even greater detriment of women and families. How ridiculous would it be to have members of the group running off to join a modern version of the circus, leaving wives and children in the lurch? The possibility of such an outcome inheres in the organization's utopian vision, which in many ways misses the heart of the problem it is designed to address.

POST UTOPIA

A civic nation is built and sustained by people who honor a common future more than a common past.
—David Hollinger, *Postethnic America: Beyond Multiculturalism*

The imperfect is our paradise.
—Wallace Stevens, "The Poems of Our Climate"

If I have done my job in this book, then utopianism as a thought process lies in tiny glittering pieces at my readers' feet. As we survey the wreckage together, I can only hope that the other constructs I have built—the alternative ways to think about feminist thought and theory, as well as other social analyses and conflicts—offer consolation for and relief from the loss of inspiring dreams and visions of the utopian past. In this era of sturdy leather boots rather than glass slippers, stepping over such utopian wreckage toward the path of realism should not seem too discouraging, even to the most idealistic of my feminist fellow travelers. But in order to put my argument to rest, and to placate my own enduring utopian longings, I want to tackle one last challenge. I want to begin suggesting an answer to the political questions scattered throughout *Higher Ground:* How do we build a movement or work toward social change based on this book's assemblage of realistic thought processes? How exactly do we think about the future we want to inhabit without falling prey to utopian thinking? What should we *do* about conflicts over values and policy? How do we enact a new social contract or a new form of citizenship that provides the context for realistic social change?

Although the complete answer to those questions lies outside the purview of this book, whose focus is on constructing idea systems rather social institutions, I cannot overlook them entirely. I recognize the limits of carefully wrought but ultimately unverifiable theory, as I witness all around me the continued existence of pain and suffering from both ill-conceived ideas and pernicious policies and practices. In order to support my claims for realism, I must also consider the actions these claims imply.

In thinking about constructing a realistic politics, I must first consider the problems and solutions already proposed in this book. We have seen, for example, the interconnection between material and discursive realities—in the formation of gender identity and even sexuality. We have seen the importance of balancing a recognition of diversity with a sense of women's commonality. We have also, however, seen the treachery of labels in constituting difference as well as in asserting commonality. For example, racial differences construct the sexual division of labor, the concept of male privilege, the definition of housewifery, and even the distinction between public and private spheres. Yet, we can also identify gender issues and experiences, such as sexual harassment, that cross racial, ethnic, and class divides (Eisenstein 1994, 200–202).

We have repeatedly noted the importance of recognizing that all solutions are partial. In seeking social change, we must remember the limitations of our political visions and actions as well as their possibilities. Like feminism, politics and governmental actions are not panaceas. Much escapes their influence. That reality, however, produces its own consolations. For example, it provides a kind of bridge between feminist theorists, like Nancy Fraser, who focus on governmental action and those, like Wendy Brown, who express a healthy skepticism about the prospects of women's involvement with the state. We need both viewpoints. At the same time.

Familiar social values and principles of social change, such as democracy and equality, also present contradictory legacies for a politics of realism. United States democracy carries the taint of imperialism and exploitative global capitalism abroad, and the stench of sexism, racism, and other forms of discrimination at home. In our democracy, some freedoms mask other oppressions; we enjoy freedom of speech, perhaps, but not freedom from want. Proclamations of equality often entail white male standards against which women and minority men are measured and inevitably found lacking. Or such anomalies produce other, more egregious ones, such as the specter of "pregnant persons" in court rulings and legislation.

Clearly, realistic political action must both recognize and transcend such histories and limitations in the political process. At the same time, it must eschew highly specific models and concrete future visions. There is too much we do not know about the problems that exist in our current situation; there is too much about the future we cannot predict. What is left to us, then, is a quest for political processes that accommodate realism's multifaceted demands. We can ask whether a particular process provides for the changing nature of social values or if it appreciates, even cultivates, diversity, ambiguity, and complexity. We can seek to establish a social and political context for general liberatory projects, since in reality feminism(s) will not prevail in the absence of overall support for social justice. We can insist that the politics of the future allow—even require—continuous reexamination and reevaluation of cherished goals and foundational principles, including any that might emerge from this book. We can devise processes that resist pre-existing categories, that lead to appropriately incremental or appropriately revolutionary changes, and that accommodate contradictions and complexities.

Critics might warn that such ideas lead us right back to utopia, but in fact I think they will not. What I propose are processes that foster change by promoting dialogue and by recruiting newcomers as well as new thinking to engage with existing views in the political arena. Such processes provide the best hedge against utopianism because they facilitate as well as adapt to change, accommodate diverse viewpoints, reexamine themselves and the policies and practices they produce, and replace utopian destinations with mutable social journeys. Besides, what choice do we have? We know that change will occur, and we need to find ways to shape it.

Snapshots of Change

Numerous contemporary political theorists concerned with race and gender, such as Howard Winant, Nancy Hirschmann, Iris Marion Young, Michael Sandel, Nancy Fraser, Drucilla Cornell, and David Hollinger, define what I consider to be realistic political processes. (Readers will undoubtedly think of others to add to the list.) Like many utopians, such theorists want to improve the American political system, which all see as flawed. Unlike utopians, however, none of them prescribes building a new social order from scratch. Rather, they propose primarily measured and incremental change that both transcends and respects history. They reject the prospect of a fantasy world. And despite their criticisms of it, they accept the potential (if not the actualization) of United States democracy, with its system of checks and balances on power, its (admittedly unrealized) principle of equality, and its acceptance of continuous political debate. Most importantly, however, all seem to value the foundation of United States democracy in a uniquely diverse population. Indeed, according to Hollinger, diversity is what makes the United States "a model of civic nationality" (1995, 141). For him and others, diversity is the fount from which the other civic virtues can flow, including (perhaps surprisingly) the virtue of a collective sense that binds a society together. *E pluribus unum.*

Without, I hope, distorting the uniqueness of these theorists' complex analyses, I would like to construct a composite of the political processes they recommend as a realistic approach to social change suitable to the complexities and contradictions of feminist thought and theory. As background for such a composite I would choose Winant's "radical democracy project," whose most compelling strategy is the infusion of social-justice projects into the general interests of the society as a whole. Winant wants to transform "the politics of exclusion" into the "politics of inclusion" by articulating "an emancipatory account of the virtues of racial diversity" (1994, 34–36). In other words, Winant transcends identity politics by recommending that liberatory issues, such as racial and gender equity, be "decentered" and intertwined with the general welfare.

Thus, he suggests that women's issues or minority issues be reframed in terms of state-formation or economic-growth concerns, such as the redistribution of resources, the broad extension of democratic rights, and societal control over the state (1994, 31). Winant's strategy eliminates accusations that such issues are special pleading without also eliminating attention to specific harms and concerns of particular groups. Adapting Winant's suggestion, I can imagine framing reproductive policies, for example, as an opportunity to define and redefine citizenship as well as an issue of women's specific rights. Likewise, daycare and welfare policies can be articulated both in terms of their impact on women's ability to engage in economic activity and in terms of the GNP. *Woman* becomes a variable rather than a fixed signifier in such a politics, since it connotes oppression in some contexts and resistance in others (Grewal and Kaplan 1994, 27).

Winant's notion of decentralizing and interconnecting social movements reinforces feminist theoretical appeals to join with various other compatible movements and social goals. It provides a rationale for crossing expected or traditional barriers, thereby subordinating divisive defenses of identity to larger causes, such as democracy and human rights (Chow 1993, 17). Winant's thesis could lead to the connection between feminist activism and antiracist and anticolonial movements worldwide, or even, with a lot more work, to alliances with groups like the Aglows. If Chandra Mohanty's notion of "strategic continuities" among women's lives is valid, such coalitions could be politically fruitful. As Mohanty explains, many women's lives can be connected through such issues as women's work, which both "draws upon and reconstructs notions of masculinity, femininity, and sexuality" (1997, 8).

In addition, Winant's democracy project requires no finite definition of a common good. That indeterminate quality is consistent with Nancy Fraser's warning against selecting *the* feminist good (1993, 20–21). Winant's advocacy of decentering suggests that numerous feminist "goods" can be discovered, articulated, and empowered simultaneously.

At the same time, Winant's emphasis on decentering is compatible with Hollinger's notion of social commonality. *Pluribus* can become *unum* as long as we abandon notions of melting pots or ideal types, either of citizens or of feminists. Instead, according to David Hollinger and Nancy Hirschmann, we must embrace the concept of diversity as a foundation of equality, whose very meaning derives "from individuals' unique and particular ways of manifesting and living out the commonly shared and similarly encoded aspects of experience" (Hirschmann 1996, 63). We must also abandon utopian, oppositional interpretations of difference. Instead, we must consider the extent to which self-interest in a diverse society is served not by the perpetual reenactment of difference but by the creation of a social context that protects diversity, promotes equality among diverse groups, and allows differences to co-exist peacefully and to interact productively. In other words, we must understand that while diversity promotes the empowerment of individuals "to create and influence their contexts," it also inspires "more self-critical, self-reflexive ways" of exerting influence through comparison of one's own values, goals, and motives with those of other people (ibid.). Thus, diversity (in the context of justice) is a necessary feature of commonality precisely because it reduces the likelihood that one group will project its dreams and desires as universal.

Also important in the transition from *pluribus* to *unum*, as we saw in chapter 6, is the analogue between diversity among persons and multiplicity within persons. That is, diversity prefigures and reflects the many identities and commitments that constitute each of us individually. Our many identities, parts, and affinities allow us to form attachments with a wide variety of other folks in varying circumstances. Our inner multiplicity undermines utopian notions of fixed identity categories. The political result, as Sandel explains, is a new "civic virtue distinctive to our time . . . the capacity to negotiate our way among the sometimes overlapping, sometimes conflicting obligations that claim us, and to live with the tension to which multiple loyalties give rise" (1996, 350). Again, a characteristic that appears to divide can actually connect people with different backgrounds, identities, and lifeworlds. Navigating both inner and outer diversity also allows citizens to determine for themselves the valuation of their own "difference," according to Drucilla Cornell (1992, 282).

What is achieved from that navigation is not uniformity, explains Hollinger, but commonality, not a flattening social consensus, but a politics that functions like a jury seeking a common outcome while acknowledging and respecting differences among themselves. "The nation can constitute a common project without effacing all of the various projects that its citizens pursue through their voluntary affiliations," Hollinger argues (1995, 157). He imagines a contested and critically revised public culture, "against which the demands of various particularisms shall be obliged to struggle within a formal constitutional framework" (ibid., 161). "Insofar as there is an ideal nation from a postethnic point of view," he continues, "it is a democratic state defined by a civic principle of nationality in the hands of an ethnoracially diverse population and possessed of [an indeterminate] national ethnos of its own" (ibid., 132).

Iris Marion Young also envisions social struggle as the underpinning of commonality. She argues that "a general perspective does not exist which all persons can adopt and from which all experiences and perspectives can be understood and taken into account" ([1989] 1990, 129). Therefore, what's needed is a "rainbow coalition" in which "each of the constituent groups affirms the presence of the others and affirms the specificity of its experience and perspective on social issues" (ibid., 131). In this "heterogeneous public," groups must justify their interests as "right or as compatible with social justice"—a variation on Hollinger's idea of a common national project—and the public as a whole must determine what is best or most just (ibid., 134).

Although "rainbow coalitions" sound a little romantic, even a little utopian, perhaps they are more realistic than they seem. Nancy Fraser's approach to welfare legislation offers an example. Fraser is well aware that feminists disagree on some very basic premises when they debate welfare policy. For example, some feminists believe that equality means treating women exactly like men, while others believe just as firmly that equality means treating women differently from men insofar as they do differ (Fraser 1997, 44–45). Instead of being stymied by that apparent dichotomy, Fraser envisions amalgamating conflicting feminist "voices" by devising seven "normative principles" for welfare reform—"some associated with the equality side of the debate . . . [and] some associated with the difference side . . . [and still others] that neither side has accorded due weight." She recommends that feminists "[break] with the assumption that gender equity can be identified with any single value or norm, whether it be equality, difference, or something else. Instead," she continues, "we should treat it as a complex notion comprising a plurality of distinct normative principles"(ibid., 45). Thus, she explores a feminist version of Hollinger's "indeterminate ethnos."

Even such lists of normative principles are not inherently utopian. Unlike Promise Keeper promises, Fraser's feminist norms are not absolutes. They vary depending on the issue. They are subject to revision. They are not fixed rules or scenarios. They take nothing, including what constitutes a feminist value, for granted.

Thus, Fraser constructs seven measures for judging welfare policies which may or may not apply to other issues. They are the antipoverty principle, the antiexploitation principle, the income-equality principle, the leisure-time-equality principle, the equality-of-respect principle, the antimarginalization principle, and the antiandrocentrism principle. Fraser then applies those norms to the two most commonly discussed feminist solutions to the welfare issue: the Universal-Breadwinner Model—which provides services, such as daycare, that enable women to take employment on terms comparable to those of employed men; and the Caregiver-Parity Model—in which women doing carework are allowed flexibility in employment and given allowances by the government to support their childbearing, childrearing, housework, and elder-care activities (1997, 45–48). She gives the Universal-Breadwinner Model good marks only on antipoverty and antiexploitation, fair marks on income equality, equality of respect, and antimarginalization, and poor marks for leisure-time equality and antiandrocentrism (1997, 55). She gives the Caregiver-Parity Model good marks on antipoverty and antiexploitation, fair marks on leisure-time equality and equality of respect, and antiandrocentrism, and poor marks on income equality and antimarginalization (ibid., 59).

The obvious result of this "thought exercise" is the basic failure of both proposed models. So, Fraser suggests another approach: eliminate the "gendered opposition between breadwinning and caregiving

. . . eliminate their gender-coding and encourage men to perform them too" (1997, 61). That model earns good marks on all seven of Fraser's issue-specific norms.

In some hands, Fraser's picture of the welfare solution, in which both men and women confront the pleasures and pains of combining caregiving and gainful employment, could be utopian. If men were going to see the benefits of caring, surely they would have done so by now. But Fraser's analysis is less a utopian blueprint than a pointer toward the kind of complex policy decisions that are required to enact fair and effective welfare policy. As we consider such policies, Fraser admonishes, we must examine all assumptions. For example, must we consider welfare dependency a social failure? In Colonial America, *dependency* denoted a form of acceptable social relations. Today, most Americans consider dependency a form of individual pathology analogous to drug addiction. Even feminists question the wisdom of a system that makes women dependent on the government (Fraser 1997, 121–49). But modern usage—which implies a utopian duality of entirely dependent welfare recipients, on the one hand, and entirely independent nonrecipients, on the other—may overlook the essential question: Who is really dependent on the government in the welfare scenario? Fraser concludes that the real "free-riders" in the current system are not the poor mothers who accept welfare but rather the "men of all classes who shirk carework and domestic labor as well as corporations who free-ride on the labor of working people, both underpaid and unpaid" (ibid., 62). What kind of welfare policy might we enact if we understood the impact of those dependencies?

Fraser also avoids utopianism by recommending that all policy making—including, presumably, her own approach to welfare reform—must involve the participation of multiple publics, including "subaltern counterpublics," in which differences (*pace* Habermas) are neither bracketed nor ignored, real conflicts of interest are recognized, and no a priori definition of the common good exists (1997, 86–87).

What Fraser's work suggests, along with Hirschmann's, Young's, and Hollinger's, is that social change requires processes that invite debate, scrutinize assumptions and terms of analysis, and establish meaningful exchanges within and among varying groups of people whose differences are neither predetermined nor disregarded. They promote the willingness of all parties to be changed by the exchange of perspectives, to distribute power and resources broadly and fairly, and to resist corruption. These processes do not yet exist in American society at large, but the tools for constructing them are already ours. They can begin with us. As we establish and move among groups with liberatory agendas, we can model the use of those tools and the enactment of those processes in the way we construct our own interactions—among ourselves and with the world. And then we can pass it along.

CONCLUSION

As I bring *Higher Ground* to a close, I imagine myself standing on a new hill. This time I am not gazing across the rolling meadows and pristine white fences of an inviting but pre-established Shaker "earthly heaven," wondering if I could belong. Now what I see is a dimly lit, veiled view of the distance. Instead of glistening visions, I see confusing intersections with no directional signs. On the stretch of road before me are lots of feet, my own and those of my fellow travelers moving toward realistic feminist social change. Instead of perfect peace in a beautiful, clean, and ordered place, we are poised, like Wallace Stevens, to find "paradise in imperfection." Unlike utopia, the feminism we seek does not depend on prescriptions of perfection. Indeed, it will be stronger if it abandons the need for ideal women or world conditions.

My encounters with utopianism have taught me to question not only unhappiness but also contentment on this journey. We have learned contentment's costs, some of which have been as painful as those resulting from turmoil, struggle, and disappointment. With no predetermined destination, we will strive to appreciate the process and hard work of our journey and to disdain utopian shortcuts. Our travels will require resilience, courage, humility, and the appreciation of uncertainties. We will try to embrace the vicissitudes of the game and avoid the predictable comforts of ritual.

On the way to the higher ground that we cannot see, we will also remember that life's loftiest goals remain perpetually unfinished. Justice, equality, decency, and goodness can never be completely achieved, not simply because human beings inevitably fall short, but also because such concepts *require* continual reinterpretation, redefinition, and reenactment. When fixed, they become illusions, dream worlds fated, like perfect flowers, to wither and to die.

By the same token, we will take no final comfort in whatever roads we choose, for the roads of realism are many. No single path guarantees a successful journey to wisdom or truth. If we're lucky, the roads we travel will lead us away from complacency. In the company of our companions, we will seek the multiple voices of realism to guide as well as challenge our feminist steps, judgments, decisions, and thought.

REFERENCES

Abraham, Ken. 1997. *Who Are the Promise Keepers?: Understanding the Christian Men's Movement.* New York: Doubleday.

Ackroyd, Peter. 1998. *The Life of Thomas More.* London: Chatto and Windus.

Adolph, Anna. 1899. *Arqtiq: A Study of Marvels at the North Pole.* Hanford, Calif.: author.

Alarcón, Norma. 1990. "The Theoretical Subject(s) of *This Bridge Called My Back* and Anglo-American Feminism." In *Making Face, Making Soul: Haciendo Caras,* edited by Gloria Anzaldúa, 356–69. San Francisco: Aunt Lute Foundation.

Albinski, Nan Bowman. 1990. "The Laws of Justice, of Nature, and of Right: Victorian Feminist Utopias." In *Feminism, Utopia, and Narrative,* edited by Libby Falk Jones and Sarah Webster Goodwin, 50–68. Knoxville: University of Tennessee Press.

Alexander, M. Jacqui, and Chandra Talpade Mohanty, eds. 1997. "Introduction: Genealogies, Colonial Legacies, Democratic Futures." In *Feminist Genealogies, Colonial Legacies, Democratic Futures,* edited by Alexander and Mohanty, xiii–xlvii. New York: Routledge.

Alexander, Thea Plym. 1971. *2150 A.D.* Tempe, Ariz.: Macro Books.

Amoros, Celia. 1993. "The Matriarchal Myth." *Literary Review* 36(3) (spring): 415–18.

Anderson, Elizabeth. 1995. "Feminist Epistemology: An Interpretation and a Defense." *Hypatia* 10(3) (summer): 50–84.

Andrews, Edward Deming. 1963. *The People Called Shakers: A Search for the Perfect Society.* New York: Dover Publications.

Andrews, Edward Deming, and Faith Andrews. 1964. *Shaker Furniture: The Craftsmanship of an American Communal Sect.* New York: Dover.

Anzaldúa, Gloria. [1987] 1993. "La Conciencia de la Mestiza: Towards a New

Consciousness." In *American Feminist Thought at Century's End: A Reader,* edited by Linda Kauffman, 427–40. Cambridge, Mass.: Blackwell.

Appleton, Jane Sophia. [1848] 1984. "Sequel to 'The Vision of Bangor in the Twentieth Century.'" In *Daring to Dream: Utopian Stories by United States Women, 1836–1919,* edited by Carol Farley Kessler, 49–64. Excerpt, Boston: Pandora Press.

Assiter, Alison. 1996. *Enlightened Women: Modernist Feminism in a Postmodern Age.* London: Routledge.

Attewell, Paul A. 1996. "The Productivity Paradox." *Chronicle of Higher Education,* 15 March, A56.

Atwood, Margaret. 1985. *The Handmaid's Tale.* New York: Fawcett.

Bader, Eleanor J. 1996. "Manage My Moods." Review of *Men Are from Mars, Women Are from Venus,* by John Gray. *On The Issues* (spring): 51–53.

Baker, Jean Harvey. 1980. "Women in Utopia: The Nineteenth-Century Experience." In *Utopias: The American Experience,* edited by Gairdner B. Moment and Otto F. Kraushaar, 56–71. Metuchen, N.J.: Scarecrow Press.

Barkun, Michael. 1993. "Reflections after Waco: Millennialists and the State." *Christian Century,* 2–9 June, 597.

Bar On, Bat-Ami. 1993. "Marginality and Epistemic Privilege." In *Feminist Epistemologies,* edited by Linda Alcoff and Elizabeth Potter, 83–101. New York: Routledge.

Barr, Marleen. 1983. "Utopia at the End of a Male Chauvinist Dystopian World: Suzy McKee Charnas's Feminist Science Fiction." In *Women and Utopia: Critical Interpretations,* edited by Barr and Nicholas D. Smith, 43–66. Lanham, Md.: University Press of America.

———. 1990. "Food for Postmodern Thought: Isak Dinesen's Female Artists as Precursors to Contemporary Feminist Fabulators." In *Feminism, Utopia, and Narrative,* edited by Libby Falk Jones and Sarah Webster Goodwin, 21–33. Knoxville: University of Tennessee Press.

Barr, Marleen, and Nicholas D. Smith. 1983. Preface to *Women and Utopia: Critical Interpretations,* edited by Barr and Smith, 1–2. Lanham, Md.: University Press of America.

Bartkowski, Frances. 1989. *Feminist Utopias.* Lincoln: University of Nebraska Press.

Baruch, Elaine Hoffman. 1984. "The Quest and the Question." Introduction to *Women in Search of Utopia: Mavericks and Mythmakers,* edited by Ruby Rohrlich and Baruch, xi–xv. New York: Shocken Books.

Bell, Diane, and Renate Klein, eds. 1996. *Radically Speaking: Feminism Reclaimed.* Victoria, Australia: Spinifex Press.

Bell, Michael Davitt. 1995. *The Problem of American Realism Studies in the Cultural History of a Literary Idea.* Chicago: University of Chicago Press.

Bellamy, Edward. [1888] 1889. *Looking Backward, 2000–1887.* Boston: Houghton Mifflin and Co.

———. 1968. "Looking Backward." In *Utopian Literature,* edited by J. W. Johnson, 229–41. New York: Modern Library.

Bem, Sandra. 1993. *The Lenses of Gender: Transforming the Debate on Sexual Inequality.* New Haven: Yale University Press.

Benhabib, Seyla. 1995. "Feminism and Postmodernism: An Uneasy Alliance." In *Feminist Contentions: A Philosophical Exchange,* edited by Seyla Benhabib, Judith Butler, Drucilla Cornell, and Nancy Fraser, 17–34. New York: Routledge.

Berke, Richard L. 1995. "Study Plays Down Sex 'Chasm' in Voting." *New York Times,* 24 Aug., A10.

Berkson, Dorothy. 1990. "'So We All Became Mothers': Harriet Beecher Stowe, Charlotte Perkins Gilman, and the New World of Women's Culture." In *Feminism, Utopia, and Narrative,* edited by Libby Falk Jones and Sarah Webster Goodwin, 100–115. Knoxville: University of Tennessee Press.

Berlant, Lauren. 1988. "The Female Complaint." *Social Text* 19/20 (fall): 237–59.

Bernstein, Susan David. 1992. "Confessing Feminist Theory: What's 'I' Got to Do with It?" *Hypatia* 7(2) (spring): 120–47.

Berry, Dawn Bradley. 1996. *The Domestic Violence Sourcebook: Everything You Need to Know.* Los Angeles: Lowell House.

Berry, John. 1993. "The Last Revelation From Waco." *Esquire,* July, 52–55+.

Bethel, Lorraine. 1979. "What Chou Mean *We,* White Girl?" *Conditions Five: The Black Women's Issue,* edited by Lorraine Bethel and Barbara Smith. 2(2) (autumn): 86–92.

Betsky, Aaron. 1994. "Riding the A Train to the Aleph: Eight Utopias." In *Heterotopia: Postmodern Utopia and the Body Politic,* edited by Tobin Siebers, 96–121. Ann Arbor: University of Michigan Press.

Bhaskar, Roy. 1989. *Reclaiming Reality: A Critical Introduction to Contemporary Philosophy.* London: Verso.

Bhavnani, Kum-Kum. 1993. "Talking Racism and the Editing of Women's Studies." In *Thinking Feminist: Key Concepts in Women's Studies,* edited by Diane Richardson and Victoria Robinson, 27–48. New York: Guilford Press.

Black, Max. 1979. "More about Metaphor." In *Metaphor and Thought,* edited by Andrew Ortony, 19–43. Cambridge: Cambridge University Press.

Bleich, David. 1989. "Sexism and the Discourse of Perfection." *ATQ* 16(3/4): 11–25.

Bloom, Allan. 1987. *The Closing of the American Mind.* New York: Simon and Schuster.

Bordo, Susan. 1990. "Feminism, Postmodernism, and Gender Scepticism." In *Feminism/Postmodernism,* edited by Linda J. Nicholson, 133–56. New York: Routledge.

Boumelha, Penny. 1988. "Realism and the Ends of Feminism." In *Grafts: Feminist Cultural Criticism,* edited by Susan Sheridan, 77–91. London: Verso.

Braidotti, Rosi, with Judith Butler. 1994. "Feminism by Any Other Name." *differences* 6(2/3) (summer/fall): 27–61.

Brewer, Priscilla J. 1993. "Tho' of the Weaker Sex: A Reassessment of Gender Equality among the Shakers." In *Women in Spiritual and Communitarian Societies in the United States,* edited by Wendy E. Chmielewski, Louis J. Kern, and Marlyn Klee-Hartzell, 133–49. Syracuse: Syracuse University Press.

Broner, Esther M. 1978. *The Weave of Women.* New York: Holt, Rinehart Winston.

Brown, Chris. 1993. "International Affairs." In *A Companion to Contemporary Political Philosophy,* edited by Robert E. Goodin and Philip Pettit, 515–19. Oxford: Blackwell.

Bruère, Martha Bensley. 1919. *Mildred Carver, USA.* New York: Macmillan.

Bryant, Dorothy. 1978. *The Kin of Ata Are Waiting for You.* New York: Random House.

Buss, David M., and Neil M. Malamuth, eds. 1996. *Sex, Power, and Conflict: Evolutionary and Feminist Perspectives.* New York: Oxford University Press.

Butler, Judith. 1990a. *Gender Trouble: Feminism and the Subversion of Identity.* New York: Routledge.

———. 1990b. "Gender Trouble, Feminist Theory, and Psychoanalytic Discourse." In *Feminism/Postmodernism,* edited by Linda J. Nicholson, 324–40. New York: Routledge.

———. 1991. "Imitation and Gender Insubordination." In *Inside/Out: Lesbian Theories, Gay Theories,* edited by Diana Fuss, 13–31. New York: Routledge.

———. 1992. "Feminist Contentions." In *Feminists Theorize the Political,* edited by Judith Butler and Joan W. Scott, 3–21. London: Routledge.

———. 1993. *Bodies That Matter: On The Discursive Limits of 'Sex.'* New York: Routledge.

Butler, Octavia. 1979. *Kindred.* New York: Doubleday.

Cameron, Barbara. 1981. "Gee, You Don't Seem Like an Indian from the Reservation." In *This Bridge Called My Back: Writings by Radical Women of Color,* edited by Cherríe Moraga and Gloria Anzaldúa, 46–52. New York: Kitchen Table: Women of Color Press.

Cameron, Deborah. 1992. "'Not Gender Difference But the Difference Gender Makes': Explanation in Research on Sex and Language." *International Journal of the Sociology of Language* 94: 13–26.

———. 1998. "Gender, Language, and Discourse: A Review Essay." *Signs* 23(4): 945–73.

Campbell, Tom D. 1993. "The Contribution of Legal Studies." In *A Companion to Contemporary Political Philosophy,* edited by Robert E. Goodin and Philip Pettit, 183–211. Oxford: Blackwell.

Canning, Kathleen. 1994. "Feminist History after the Linguistic Turn: Historicizing Discourse and Experience." *Signs* 19(2): 368–404.

Capasso, Ruth Carver. 1994. "Islands of Felicity: Women Seeing Utopia in Seventeenth-Century France." In *Utopian and Science Fiction by Women,* edited by Jane L. Donawerth and Carol A. Kolmerten, 35–53. Syracuse: Syracuse University Press.

Caraway, Nancie. 1991. "The Challenge and Theory of Feminist Identity Politics: Working on Racism." *Frontiers* 12(2): 109–29.

Carter, Angela. [1982] 1997. *The Passion of New Eve.* London: Virago.

Cavendish, Margaret. 1688. *The Description of a New World, Called the Blazing-World.* London: A. Maxwell.

Charnas, Suzy McKee. 1978. *Motherlines.* New York: Berkley.

Charoula. 1977. "Dyke Separatist Womanifesto." *Tribad: A Lesbian Separatist Newsjournal* 1(1): 1–4.

Chmielewski, Wendy E. 1993. "Sojourner Truth: Utopian Vision and Search for Community, 1797–1883." In *Women in Spiritual and Communitarian Societies in the United States,* edited by Wendy E. Chmielewski, Louis J. Kern, and Marlyn Klee-Hartzell, 21–37. Syracuse: Syracuse University Press.

Chodorow, Nancy J. 1978. *The Reproduction of Mothering: Psychoanalysis and the Sociology of Gender.* Berkeley: University of California Press.

———. 1995. "Gender as a Personal and Cultural Construction." *Signs* 20(3) (spring): 516–44.

Chow, Rey. 1993. *Writing Diaspora.* Bloomington: Indiana University Press.

Christensen, Kimberly. 1997. "'With Whom Do You Believe Your Lot Is Cast?': White Feminists and Racism." *Signs* 22(3) (spring): 617–48.

Chrystos. 1981. "I Don't Understand Those Who Have Turned Away from Me." In *This Bridge Called My Back: Writings by Radical Women of Color,* edited by Cherríe Moraga and Gloria Anzaldúa, 68–70. New York: Kitchen Table: Women of Color Press.

Cixous, Hélène. [1975] 1992. "The Laugh of the Medusa." In *Modern Feminisms: Political, Literary, Cultural,* edited by Maggie Humm, 196–202. New York: Columbia University Press.

Clark, Cheryl. [1979] 1983. "Lesbianism: An Act of Resistance." In *This Bridge Called My Back: Writings by Radical Women of Color,* edited by Cherríe Moraga and Gloria Anzaldúa, 128–37. New York: Kitchen Table: Women of Color Press.

Cliff, Michelle. 1980. *Claiming an Identity They Taught Me to Despise.* Watertown, Mass.: Persephone Press.

Collier, Andrew. 1998. "Critical Realism." In *Routledge Encyclopedia of Philosophy,* edited by Edward Craig, 720–22. London: Routledge.

Collins, Patricia Hill. 1990. *Black Feminist Thought: Knowledge, Consciousness, and the Politics of Empowerment.* Boston: Unwin Hyman.

———. 1997. "Comment on Hekman's 'Truth and Method: Feminist Standpoint Theory Revisited': Where's the Power?" *Signs* 22(2) (winter): 375–81.

Collins, Patricia Hill, Lionel A. Maldonado, Dana Y. Takagi, Barrie Thorne, Lynn Weber, and Howard Winant. 1995. "Symposium: On West and Fenstermaker's 'Doing Difference.'" *Gender and Society* 9(4) (Aug.): 491–513.

Combahee River Collective. [1977] 1981. "A Black Feminist Statement." In *This Bridge Called My Back: Writings by Radical Women of Color,* edited by Cherríe Moraga and Gloria Anzaldúa, 210–18. New York: Kitchen Table: Women of Color Press.

Connell, R. W. 1987. *Gender and Power: Society, the Person, and Sexual Politics.* Stanford, Calif.: Stanford University Press.

———. 1997. "Comment on Hawkesworth's 'Confounding Gender': Restructuring Gender." *Signs* 22(3) (spring): 702–7.

———. 1998. "Reply: Symposium on R. W. Connell's *Masculinities.*" *Gender and Society* 12(4) (Aug.): 474–77.

Cornell, Drucilla. 1991. *Beyond Accommodation: Ethical Feminism, Deconstruction, and the Law.* London: Routledge.

———. 1992. "Gender, Sex, and Equivalent Rights." In *Feminists Theorize the Political,* edited by Judith Butler and Joan W. Scott, 280–96. New York: Routledge.

Craig, Edward. 1998. "Realism and Anti-Realism." In *Routledge Encyclopedia of Philosophy,* edited by Craig, 115–19. London: Routledge.

Craige, Betty Jean. 1994. "Multiculturalism and the Vietnam Syndrome." *Chronicle of Higher Education,* 12 Jan., B3.

Daly, Martin, and Margo Wilson. 1988. *Homocide.* New York: Aldine De Gruyter.

Dancy, Jonathan. 1998. "Moral Realism." In *Routledge Encyclopedia of Philosophy,* edited by Edward Craig, 534–39. London: Routledge.

D'Aulnoy, Marie-Catherine. 1690. "L'isle de la félicité." Paris: Louis Sevestre.

Davis, Nancy J., and Robert V. Robinson. 1997. "A War for America's Soul? The American Religious Landscape." In *Cultural Wars in American Politics: Critical Reviews of a Popular Myth,* edited by Rhys H. Williams, 39–61. New York: Aldine De Gruyter.

Deseger, Peter. 1994. "Performativity Trouble: Postmodern Feminism and Essential Subjects." *Political Research Quarterly* 47(3) (Sept.): 655–73.

Dill, Bonnie Thornton. 1983. "Race, Class, and Gender: Prospects for an All-Inclusive Sisterhood." *Feminist Studies* 9(1): 131–50.

Dimaggio, Paul, John Evans, and Bethany Bryson. 1997. "Have Americans' Social Attitudes Become More Polarized?" In *Cultural Wars in American Politics: Critical Reviews of a Popular Myth,* edited by Rhys H. Williams, 63–99. New York: Aldine De Gruyter.

Dinesen, Isak. [1953] 1974. "Babette's Feast." *Anecdotes of Destiny.* Reprint, New York: Vintage.

Dinnerstein, Dorothy. 1976. *The Mermaid and the Minotaur: Sexual Arrangements and Human Malaise.* New York: Harper and Row.

Donawerth, Jane L., and Carol A. Kolmerten. 1994. Introduction to *Utopian and Science Fiction by Women,* edited by Donawerth and Kolmerten, 1–14. Syracuse: Syracuse University Press.

Donovan, Josephine. 1985. *Feminist Theory: The Intellectual Traditions of American Feminism.* New York: F. Ungar.

Dower, John W. 1995. "How a Genuine Democracy Should Celebrate Its Past." *Chronicle of Higher Education,* 16 June, B1–2.

Downing, Nancy E., and Kristin L. Roush. 1985. "From Passive Acceptance to Active Commitment: A Model of Feminist Identity Development for Women." *The Counseling Psychologist* 13(4) (Oct.): 695–709.

Downs, Laura Lee. 1988. "If 'Woman' Is Just an Empty Category, Then Why Am I Afraid to Walk Alone at Night? Identity Politics Meets the Postmodern Subject." *Comparative Studies in Society and History* 35(7): 414–37.

———. 1993. "If 'Woman' Is Just an Empty Category, Then Why Am I Afraid to Walk Alone at Night? Identity Politics Meets the Postmodern Subject." *Comparative Studies in Society and History* 35(2) (Apr.): 414–37.

Dunne, Linda. 1994. "Mothers and Monsters in Sarah Robinson Scott's *Millennium Hall.*" In *Utopian and Science Fiction by Women,* edited by Jane L. Donawerth and Carol A. Kolmerten, 54–72. Syracuse: Syracuse University Press.

Duran, Jane. 1991. *Toward a Feminist Epistemology.* Savage, Md.: Rowman and Littlefield.

Duxbury, Neil. 1992. "The Reinvention of American Legal Realism." *Legal Studies* 12(2) (July): 137–77.

———. 1998. "Legal Realism." In *Routledge Encyclopedia of Philosophy,* edited by Edward Craig, 521–25. London: Routledge.

Dworkin, Andrea. 1981. *Men Possessing Women.* New York: Putnam.

———. 1988. *Letters from a War Zone: Writings 1976–1989.* New York: Dutton.

Eisenstein, Zillah R. 1994. *The Color of Gender: Reimaging Democracy.* Berkeley: University of California Press.

Eisler, Riane. 1987. *The Chalice and the Blade.* San Francisco: Harper and Row.

Elgin, Suzette Haden. 1984–94. *Native Tongue.* 3 vols. New York: DAW.

———. 1992. "Washing Utopian Dishes, Scrubbing Utopian Floors." *Women and Language* 17(1): 43–47.

Eliade, Mircea. 1966. "Paradise and Utopia: Mythical Geography and Eschatology." In *Utopias and Utopian Thought,* edited by Frank E. Manuel, 260–80. Boston: Houghton Mifflin.

Elshtain, Jean Bethke. 1986. "The New Feminist Scholarship." *Salmagundi* 70/71: 3–26.

———. 1995. *Democracy on Trial.* New York: BasicBooks.

Evans, Frederick W. 1890. *Two Orders: Shakerism and Republicanism: The American Church and American Civil Government, Coequal and Separate: The New Heavens and Earth.* Pittsfield, Mass.: Sun Printing Press.

Fairbairn, Zoe. 1979. *Benefits.* London: Virago.

Faludi, Susan. 1991. *Backlash: The Undeclared War against American Women.* New York: Crown.

Felder, Raoul, and Barbara Victor. 1996. *Getting Away with Murder: Weapons for the War against Domestic Violence.* New York: Simon and Schuster.

Fellowship for Intentional Community. 1996. *Communities Directory: A Guide to Cooperative Living.* Rev. ed. Rutledge, Mo.: Fellowship for Intentional Community.

Ferguson, Ann. 1994. "Twenty Years of Feminist Philosophy." *Hypatia* 9(3): 197–215.

Firestone, Shulamith. 1971. *The Dialectic of Sex: The Case for Feminist Revolution.* New York: Bantam.

Fitting, Peter. 1990. "The Turn from Utopia in Recent Feminist Fiction." In *Feminism, Utopia, and Narrative,* edited by Libby Falk Jones and Sarah Webster Goodwin, 141–58. Knoxville: University of Tennessee Press.

Flanders, Laura. 1994. "The 'Stolen Feminism' Hoax: Anti-Feminist Attack Based on Error-Filled Anecdotes." In *Extra!* (Sept./Oct.). Available *From the Women's Desk* at www.igc.org/fair/extra/9409/stolen-feminism-hoax.html.

Flax, Jane. 1990. "Postmodernism and Gender Relations in Feminist Theory." In *Feminism/Postmodernism,* edited by Linda J. Nicholson, 39–62. New York, Routledge.

———. 1992. "The End of Innocence." In *Feminists Theorize the Political,* edited by Judith Butler and Joan W. Scott, 445–63. London: Routledge.

Forrest, Katherine V. 1984. *Daughters of a Coral Dawn.* Tallahassee: Naiad Press.

Fowlkes, Diane L. 1997. "Moving from Feminist Identity Politics to Coalition Politics through a Feminist Materialist Standpoint of Intersubjectivity in Gloria Anzaldúa's *Borderlands/La Frontera: The New Mestiza.*" *Hypatia* 12(2) (spring): 105–24.

Fraser, Nancy. 1993. "Rethinking the Public Sphere: A Contribution to the Critique of Actually Existing Democracy." In *The Phantom Public Sphere,* edited by Bruce Robbins, 1–32. Minneapolis: University of Minnesota Press.

———. 1995. "False Antitheses." In *Feminist Contentions: A Philosophical Exchange,* edited by Seyla Benhabib, Judith Butler, Drucilla Cornell, and Nancy Fraser, 59–74. New York: Routledge.

———. 1997. *Justice Interruptus: Critical Reflections on the "Postsocialist" Condition.* New York: Routledge.

Fraser, Nancy, and Linda J. Nicholson. 1990. "Social Criticism without Philosophy: An Encounter between Feminism and Postmodernism." In *Feminism/ Postmodernism,* edited by Linda J. Nicholson, 19–38. New York, Routledge.

Freeman, Jo. [Joreen, pseud.]. [1972] 1973. "The Tyranny of Structurelessness." In *Radical Feminism,* edited by Anne Koedt, Ellen Levine, and Anita Rapone, 285–99. New York: Quadrangle Books.

Freibert, Lucy M. 1993. "Creative Women of Brook Farm." In *Women in Spiritual and Communitarian Societies in the United States,* edited by Wendy E. Chmielewski, Louis J. Kern, and Marlyn Klee-Hartzell, 75–88. Syracuse: Syracuse University Press.

French, Marilyn. 1985. *Beyond Power: On Women, Men, and Morals.* New York: Ballantine Books.

Friedan, Betty. [1963] 1984. *The Feminine Mystique.* New York: DAW.

———. 1981. *The Second Stage.* New York: Summit Books.

Friedman, Susan Stanford. 1985. "Authority in the Feminist Classroom: A Contradiction in Terms?" In *Gendered Subjects: The Dynamics of Feminist*

Teaching, edited by Margo Culley and Catherine Portuges, 203–8. Boston: Routledge and Kegan Paul.

———. 1995. "Beyond White and Other: Relationality and Narratives of Race in Feminist Discourse." *Signs* 21(1) (autumn): 1–49.

Frye, Marilyn. [1990] 1992. "Willful Virgin or Do You Have to Be a Lesbian to Be a Feminist?" In *Willful Virgin: Essays in Feminism, 1976–1992,* by Frye, 124–37. Freedom, Calif.: Crossing Press.

———. 1996. "The Necessity of Differences: Constructing a Positive Category of Women." *Signs* 21(4) (summer): 991–1010.

Frye, Northrop. 1966. "Varieties of Literary Utopias." In *Utopias and Utopian Thought,* edited by Frank E. Manuel, 25–49. Boston: Houghton Mifflin.

Fuss, Diana J. 1989. "'Essentially Speaking': Luce Irigaray's Language of Essence." *Hypatia* 3(3) (winter): 94–112.

Gage, Carolyn. 1993. "Invitation to a Trashing." *Off Our Backs* 23(4) (Apr.): 16–17.

Gates, Henry Louis, Jr. 1994. "Black Studies: Myths or Realities?" *Essence,* Feb., 138.

Gearhart, Sally. 1979. *The Wanderground: Stories of the Hill Women.* Watertown, Mass.: Persephone.

Gilligan, Carol. 1982. *In a Different Voice: Psychological Theory and Women's Development.* Cambridge: Harvard University Press.

———. 1995. "Hearing the Difference: Theorizing Connection." *Hypatia* 10(2): 120–27.

Gilman, Charlotte Perkins. [1898] 1966. *Women and Economics.* Reprint, with an introduction and notes by Carl N. Degler, New York: Harper and Row.

———. 1907. *A Woman's Utopia.* Box 21, Folder 260. Arthur and Elizabeth Schlesinger Library, Radcliffe College.

———. [1910] 1980. *Moving the Mountain.* In *The Charlotte Perkins Gilman Reader,* edited by Ann J. Lane, 178–88. Reprint, New York: Pantheon Books.

———. [1915] 1979. *Herland.* Reprint, with an introduction by Ann J. Lane, New York: Pantheon.

Goheen, Robert F. 1969. *The Human Nature of a University.* Princeton: Princeton University Press.

Golden, Marita. 1995. Introduction to *Skin Deep: Black Women and White Women Write about Race,* edited by Marita Golden and Susan Richards Shreve, 1–5. New York: Nan A. Talese.

Golding, William. 1954. *Lord of the Flies.* London: Faber and Faber.

Gomez, Jewelle. 1991. *The Gilda Stories: A Novel.* Ithaca, N.Y.: Firebrand.

Goodwin, Sarah Webster. 1990. "Feminism and Utopian Discourse in *Pride and Prejudice, Villette,* and 'Babette's Feast.'" In *Feminism, Utopia, and Narrative,* edited by Libby Falk Jones and Sarah Webster Goodwin, 1–20. Knoxville: University of Tennessee Press.

Gordon, Linda. 1991. "On 'Difference.'" *Genders* 10 (spring): 91–111.

Gorelick, Sherry. 1991. "Contradictions of Feminist Methodology." *Gender and Society* 5(4) (Dec.): 459–77.

Gottlieb, Beatrice. 1997. "The Problem of Feminism in the Fifteenth Century." *The Selected Writings of Christine de Pisan: New Translations, Criticism,* edited by Renate Blumenfeld-Kosinski, translated by Renate Blumenfeld-Kosinski and Kevin Brownlee, 274–97. New York: Norton.

Govier, Trudy. 1992. "Trust, Distrust, and Feminist Theory." *Hypatia* 7(1) (winter): 16–33.

Grant, Judith. 1993. *Fundamental Feminism: Contesting the Core Concepts of Feminist Theory.* New York: Routledge.

Gray, John. 1992. *Men Are from Mars, Women Are from Venus: A Practical Guide for Improving Communication and Getting What You Want in Your Relationships.* New York: HarperCollins.

Green, Michelle Erica. 1994. "'There Goes the Neighborhood': Octavia Butler's Demand for Diversity in Utopias." In *Utopian and Science Fiction by Women,* edited by Jane L. Donawerth and Carol A. Kolmerten, 166–89. Syracuse: Syracuse University Press.

Greer, Germaine. 1984. *Sex and Destiny: The Politics of Human Fertility.* New York: Harper and Row.

———. 1990. *Daddy, We Hardly Knew You.* New York: Knopf.

Grewal, Inderpal, and Caren Kaplan, eds. 1994. *Scattered Hegemonies: Postmodernity and Transnational Feminist Practices.* Minneapolis: University of Minnesota Press.

Griffin, Susan. 1981. *Pornography and Silence: Culture's Revenge Against Nature.* New York: Harper and Row.

———. 1982. "The Way of All Ideology." In *Made from This Earth: An Anthology of Writings,* edited by Griffin, 161–81. New York: Harper and Row.

Griffith, Mary. [1836] 1984. *Three Hundred Years Hence.* In *Daring to Dream: Utopian Stories by United States Women, 1836–1919,* edited by Carol Farley Kessler, 29–48. Excerpt, Boston: Pandora Press.

Griffith, R. Marie. 1997. "The Affinities between Feminists and Evangelical Women." *Chronicle of Higher Education,* 17 Oct., B6–7.

Grinde, Donald A., Jr., and Bruce E. Johansen. 1991. *Exemplar of Liberty: Native America and the Evolution of Democracy.* Los Angeles: American Indian Studies Center.

Gross, Elizabeth. 1987. "Philosophy, Subjectivity, and the Body: Kristeva and Irigaray." In *Feminist Challenges: Social and Political Theory,* edited by Carole Pateman and Elizabeth Gross, 125–43. Boston: Northeastern University Press.

Grosz, Elizabeth. 1993. "Bodies and Knowledge: Feminism and the Crisis of Reason." In *Feminist Epistemologies,* edited by Linda Alcoff and Elizabeth Potter, 187–215. New York: Routledge.

Gubar, Susan. 1986. "Feminism and Utopia." *Science Fiction Studies* 13: 79–83.

———. 1995. "Feminist Misogyny: Mary Wollstonecraft and the Paradox of 'It Takes One to Know One.'" In *Feminism beside Itself,* edited by Diane Elam and Robyn Wiegman, 133–54. New York: Routledge.

Hackney, Sheldon. 1994. "Organizing a National Conversation." *Chronicle of Higher Education,* 20 Apr., A56.

Haraway, Donna J. 1991. "Situated Knowledges: The Science Question in Feminism and The Privilege of Partial Perspective." In *Simians, Cyborgs, and Women,* edited by Haraway, 183–201. New York: Routledge.

Harding, Sandra. 1991. "Reinventing Ourselves as Other: More New Agents of History and Knowledge." In *American Feminist Thought at Century's End: A Reader,* edited by Linda S. Kauffman. 1993, 140–64. Cambridge, Mass.: Blackwell.

———. 1993a. "Reinventing Ourselves as Other: More New Agents of History and Knowledge." In *American Feminist Thought at Century's End,* edited by Linda Kauffman, 140–64. Cambridge, Mass.: Blackwell.

———. 1993b. "Rethinking Standpoint Epistemology: 'What is Strong Objectivity?'" In *Feminist Epistemologies,* edited by Linda Alcoff and Elizabeth Potter, 49–82. New York: Routledge.

———. 1997. "Comment on Hekman's 'Truth and Method: Feminist Standpoint Theory Revisited': Whose Standpoint Needs the Regimes of Truth and Reality?" *Signs* 22(2) (winter): 382–91.

Hare-Mustin, Rachel, and Jeanne Marecek. 1988. "The Meaning of Difference: Gender Theory, Postmodernism and Psychology." *American Psychologist* 43(6): 455–64.

Hartsock, Nancy. 1987. "Rethinking Modernism: Minority vs. Majority Theories." *Cultural Critique* 7 (fall): 187–206.

Hawkesworth, Mary E. 1989. "Knowers, Knowing, Known: Feminist Theory and Claims of Truth." *Signs* 14(3) (spring): 533–57.

———. 1997. "Confounding Gender." *Signs* 22(3) (spring): 649–85.

Heath, Robert L. 1986. *Realism and Relativism: A Perspective on Kenneth Burke.* Macon, Ga.: Mercer University Press.

Hekman, Susan. 1997. "Truth and Method: Feminist Standpoint Theory Revisited." *Signs* 22(2) (winter): 341–65.

Hinds, William Alfred. 1973. *American Communities.* Secaucus, N.J.: Citadel Press.

Hirschman, Linda. 1994. "The Big Lie." *Democratic Culture* 3(2) (fall): 13.

Hirschmann, Nancy J. 1996. "Toward a Feminist Theory of Freedom." *Political Theory* 24(1) (Feb.): 46–67.

Hoagland, Sarah Lucia. 1988. *Lesbian Ethics: Toward New Value.* Palo Alto, Calif.: Institute of Lesbian Studies.

Hoagland, Sarah Lucia, and Julia Penelope, eds. 1988. *For Lesbians Only: A Separatist Anthology.* London: Onlywomen.

Hoard, Dorothy. 1983. *A Guide to Bandelier National Monument.* Rev. ed., Los Alamos, N.M.: Los Alamos Historical Society.

Hobbes, Thomas. [1651] 1996. *Leviathan,* edited and with an introduction by J. C. A. Gaskin. Oxford: Oxford University Press.

Hoff, Joan. 1994. "Gender as a Postmodern Category of Paralysis." *Women's Studies International Forum* 17(4): 443–47.

Hogeland, Lisa Maria. 1994. "'Men Can't Be All That Bad': Realism and Feminist Fiction in the 1970's" *American Literary History* 6(2) (summer): 287–306.

Hollinger, David A. 1995. *Postethnic America: Beyond Multiculturalism.* New York: BasicBooks.

Holloway, Mark. 1951. *Heavens on Earth: Utopian Communities in America, 1680–1880.* New York: Library Publishers.

———. 1966. Introduction to *The Communistic Societies of the United States from Personal Observations,* by Charles Nordhof, v–xi. New York: Dover Publications.

hooks, bell. 1990. "Radical Black Subjectivity." In *Yearning: Race, Gender, and Cultural Politics,* by hooks, 15–22. Boston: South End Press.

———. 1991. "Sisterhood: Political Solidarity between Women." In *A Reader in Feminist Knowledge,* edited by Sneja Marina Gunew, 27–41. New York: Routledge.

Horgan, Edward R. 1982. *The Shaker Holy Land: A Community Portrait.* Harvard, Mass.: Harvard Common Press.

Howells, William Dean. 1894. *A Traveler from Altruria.* New York: Harper and Brothers.

Howland, Marie Stevens Case. [1874] 1984. *Papa's Own Girl.* In *Daring to Dream: Utopian Stories by United States Women, 1836–1919,* edited by Carol Farley Kessler, 95–103. Excerpt, Boston: Pandora Press.

Hunter, James Davison. 1991. *Culture Wars: The Struggle to Define America.* New York: BasicBooks.

Huxley, Aldous. 1932. *Brave New World.* Bath: Lythway Press.

Irigaray, Luce. [1977] 1992. "This Sex Which Is Not One." In *Modern Feminisms: Political, Literary, Cultural,* edited by Maggie Humm, 204–6. New York: Columbia University Press.

———. 1985. *This Sex Which Is Not One.* Translated by Catherine Porter with Carolyn Burke. Ithaca: Cornell University Press.

Jacobs, Wilbur R. 1992. "Commentary: The American Indian Legacy of Freedom and Liberty." *American Indian Culture and Research Journal* 16(4): 185–93.

Jacoby, Russell. 1994. "The Most Radical Afrocentric Ideologue Is Culturally an American." *Chronicle of Higher Education,* 30 Mar., B5.

Jagger, Alison. 1983. *Feminist Politics and Human Nature.* Totowa, N.J.: Rowman and Allanheld.

Jagose, Annamarie. 1994. *Lesbian Utopics.* New York: Routledge.

Jameson, Fredric. 1985. "Periodizing the 60s." *The 60s without Apology,* edited by Sohnya Sayres et al., 178–209. Minneapolis: University of Minnesota Press.

Janack, Marianne. 1997. "Standpoint Epistemology without the 'Standpoint'?: An Examination of Epistemic Privilege and Epistemic Authority." *Hypatia* 12(2) (spring): 125–39.

Johansen, Bruce E. 1982. *Forgotten Founders: Benjamin Franklin, the Iroquois, and the Rationale for the American Revolution.* Ipswich, Mass.: Gambit Publishers.

Johnson, Barbara. 1992. "The Postmodern in Feminism." *Harvard Law Review* 105(5) (Mar.): 1076–83.

Johnson, J. W., ed. 1968. *Utopian Literature: A Selection.* New York: Modern Library.

Johnson, Samuel. [1759] 1886. *Rasselas, Prince of Abyssinia.* Boston: Ginn and Co.

Johnson, Sonia. 1989. "Rearing Nice Sons Can't Change the World." In *Wildfire: Igniting the She/volution,* by Johnson, 177–79. Albuquerque: Wildfire Books.

Jones, Alice Ilgenfritz, and Ellen Merchant. [1893] 1991. *Unveiling a Parallel: A Romance.* Reprint, with an introduction and edited by Carol A. Kolmerten, Syracuse: Syracuse University Press.

Jones, Libby Falk. 1990. "Gilman, Bradley, Piercy, and the Evolving Rhetoric of Feminist Utopias." In *Feminism, Utopia, and Narrative,* edited by Jones and Sarah Webster Goodwin, 116–29. Knoxville: University of Tennessee Press.

Jones, Lillian B. 1916. *Five Generations Hence.* Fort Worth, Tex.: Dotson Jones.

Kanter, Rosabeth Moss. 1972. *Commitment and Community: Communes and Utopias in Sociological Perspective.* Cambridge: Harvard University Press.

Kauffman, L. A. 1990. "The Anti-Politics of Identity." *Socialist Review* 20(1) (Jan.): 67–80.

Kauffman, Linda S. 1992. "The Long Goodbye: Against Personal Testimony, or An Infant Grifter Grows Up." *American Feminist Thought at Century's End: A Reader,* edited by Kauffman. 1993, 258–78. Cambridge, Mass.: Blackwell.

Keller, Evelyn Fox, and Helene Moglen. 1987. "Competition: A Problem for Academic Women." In *Competition: A Feminist Taboo?,* edited by Helen Longino and Valerie Miner, 21–37. New York: Feminist Press.

Kessler, Carol Farley. 1984a. "Introduction: Feminist Utopias by United States Women." In *Daring to Dream: Utopian Stories by United States Women, 1836–1919,* edited by Kessler, 1–25. Boston: Pandora Press.

———, ed. and comp. 1984b. *Daring to Dream: Utopian Stories by United States Women, 1836–1919.* Boston: Pandora Press.

Kesten, Seymour R. 1993. *Utopian Episodes: Daily Life in Experimental Colonies Dedicated to Changing the World.* Syracuse: Syracuse University Press.

Khanna, Lee Cullen. 1990. "Women's Utopias: New Worlds, New Texts." In *Feminism, Utopia, and Narrative,* edited by Libby Falk Jones and Sarah Webster Goodwin, 130–40. Knoxville: University of Tennessee Press.

———. 1994. "The Subject of Utopia: Margaret Cavendish and Her Blazing-World." In *Utopian and Science Fiction by Women,* edited by Jane L. Donawerth and Carol A. Kolmerten, 15–34. Syracuse: Syracuse University Press.

Kimmel, Michael S. 1997. "Promise Keepers: Patriarchy's Second Coming as Masculine Renewal." *Tikkun* 12(2) (Mar.): 46–50.

Kiser, Edgar V., and Kathryn A. Baker. 1984. "Feminist Ideology and Utopian Literature." *Quarterly Journal of Ideology* (Oct.): 29–36.

Kitch, Sally L. 1987. "Feminist Literary Criticism as Irony." *Rocky Mountain Review of Language and Literature.* 41(1/2): 7–19.

———. 1989a. "'As a Sign That All May Understand'" Shaker Gift Drawings and Female Spiritual Power." *Winterthur Portfolio* 24(1) (spring): 1–28.

———. 1989b. *Chaste Liberation: Celibacy and Female Cultural Status.* Urbana: University of Illinois Press.

———. 1993. *This Strange Society of Women: Reading the Letters and Lives of the Woman's Commonwealth.* Columbus: Ohio State University Press.

Klee-Hartzell, Marlyn. 1993. "Family Love, True Womanliness, Motherhood, and the Socialization of Girls in the Oneida Community, 1848–1880." In *Women in Spiritual and Communitarian Societies in the United States,* edited by Wendy E. Chmielewski, Louis J. Kern, and Marlyn Klee-Hartzel, 182–200. Syracuse: Syracuse University Press.

Kolmerten, Carol A. 1990. *Women in Utopia: The Ideology of Gender in the American Owenite Communities.* Bloomington: Indiana University Press.

———. 1993. "Women's Experiences in the American Owenite Communities." In *Women in Spiritual and Communitarian Societies in the United States,* edited by Wendy E. Chmielewski, Louis J. Kern, and Marlyn Klee-Hartzell, 38–51. Syracuse: Syracuse University Press.

———. 1994. "Texts and Contexts: American Women Envision Utopia, 1890–1920." In *Utopian and Science Fiction by Women,* edited by Jane L. Donawerth and Carol A. Kolmerten, 107–25. Syracuse: Syracuse University Press.

Kolodny, Annette. 1998. "If Harsh Realities Prevail, We Will All Continue to Lose." *Chronicle of Higher Education,* 6 Mar., B5.

Kristeva, Julia. [1979] 1992. "Women's Time." In *Modern Feminisms: Political, Literary, Cultural,* edited by Maggie Humm, 216–18. New York: Columbia University Press.

Kruks, Sonia. 1995. "Identity Politics and Dialectical Reason: Beyond an Epistemology of Provenance." *Hypatia* 10(2) (spring): 1–22.

Lamott, Anne. 1995. *Bird by Bird.* New York: Anchor Books.

Lane, Mary E. Bradley. [1880–81] 1984. *Mizora: A Prophecy.* In *Daring to Dream: Utopian Stories by United States Women, 1836–1919,* edited by Carol Farley Kessler, 117–37. Excerpt, Boston: Pandora Press.

Lauret, Maria. 1994. *Liberating Literature: Feminist Fiction in America.* New York: Routledge.

Lefkowitz, Mary. 1996. *Not Out of Africa: How Afrocentrism Became an Excuse to Teach Myth as History.* New York: BasicBooks.

Le Guin, Ursula. [1969] 1976. *The Left Hand of Darkness.* Reprint, New York: Ace.

———. 1974. *The Dispossessed.* New York: Avon Books.

———. 1985. *Always Coming Home.* Toronto: Bantam.

Leidner, Robin. 1991. "Stretching the Boundaries of Liberalism: Democratic Innovation in a Feminist Organization." *Signs* 16(2): 263–89.

———. 1993. "Constituency, Accountability, and Deliberation: Reshaping Democracy in the National Women's Studies Association." *NWSA Journal* 5(3): 4–27.

———. 1994. "Response to Gerber's 'Reshaping Democracy' and Sirianni's 'Feminist Pluralism and Democratic Learning.'" *NWSA Journal* 6(1): 103–6.

Lerner, Gerda. 1986. *The Creation of Patriarchy.* New York: Oxford University Press.

Lessing, Doris. 1992. *Canopus in Argus* series. New York: Vintage. (*The Memoirs of a Survivor* [1975], *Archives, Re: Colonized Planet 5, Shikasta* [1979], *The Marriages between Zones Three, Four, and Five* [1980], *The Sirian Experiments* [1981].)

Levine, Lawrence W. 1996. *The Opening of the American Mind: Canons, Culture, and History.* Boston: Beacon Press.

Lewes, Darby. 1995. *Dream Revisionaries: Gender and Genre in Women's Utopian Fiction, 1870–1920.* Tuscaloosa: University of Alabama Press.

Limerick, Patricia Nelson. 1997. "The Startling Ability of Culture to Bring Critical Inquiry to a Halt." *Chronicle of Higher Education*, 24 Oct., A76.

Longino, Helen. 1993. "Subjects, Power, and Knowledge: Description and Prescription in Feminist Philosophies of Science." In *Feminist Epistemologies*, edited by Linda Alcoff and Elizabeth Potter, 101–20. New York: Routledge.

Lorde, Audre. 1979. "Man Child: A Black Lesbian Feminist's Response." *Conditions* 4: 30–36.

———. [1980] 1981. "The Master's Tools Will Never Dismantle the Master's House." In *This Bridge Called My Back: Writings by Radical Women of Color*, edited by Cherríe Moraga and Gloria Anzaldúa, 98–101. New York: Kitchen Table: Women of Color Press.

Love, David A. 1997. "Keeping an Eye on the Promise Keepers." *Emerge* 8(6) (Apr.): 76.

Love, Nancy S. 1991. "Politics and Voice(s): An Empowerment/Knowledge Regime." *differences* 3(1) (spring): 85–103.

Lubiano, Wahneema. 1992. "Black Ladies, Welfare Queens, and State Minstrels: Ideological War by Narrative Means." In *Race-ing Justice, En-Gendering Power: Essays on Anita Hill, Clarence Thomas, and the Construction of Social Reality*, edited by Toni Morrison, 323–63. New York: Pantheon.

Lugones, Maria. 1990. "Playfulness, 'World'-Travelling, and Loving Perception." In *Lesbian Philosophies and Culture*, edited by Jeffner Allen, 160–79. Albany: State University of New York Press.

———. 1994. "Purity, Impurity and Separation." *Signs* 19(2) (winter): 458–79.

Lugones, Maria, and Pat Alake Rosezelle. 1992. "Sisterhood and Friendship as Feminist Models." In *The Knowledge Explosion: Generations of Feminist Scholarship*, edited by Cheris Kramarae and Dale Spender, 406–12. New York: Teachers College Press.

Mama, Anima. 1997. "Sheroes and Villains: Conceptualizing Colonial and Contemporary Violence against Women in Africa." In *Feminist Genealogies,*

Colonial Legacies, Democratic Futures, edited by M. Jacqui Alexander and Chandra Talpade Mohanty, 46–62. New York: Routledge.

Manuel, Frank E. 1966. Introduction to *Utopias and Utopian Thought,* edited by Manuel, i–xxi. Boston: Houghton Mifflin.

Marcus, Laura. 1992. "Feminist Aesthetics and the New Realism." In *New Feminist Discourses: Critical Essays on Theories and Texts,* edited by Isobel Armstrong, 11–25. London: Routledge.

Marcus, Sharon. 1992. "Fighting Bodies, Fighting Words: A Theory and Politics of Rape Prevention." In *Feminists Theorize the Political,* edited by Judith Butler and Joan W. Scott, 385–403. New York: Routledge.

Martin, Biddy, and Chandra Talpade Mohanty. 1986. "Feminist Politics: What's Home Got to Do with It?" In *Feminist Studies/Critical Studies,* edited by Teresa de Lauretis, 191–212. Bloomington: Indiana University Press.

Martin, Jane Roland. 1994. "Methodological Essentialism, False Difference, and Other Dangerous Traps." *Signs* 19(3) (spring): 630–57.

McClintock, Anne. 1995. *Imperial Leather: Race, Gender, and Sexuality in the Colonial Conquest.* New York: Routledge.

McDonald, Christie. 1995. "Personal Criticism: Dialogue of Differences." In *Feminism beside Itself,* edited by Diane Elam and Robyn Wiegman, 237–59. New York: Routledge.

McDonald, Marci. 1997. "My Wife Told Me to Go." *US News and World Report,* 6 Oct., 28–30.

McDowell, Deborah E. 1990. "The Changing Same." In *Reading Black, Reading Feminist: A Critical Anthology,* edited by Henry Louis Gates, Jr., 91–115. New York: Meridian.

McNeil, Maureen. 1992. "Pedagogical Praxis and Problems: Reflections on Teaching about Gender Relations." In *Working Out: New Directions of Women's Studies,* edited by Hilary Hinds, Ann Phoenix, and Jackie Stacey, 18–27. London: Falmer Press.

Meijer, Maaike. 1993. "Countering Textual Violence: On the Critique of Representation and the Importance of Teaching Its Methods." *Women's Studies International Forum* 16(4): 367–78.

Mellor, Anne K. 1982. "On Feminist Utopias." *Women's Studies* 9: 241–62.

Menon, Ritu. 1996. "Beijing's Lessons." Review of *The Challenge of Local Feminisms: Women's Movements in Global Perspective,* edited by Amrita Basu. *Women's Review of Books* 13(12) (Sept.): 15–16.

Merton, Thomas. 1950. Introduction to *The City of God,* by Saint Augustine. Translated by Marcus Dods, ix–xv. New York: Modern Library.

Michie, Helena. 1992. Introduction to *Sororophobia: Differences among Women in Literature and Culture,* by Michie, 3–14. New York: Oxford University Press.

Mies, Maria. 1989. "Self-Determination: The End of a Utopia?" *Resources for Feminist Research* 18(3) (Sept.): 51–56.

Millett, Kate. 1970. *Sexual Politics.* Garden City, N.Y.: Doubleday.

————. 1979. *The Basement: Meditations on a Human Sacrifice.* New York: Simon and Schuster.

Minkowitz, Donna. 1995. "In the Name of the Father." *Ms,* Nov./Dec., 64–71.

Mitchell, Juliet. 1975. *Psychoanalysis and Feminism.* New York: Vintage.

Mohanty, Chandra Talpade. 1991. "Under Western Eyes: Feminist Scholarship and Colonial Discourses." In *Cartographies of Struggle: Third World Women and the Politics of Feminism,* edited by Chandra Mohanty, Ann Russo, and Lourdes Torres, 51–80. Bloomington: Indiana University Press.

————. 1992. "Feminist Encounters: Locating the Politics of Experience." In *Destabilizing Theory,* edited by Michele Barrett and Anne Phillips, 74–92. Stanford, Calif.: Stanford University Press.

————. 1997. "Women Workers and Capitalist Scripts: Ideologies of Domination, Common Interests, and the Politics of Solidarity." In *Feminist Genealogies, Colonial Legacies, Democratic Futures,* edited by M. Jacqui Alexander and Chandra Talpade Mohanty, 3–29. New York: Routledge.

Moi, Toril. 1993. "Beauvoir's Utopia: The Politics of the Second Sex." *The South Atlantic Quarterly* 92(2) (spring): 311–60.

Moore, Henrietta. 1994. "'Divided We Stand': Sex, Gender and Sexual Difference." *Feminist Review* 47 (summer): 78–95.

Moore, M. Louise. 1892. *Al Modad; or Life Scenes beyond the Polar Circumflex, A Religio-Scientific Solution of the Problems of Present and Future Life.* Shell Bank, Cameron Parish, La.: Moore and Beauchamp.

Morales, Rosario. 1981. "I Am What I Am." In *This Bridge Called My Back: Writings by Radical Women of Color,* edited by Cherríe Moraga and Gloria Anzaldúa, 14–15. New York: Kitchen Table: Women of Color Press.

Moya, Paula M. L. 1997. "Postmodernism, 'Realism,' and the Politics of Identity: Cherríe Moraga and Chicana Feminism." In *Feminist Genealogies, Colonial Legacies, Democratic Futures,* edited by M. Jacqui Alexander and Chandra Talpade Mohanty, 125–50. New York: Routledge.

Mullen, John D. 1995. *Hard Thinking: The Reintroduction of Logic to Everyday Life.* Boston: Rowman and Littlefield.

Mullin, Amy. 1995. "Selves, Diverse and Divided: Can Feminists Have Diversity without Multiplicity?" *Hypatia* 10(4) (fall): 1–31.

Muncy, Raymond Lee. 1973. *Sex and Marriage in Utopian Communities: Nineteenth-Century America.* Bloomington: Indiana University Press.

Nelson, Julie A. 1992. "Thinking about Gender." *Hypatia* 7(3) (summer): 138–54.

Nelson, Lynn Hankinson. 1990. *Who Knows: From Quine to a Feminist Empiricism.* Philadelphia: Temple University Press.

————. 1993. "Epistemological Communities." In *Feminist Epistemologies,* edited by Linda Alcoff and Elizabeth Potter, 121–59. New York: Routledge.

New York Times. 1996. "The Elections." 7 November, B5.

Nicholson, Linda. 1994. "Interpreting Gender." *Signs* 20(1) (autumn): 79–105.

Nordhoff, Charles. [1875] 1966. *The Communistic Societies of the United States from Personal Observations.* New York: Dover Publications.

Omolade, Barbara. 1993. "A Black Feminist Pedagogy." *Women's Studies Quarterly* 3 and 4: 31–38.

Orwell, George. 1949. *Nineteen Eighty-Four.* New York: Milestone Editions.

Oyewumi, Oyeronke. 1998. "De-confounding Gender: Feminist Theorizing and Western Culture, a Comment on Hawkesworth's 'Confounding Gender.'" *Signs* 23(4) (summer): 1049–62.

Paglia, Camille. 1992. "Sexual Personae: The Cancelled Preface." In *Sex, Art, and American Culture: Essays,* by Paglia, 101–24. New York: Vintage.

Patai, Daphne. 1983. "Beyond Defensiveness: Feminist Research Strategies." In *Women and Utopia: Critical Interpretations,* edited by Marleen Barr and Nicholas D. Smith, 148–69. Lanham, Md.: University Press of America.

Patai, Daphne, and Noretta Koertge. 1994. *Professing Feminism: Cautionary Tales from the Strange World of Women's Studies.* New York: BasicBooks.

Paul, Richard. 1990. *Critical Thinking.* Santa Rosa, Calif.: Foundation for Critical Thinking.

Pearson, Carol. 1977. "Women's Fantasies and Feminist Utopias." *Frontiers* 2(3): 50–61.

Peel, Ellen. 1990. "Utopian Feminism, Skeptical Feminism, and Narrative Energy." In *Feminism, Utopia, and Narrative,* edited by Libby Falk Jones and Sarah Webster Goodwin, 34–49. Knoxville: University of Tennessee Press.

Pfaelzer, Jean. 1990. "Response: What Happened to History?" In *Feminism, Utopia, and Narrative,* edited by Libby Falk Jones and Sarah Webster Goodwin, 191–200. Knoxville: University of Tennessee Press.

Piercy, Marge. 1975. *Woman on the Edge of Time.* New York: Knopf.

Pollitt, Katha. 1994. "Feminism at the Crossroads." *Dissent* 41(2) (spring): 192–95.

Pope, Christie Farnham. 1994. "The Challenges Posed by Radical Afrocentrism." *Chronicle of Higher Education,* 30 Mar., B1–3.

Rapping, Elayne. 1996. "Politics and Polemics." Review of *Radically Speaking: Feminism Reclaimed,* edited by Diane Bell and Renate Klein. *Women's Review of Books* 14(1) (Oct.): 9–10.

Reif, Joan. 1991. "Rehearsing the Future: Utopia and Dystopia in Women's Writing, 1960–1990." Ph.D. diss., University of Exeter.

Remnick, David. 1994. "Visible Man." *The New Yorker,* 14 Mar., 34–38.

Rhode, Deborah L. 1990. Introduction to *Theoretical Perspectives on Sexual Difference,* edited by Rhode, 1–9. New Haven: Yale University Press.

Rhodes, Jewell Parker. 1983. "The Left Hand of Darkness: Androgyny and the Feminist Utopia." In *Women and Utopia: Critical Interpretations,* edited by Marleen Barr and Nicholas D. Smith, 108–20. Lanham, Md.: University Press of America.

Rich, Adrienne. 1976. *Of Woman Born: Motherhood as Experience and Institution.* New York: Norton.

Richards, Janet Radcliffe. 1980. *The Sceptical Feminist: A Philosophical Enquiry.* London: Routledge and Kegan Paul.

Richberg, Eloise O. 1900. *Reinstern.* Cincinnati, Ohio: Editor Publishing.

Rosen, Jeffrey. 1998. "Damage Control." *New Yorker,* 23 Feb. and 3 Mar.: 58–68.

Ross, Ellen. 1992. "New Thoughts on 'The Oldest Vocation': *Mothers of Incest Survivors* by Janis Johnson, *Apache Mothers and Daughters* by Ruth Boyer and Narcissus Duffy Gayton, *The Anchor of My Life* by Linda Rosenzweig, and Others." *Signs* 20(2) (winter): 397–413.

Rothman, Barbara Katz. 1989. *Recreating Motherhood: Ideology and Technology in a Patriarchal Society.* New York: W. W. Norton.

———. 1994. "Beyond Mothers and Fathers: Ideology in a Patriarchal Society." In *Mothering: Ideology, Experience, and Agency,* edited by Evelyn Nakano Glenn, Grace Chang, and Linda Rennie Forcey, 139–57. New York: Routledge, 1994.

Ruddick, Sara. 1989. *Maternal Thinking: Toward a Politics of Peace.* Boston: Beacon.

Rupp, Leila J., and Verta Taylor. 1999. "Forging Feminist Identity in an International Movement: A Collective Identity Approach to Twentieth-Century Feminism." *Signs* 24(2): 380–86.

Russ, Joanna. 1975. *The Female Man.* New York: Bantam.

Sandel, Michael J. 1996. *Democracy's Discontent: America in Search of a Public Philosophy.* Cambridge, Mass.: Belknap Press of Harvard University Press.

Sanders, Scott Russell. 1999. "Teaching Thoughtful Students the Rudiments of Hope." *Chronicle of Higher Education,* 9 Apr., B4.

Sandoval, Chela. 1991. "U.S. Third World Feminism: The Theory and Method of Oppositional Consciousness in the Postmodern World." *Genders* 10 (spring): 1–24.

Sargent, Lyman Tower. 1983. "A New Anarchism: Social and Political Ideas in Some Recent Feminist Eutopias." In *Women and Utopia: Critical Interpretations,* edited by Marleen Barr and Nicholas D. Smith, 3–33. Lanham, Md.: University Press of America.

Sargent, Pamela. 1986. *The Shore of Women.* New York: Crown.

Sargisson, Lucy. 1996. *Contemporary Feminist Utopianism.* London: Routledge.

Schiappa, Edward. 1993. "Burkean Tropes and Kuhnian Science: A Social Constructionist Perspective on Language and Reality." *Journal of Advanced Composition* 13(2) (fall): 401–22.

Schmitt, Richard. 1997. *Introduction to Marx and Engels: A Critical Reconstruction.* Boulder, Colo.: Westview.

Schweickart, Patsy. 1990. "Reflections on NWSA '90," *NWSAction* 3(4) (winter): 3–4, 9–10.

Scott, Joan W. 1992. "'Experience.'" In *Feminists Theorize the Political,* edited by Judith Butler and Scott, 22–40. London: Routledge.

Scott, Sarah Robinson. [1762] 1955. *A Description of Millenium Hall.* Reprint, edited by Walter M. Crittenden, New York: Bookman Associates.

Scruton, Roger. 1982. *A Dictionary of Political Thought*. New York: Harper and Row.

Scully, Diana, and Joseph Marolla. [1985] 1996. "Riding the Bull at Gilley's: Convicted Rapists Describe the Rewards of Rape." In *Social Deviance*, edited by Erich Goode, 288–303. Boston: Allyn and Bacon.

Sheer, Arlene. 1984. "Findhorn, Scotland: The People Who Talk to Plants." In *Women in Search of Utopia: Mavericks and Mythmakers*, edited by Ruby Rohrlich and Elaine Hoffman Baruch, 146–56. New York: Shocken Books.

Shklar, Judith N. 1966. "The Political Theory of Utopia: From Melancholy to Nostalgia." In *Utopias and Utopian Thought*, edited by Frank E. Manuel, 101–15. Boston: Houghton Mifflin.

———. 1994. "What Is the Use of Utopia?" In *Heterotopia: Postmodern Utopia and the Body Politic*, edited by Tobin Siebers, 40–57. Ann Arbor: University of Michigan Press.

Shrewsbury, Carolyn M. 1993. "What Is Feminist Pedagogy?" *Women's Studies Quarterly* 21(3/4) (fall): 8–16.

Shugar, Dana R. 1995. *Sep-a-ra-tism and Women's Community*. Lincoln: University of Nebraska Press.

Siebers, Tobin. 1994. "Introduction: What Does Postmodernism Want? Utopia." In *Heterotopia: Postmodern Utopia and the Body Politic*, edited by Siebers, 1–38. Ann Arbor: University of Michigan Press.

Slonczewski, Joan. 1986. *A Door into Ocean*. New York: Arbor House.

Smith, Christian, et al. 1997. "The Myth of Culture Wars: The Case of American Protestantism." In *Cultural Wars in American Politics: Critical Reviews of a Popular Myth*, edited by Rhys H. Williams, 175–95. New York: Aldine De Gruyter.

Smyth, Ailbhe. 1992. "A (Political) Postcard from a Peripheral Pre-Postmodern State (Of Mind) or How Alliteration and Parentheses Can Knock You Down Dead in Women's Studies." *Women's Studies International Forum* 15(3): 331–37.

Snitow, Ann. 1992. "Feminism and Motherhood: An American Reading." *Feminist Review* 40 (spring): 32–51.

Sommers, Christina Hoff. 1994. *Who Stole Feminism?: Women Who Betrayed Women*. New York: Simon and Schuster.

Soper, Kate. 1995. Review of *Bodies That Matter: On the Discursive Limits of 'Sex,'* by Judith Butler; *Outside in the Teaching Machine*, by Gayatri Chakaravorty Spivak; and *Postmodern Revisionings of the Political*, by Anna Yeatman. *Feminist Review* 51: 117–20.

Spivak, Gayatri. 1989. "A Literary Representation of the Subaltern: A Woman's Text from the Third World." In *In Other Worlds: Essays in Cultural Politics*, by Spivak, 241–68. New York: Routledge.

Staton, Mary. 1975. *From the Legend of Biel*. New York: Ace.

Steinem, Gloria. [1972] 1983. "Sisterhood." In *Outrageous Acts and Everyday Rebellions*, by Steinem, 112–18. New York: Holt.

Steinfels, Peter. 1998. "Beliefs." *New York Times*, 24 Jan., A13.

Stevens, Wallace. 1942. "The Poems of Our Climate." In *Parts of a World* by Stevens. New York: A. A. Knopf.

Stimpson, Catharine R. 1994. "A Conversation, Not a Monologue." *Chronicle of Higher Education,* 16 Mar., B1–2.

———. 1996. "Women's Studies and Its Discontents." *Dissent* (winter): 67–75.

Suarez, Ray. 1998. "Too Many in Academe Stayed Grandly above the Fray." *Chronicle of Higher Education,* 6 Mar., B8.

Sullivan, E. D. S. 1983. "Place in No Place: Examples for the Ordered Society in Literature" In *The Utopian Vision: Essays on Quincentennial of Sir Thomas More,* edited by Sullivan, 29–49. Calif.: San Diego State University Press.

Surtz, Edward. 1967. "Thomas More." In *The Encyclopedia of Philosophy,* edited by Paul Edward, 389–92. New York: MacMillan and Free Press.

Swift, Jonathan. [1726] 1976. *Gulliver's Travels.* Delmar, N.Y.: Scholars' Facsimilies and Reprints.

Takagi, Dana. 1995. "Symposium: On West and Fenstermaker's 'Doing Difference.'" *Gender and Society* 9(4) (Aug.): 491–513.

Tannen, Deborah. 1990. *You Just Don't Understand: Women and Men in Conversation.* New York: Morrow.

———. 1994a. *Gender and Discourse.* Oxford: Oxford University Press.

———. 1994b. "The Triumph of the Yell." *New York Times,* 14 Jan., A29.

Tillich, Paul. 1966. "Critique and Justification of Utopia." In *Utopias and Utopian Thought,* edited by Frank E. Manuel, 296–309. Boston: Houghton Mifflin.

Tirrell, Lynne. 1993. "Definition and Power: Toward Authority without Privilege." *Hypatia* 8(4) (fall): 1–34.

Tompkins, Jane. 1994. "'Indians': Textualism, Morality, and the Problem of History." In *Styles of Cultural Activism: From Theory and Pedagogy to Women, Indians, and Communism,* edited by Philip Goldstein, 184–202. Newark: University of Delaware Press.

Tong, Rosemarie. 1989. *Feminist Thought: A Comprehensive Introduction.* Boulder: Westview.

———. 1998. *Feminist Thought: A More Comprehensive Introduction.* 2nd ed. Boulder: Westview.

Treichler, Paula A. 1994. "A Room of Whose Own?: Lessons from Feminist Classroom Narratives." In *Changing Classroom Practices: Resources for Literary and Cultural Studies,* edited by David B. Downing, 75–103. Urbana, Ill.: National Council of Teachers of English.

Uchida, Aki. 1992. "When 'Difference' Is 'Dominance': A Critique of the 'Anti-Power-Based' Cultural Approach to Sex Differences." *Language in Society* 21: 547–68.

Voltaire. [1759] 1995. *Candide.* Edited and with an introduction by Haydn Mason. London: Bristol Classical.

Waisbrooker, Lois. 1894. *A Sex Revolution.* Topeka, Kans.: author.

Wagner, Sally Roesch. 1992. "The Influence on Women's Rights." Reprint in

Indian Roots of American Democracy, edited by José Barreiro, 115–34. Ithaca: Cornell University Press.

Walker, Alice. 1983. *In Search of Our Mothers' Gardens: Womanist Prose.* San Diego: HBJ.

Walsh, Chad. 1962. *From Utopia to Nightmare.* New York: Harper and Row.

Washburn, Michael. 1994. "Reflections on a Psychoanalytic Theory of Gender Difference." *Journal of the American Academy of Psychoanalysis* 22(1): 1–28.

Watt, Shantu, and Juliet Cook. 1991. "Racism: Whose Liberation? Implication for Women's Studies." In *Out of the Margins: Women's Studies in the Nineties,* edited by Jane Aaron and Sylvia Walby, 131–42. London: Falmer Press.

Weinbaum, Batya. 1984. "Twin Oaks: A Feminist Looks at Indigenous Socialism in the United States." In *Women in Search of Utopia: Mavericks and Mythmakers,* edited by Ruby Rohrlich and Elaine Hoffman Baruch, 157–67. New York: Shocken Books.

Wells, H. G. [Herbert George]. 1895. *The Time Machine.* New York: H. Holt.

West, Candace, and Sarah Fenstermaker. 1995. "Doing Difference." *Gender and Society* 9(1) (Feb.): 8–37.

White, Thomas I. 1983. "Opposing Necessity and Truth: The Argument against Politics in Doris Lessing's Utopian Vision." In *Women and Utopia: Critical Interpretations,* edited by Marleen Barr and Nicholas D. Smith, 134–47. Lanham, Md.: University Press of America.

Whitehead, Alfred North. 1927. *Symbolism: Its Meaning and Effect.* New York: Macmillan.

Wiegman, Robyn. 1995. *American Anatomies: Theorizing Race and Gender.* Durham: Duke University Press.

Williams, Patricia. 1995. "Quayle Has a Cow." In *The Rooster's Egg: On the Persistence of Prejudice,* by Williams, 150–68. Cambridge: Harvard University Press.

Williams, Rhys H. 1997. "Culture Wars, Social Movements, and Institutional Policies." In *Cultural Wars in American Politics: Critical Reviews of a Popular Myth,* edited by Williams, 283–95. New York: Aldine De Gruyter.

Wilson, James Q. 1993. *The Moral Sense.* New York: Free Press.

Winant, Howard. 1994. *Racial Conditions: Politics, Theory, Comparisons.* Minneapolis: University of Minnesota Press.

———. 1995. "Symposium: On West and Fenstermaker's 'Doing Difference.'" *Gender and Society* 9(4) (Aug.): 503–6.

Winslow, Helen. 1909. *A Woman for Mayor.* Boston: Arena.

Wittig, Monique. [1969] 1973. *Les Guérillères.* Translated by David Le Vay as *The Guérillère.* New York: Avon.

Wright, Lawrence. 1993. "Orphans of Jonestown." *The New Yorker,* 22 Nov., 66–89.

Young, Iris Marion. [1989] 1990. "Polity and Group Difference: A Critique of the Ideal of Universal Citizenship." In *Feminism and Political Theory,* edited by Cass R. Sunstein, 117–41. Chicago: University of Chicago Press.

————. 1994. "Gender as Seriality: Thinking about Women as a Social Collective." *Signs* 19(3) (spring): 713–38.

Young-Eisendrath, Polly. 1988. "The Female Person and How We Talk about Her." In *Feminist Thought and the Structure of Knowledge,* edited by Mary McCarrey Gergen, 152–72. New York: New York University Press.

Zaki, Hoda. 1984. "Utopia and Ideology." *Women's Studies* 14: 119–33.

INDEX